Take This Job and Love It!

by
Rich Wolfe

Take This Job and Love It

©2015 Rich Wolfe

Published by Lone Wolfe Press, a division of Richcraft. Distribution, marketing, publicity, interviews, and book signings handled by Wolfegang Marketing Systems, Ltd.—But Not Very.

Color photographs © *Sports Illustrated* and reprinted with permission. This book is not affiliated with or endorsed by the University of Michigan or the NCAA.

No part of this book may be reproduced, stored in a retrieval system, or transmitted, in any form or by any means, electronic, mechanical, photocopying, recording, or otherwise, without the prior permission of Rich Wolfe.

Cover Art: Ed Hansen
Layout: Dave Reed
Author's agent: T. Roy Gaul

Rich Wolfe can be reached at 602-738-5889

ISBN: 978-0-9963247-4-8

DEDICATION

John Hrycko

Of Dowagiac, Michigan

A Great Guy and Great Friend

ACKNOWLEDGMENTS

Wonderful people helped make this book a reality starting with Shaun and Linda Fitzmaurice for their super hospitality in Richmond, Virginia; Johnny Rocket in Eau Claire, Michigan; Wendy Legler at Votype in Scots Valley, Ca. and Tom Bast and Terry Hutchens in Indianapolis.

Let's not forget Dave Hochman, the trivia wizard from Ann Arbor and Tempe, Arizona along with his buddy Dave Mann of Detroit City. In addition, Auday Arabo of AFPD in West Bloomfield Hills and Ellie Beauchamp of the beautiful Embassy Suites in Livonia, Michigan. Her hospitality at that terrific property made my four months in the Detroit area so much more enjoyable and their business center so much easier to put this book together!

Special thanks to Terry Mc Donnell at Sports Illustrated along with the talented Mike Rosenberg and Austin Murphy.

Wonderful contributions from Birmingham native Jon Spolestra of Portland, Oregon-the second best marketing man in America – as well as Steve Silverman in Chicago and Gideon Rubin in Menlo Park.

How about a big thank you to longtime friend David Gray at Gray & Company in Cleveland as well as Ed Hansen in Des Plaines, Illinois.

A giant tip of the Hatlo hat must go to Dale Ratermann at his new digs down in Ponte Vedra, Florida and to the highly regarded and highly retired Bruce Madej of Belleville, Mi. Now I understand why he had such a great reputation within the U of M Athletic Department.

And an extra special thank you to Jon Stevens of Columbus, Ohio and author and sports marketing consultant extraordinaire Ken Magee of Ann Arbor whose Michigan memorabilia collection is mind-boggling.

A final bow to Jim Harbaugh's Wolverine teammates. Their great stories of sacrifice, effort, pain, laughter and camaraderie almost made me jealous that I wasn't part of it all. Thanks, everybody!

CHAT ROOMS

Dedication 3
Acknowledgments. 5
Preface 9

CHAPTER 1   AN ECLECTIC BEGINNING   15
Put Me in Coach. 16
If You're Lucky Enough to Be Jim Harbaugh's Friend,
You're Lucky Enough 24
A Tiger's Tale 41
Big Jon, Big Bad Jon 46
A Hard Way to Make an Easy Living 58
Sometimes God Just Hands Ya One 67
Sooner Later. 81

CHAPTER 2   SWEET HOME ANN ARBOR:
THE BIG TEN, THE BIG HOUSE, THE BIG TIME   85
A Roomie with a View. 86
Jim Harbaugh was a Human Red Bull. 102
Where the Past is Present 106
The Days are Long, The Years are Short 129
All It Takes Is All Ya Got 135
Down at the Corner of What and If 139
Hoops: There It Is 142
Short Stories from Long Memories 146

CHAPTER 3   BEAR DOWN CHICAGO BEARS!!   161
Da Coach 162
The Write Guy 167
Catch This 171
When Chicago Calls, Ya Gotta Accept the Charges 174

CHAPTER 4   CALIFORNIA DREAMIN'   193
A Coach is a Teacher with a Death Wish 194
His Future is History. 200
It's Not How Big You Are, It's How Good You Are 205
Is Arizona a Four-Year School Now? 212
Straight Outta Oakland 219
A Play-Tonic Relationship 223
Lotsa Luck 227

CHAPTER 5   AN ECLECTIC ENDING   231

The Harbaughs' Old Kentucky Home 232

That's Bob with One "O" 236

The Son Also Rises 238

Buenas Noches, Coaches 241

Racecar Spelled Backwards is Racecar 246

Behold the Maize and Blue 248

Jim Harbaugh is Just a Regular Guy
Who Some Days Wears a Cape 255

When the One Great Scorer Comes to Mark Against Your Name,
He'll Mark Not If You Won or Lost But How You Played the Game . . 265

PREFACE

"Meet me at Fazoli's at noon."

That's what the man on the phone said on a beautiful spring Tuesday in 1992. The man was Jack Harbaugh, the head football coach at Western Kentucky University in Bowling Green. Just two days prior the Louisville *Courier-Journal* reported that football at WKU might be dropped. I had just finished a sports marketing consulting job in Louisville and had called Jack to offer some free advice.

It was a wonderful lunch. I was pleasantly surprised at how nice Jack Harbaugh was, how smart he was, but the thing that impressed me the most was how knowledgeable he was about baseball, particularly the Cleveland Indians. Normally people that are active in sports as players or coaches have very limited knowledge of the history of that sport or any other sport. So we had a fun early afternoon talking business and talking Cleveland Indians baseball. Hopefully, I gave him some ideas that helped, although nothing helped him like the fact that his son, Jim, an NFL quarterback, later helped him on the recruiting trail.

We parted our ways, not knowing at the end of 1992 that Western Kentucky football would be getting back on a firm foundation, and I was going to become an owner of a minor league basketball team with Rick Barry as my coach.

The next time I talked to Jack was the very next year when, after watching a Chicago Bears exhibition game with Jim at quarterback, I called Jack and said he'd better increase the life insurance policy on Jim because, if the Bears blockers didn't get better, Jim wasn't going to be alive by Christmas time.

Another fun adventure with Jack was in 2004. I was in Wisconsin signing Green Bay Packers books that I'd written. I had to go to Chicago to sign Chicago Cubs books at Nordstrom in

Oak Brook, when I remembered that Jack had moved to Milwaukee. Western Kentucky had won their division national championship a year or two before, and he moved to Milwaukee as associate athletic director of Marquette University to be closer to his daughter.

I called Jack and said, "Let's have dinner tonight. I'm coming through Milwaukee, and there's something I want to talk to you about."

He said, "That would be great." Then he said, "Oh, wait a minute. I can't do it. Jackie (his wife) and I are babysitting at our daughter's house tonight. They're going to the Milwaukee Bucks game." Then suddenly he said, "Well, why don't you just meet us over at their house? I'll give you the address, and we'll have some fun."

I met him at his daughter's house...We're sitting in the kitchen... About halfway through our three-hour session, he said, "What is it you wanted to talk to me about?" I said, "Well, Notre Dame, my alma mater, today was in Buffalo talking to Tom Clements, the quarterback coach of the Buffalo Bills and a former star quarterback at Notre Dame about the head coaching job. Tomorrow they're going to Boston to talk to Charlie Weis for the second time, the offensive coordinator for the Patriots. I don't think either one of them is equipped to be head coach at Notre Dame. My idea is that Notre Dame should hire your son John as head coach, your son Jim as offensive coordinator, and you, Jack, as recruiting coordinator, since you know every high school coach in the country."

Jack broke out laughing.

I said, "Jack, don't laugh. I'm serious."

"Oh," he said, "I know you are."

I said, "Well, would it work?"

Jack stopped smiling, his eyes narrowed, and he said, "My sons can coach."

I said, "So you think it would work?"

He said, "Of course, it will work. Here's what you do. Tomorrow before or after your signing, call Bryan Harlan, my sons' agent, and run this by him. I think it's a pretty good idea, and I think it would work."

Bryan Harlan's father Bob was the popular president of the Green Bay Packers and his brother, Kevin Harlan, a popular network sportscaster. After talking with Bryan Harlan the next day, Bryan called Notre Dame and basically was blown off. I called three higher-ups at Notre Dame that I knew pretty well, and I was laughed at as well. After five years of Charlie Weis, who's laughing now?

Anyway, I've always wanted to do a book on the Harbaughs because I find the whole family to be very interesting and Jack Harbaugh to be a terrific guy.

There is a big problem in doing a book about a person who has one or more characteristics that really stand out. In this case, it's Jim's competitiveness. Everyone dwelled on that. Since this is a book of tributes from Jim Harbaugh's friends, obviously there's going to be some repetition. Repetition is usually a problem. For example, in my Mike Ditka book, seven people described a run Ditka made in Pittsburgh the week of JFK's assassination as the greatest run they'd ever seen, yet only one of those made the book. The editor didn't understand that when the reader was through with the book, few would remember the importance, the singularity of that catch and run. However, if most of the seven stories had remained intact, everyone would realize that one play summarized Ditka's persona and his career. So too the reputation with Jim Harbaugh and his competitiveness, except many times greater. It was overwhelming. Many pages were deleted from this book because there were constant similar testimonials. Even so, many remain.

In doing more than four dozen books, I've never encountered as much repetition. It's been close several times. It's a real tribute to Harbaugh, but a real challenge to the editors.

I write books only on people who seem admirable from a distance. The fear, once you start a project, is the subject will turn out to be a jerk. Not true with Harbaugh. As you will soon find out, you would want your coach to possess the qualities that have made Jim Harbaugh a success.

Growing up on a farm in Iowa, I avidly read all of the Horatio Alger-style books of John R. Tunis, the Frank Merriwell collection, and Clair Bee's Chip Hilton series, all which preach the values of hard work, perseverance, full obedience, and sportsmanship, where sooner or later, one way or another, some forlorn, underweight underdog will succeed beyond his wildest dreams in the arena of life. Frank Merriwell, thy name is Jim Harbaugh. Jim Harbaugh was better than Frank Merriwell. He was real life...harder working than Roy Hobbs...a Rudy with talent. Harbaugh was manna from heaven for the University of Michigan and Wolverines fans and many other fervent college football fans.

From the age of 10, I've been a serious collector of books, mainly sports book. During that time—for the sake of argument, let's call it 30 years—my favorite book style is the "eavesdropping" type where the subject talks in his own words. In his own words, without the "then he said" or "the air was so thick you could cut it with a butter knife" voice of verbiage that makes it hard to get to the meat of the matter...books like Lawrence Ritter's *The Glory of Their Times: The Story of the Early Days of Baseball Told by the Men Who Played It* or Donald Honig's *Baseball When the Grass Was Real*. Thus I adopted that style when I started compiling the oral histories of the Vin Scullys and Bobby Knights of the world.

There's a big difference in doing a book on Mike Ditka or Harry Caray and doing one on Jim Harbaugh. Ditka and Caray were born long before Jim Harbaugh, thus they had many more years to create their stories and build on their legends. Furthermore, unlike Harbaugh, they both liked to enjoy liquid fortification against the unknown, which leads to even wilder tales.

I don't even pretend to be an author. This book with its unusual format is designed solely for fans. I don't really care what the publishers, editors, or critics think, but I am very concerned that Harbaugh fans have an enjoyable read and get their money's worth. Sometimes, the person being interviewed will drift off the subject, but if the feeling is that the reader would enjoy their digression, it stays in the book.

In an effort to include more material, the editor decided to merge some of the paragraphs and omit some of the punctuation which allows the reader to receive an additional 10,000 words, an equivalent of 25-30 pages. More bang for buck... more fodder for English teachers...fewer dead trees.

It's also interesting—as you'll find in this book—how some people will view the same happening in completely different terms.

Jim Harbaugh is a man in a society where orthodox behavior has stifled creativity, adventure and fun...a society where posturing and positioning one's image in order to maximize income has replaced honesty and bluntness...Jim Harbaugh is a principled man in a world of rapidly dwindling principles... a difference maker on an indifferent planet...a coach the way coaches used to be in an America that's not the way it used to be...a loyal man to colleagues, teammates, and friends in an age when most people's loyalties are in their wallet...a man who is fighting the good fight and living the good life.

Go now.

Chapter 1

AN ECLECTIC
BEGINNING

SUSAN
HAMILTON

LYNDA
HANSELMAN

JAMES
HARBAUGH

43

PUT ME IN COACH

ROB LILLIE

Rob Lillie, 69, taught and coached at Tappan Junior High School in Ann Arbor for 43 years. During his time at Tappan, he coached many Michigan coaches' sons, including John and Jim Harbaugh. He also coached Olympic swimming gold-medalist Annette Salmeen, and President Clinton economic adviser Gene Sperling. In 2010, the school district honored him by naming the gym the "Lillie Gymnasium."

Jim Harbaugh first got my attention when two boys came from St. Francis, which is the Catholic school right across the street from Tappan Junior High. When Jim was in eighth grade and John was in ninth grade, I had both of them. The first year, we had scaled back a lot. So we only had ninth grade football. We no longer had a team for the eighth grade. John was my quarterback. That team was exceptional, even though we had no linemen. Out of the 35 kids on the team, we probably had 25 or more that were only big enough to be maybe a running back. So everybody had to take their turns being a lineman.

Until one day the kids said, "Well, have you ever seen John hit?" I go, "No, but he's a quarterback and I don't want to get him hurt." They said, "He'll knock your socks off." Before long, he was going both ways. John was quiet—a nice, polite kid and wonderful at the same time. I also had Jim in gym class. He was a young, wild stallion. He was into everything, wanting to do everything. He would tell you how good he was, but he could back up everything he said. Jim goes, "Well, I want to play football." I said, "Well, you can't until you're in ninth grade." He said, "But I can beat...I'm better than these guys." I said, "You don't understand. Only ninth graders can play." The school had a soccer team and the coach said, "Jim, we need a goalie." Jim goes, "I can do that." That's what he said to everything. "I can do that." He played soccer in eighth grade and they won the championship.

Then it came around to springtime. Jim goes, "Well, I want to play **BASEBALL***." And I said, "Jim, remember football in the fall was only for ninth graders? Baseball is the same way." "But I'm better than all of those guys." I said, "Can't do it. But I'm the track coach. Why don't you come out?" "I can do that." He came out and ran track for me. I'm looking for a high hurdler. I would teach in my gym class how to do the different events— how to hurdle and long jump and high jump and everything. I said, "You know, Jim, you've got long legs. I need a second high hurdler." "Well, I've never done it, but I can do that." He started working, and he would not quit. He was not going to quit at whatever he did. He kept getting better and better. Tommy Rush was my star hurdler from the year before. Tommy would beat Jim. By the end of the year, Jim beat him in the city championship.

Jim was just a year behind John. I had him the following year in football. Right away, Jim is out there. I go, "Wow, okay Jim, now is your time to shine." He was my quarterback. We would end gym class, go out and have passing contests and kicking contests. Of course, he was right up there. He wants to do everything. He becomes my No. 1 quarterback. Like John the year before, I go, "Well, I don't want you to get hurt." He goes, "Coach, I am not going to get hurt. I want to play on defense, too." I said, "Well, what do you play?" "I want to be a linebacker." He played linebacker on defense and quarterback on offense. We just took off and started winning. It got down to the big game with the cross-town rival, and Jim comes in one

*Since 1997, participation in Little League **BASEBALL** is down 25 percent from 2.6 million to way less than 2 million.

day—the kids would oftentimes come in during my off period down by the locker room and the equipment room—and he goes, "I'm getting phone calls from this other team. They're telling me how they're going to break my leg and break my arm." I tell their athletic director. But Jim says, "They won't even touch me." He played great, no broken bones, and we won.

One thing I do remember, sometimes some of his own players would come to me and they'd say, "You've got to do something about Harbaugh. He's trying to tell us what to do and whatever." I'd get Jim aside, and I'd say, "Jim, I know you know what you're talking about. But let me tell the kids what to do, because they don't like it. They think you're just cocky and they don't want to listen to you tell them." He said, "Okay, I can do that." That was the end of it. No problem.

Jim was on the basketball team, and he was a really good basketball player. But he wasn't our best one. Again, we're working for the championship. He comes down to the equipment room one day when the other gym teacher and I are in there. We go, "Jim, we want to know something. We're playing for the championship, and the game is tied. Somebody gets fouled and there is no time on the clock. Or, you're one point behind and somebody gets fouled. Who would you want shooting the free throws?" Now this other kid was really, really good. Jim goes, "Oh, that's easy." He goes, "Me." I go, "What? Why you?" He goes, "Because I know I'd make them." Some kids resented his cocky attitude, but he was not cocky, just supremely confident. He knew what he could do and wanted to show it.

He was great. I'd say he was about as good as you're going to get. I had other athletes that were probably equally as good at that stage, but his attitude and field awareness and everything was better. I knew he was going to go on to big things. When he went up to the high school in tenth grade, he was on the JV team. Of course, I would go up and watch the JV games, and the varsity games, because there were a lot of kids on the team that I had in junior high. They pulled up Jim to the varsity. We were playing Ypsilanti, which was a big rival in the town next door to us. They had tremendous athletes. In fact, their star ended up going to Notre Dame and playing as a defense back. But he was their quarterback at that time. Anyway, we're playing. I'm doing the down marker on the sidelines, so I'm right there when they put Jim in as the quarterback. He throws a couple of completions. You could just see these kids from Ypsi just starting to drool. Ypsi had this one kid whose last name was Armstrong. He played at Pitt. He was like 6-foot-7 and 250 pounds, a defensive end. Jim goes back to pass and Armstrong comes flying in from the back side and just cold-cocks Jim. Just creams him. Jim immediately hops to his feet. You could tell he was barely breathing. Jim helps Armstrong up and pats him on the back. Jim goes back into the huddle and you could see him bend over on his knees to catch his breath or vomit or whatever. But Jim wasn't going to give in and tell anybody that he wasn't tough enough.

He just had a persona about him. He had been around football his whole life. It wasn't going to stop. He had a passion to be great. He wasn't going to let anything get in the way of that. His passion is a matter of him growing up in that arena, with his dad and the different coaches, and seeing the elite players there at an early age, seeing how they presented themselves, and how the great ones acted. I think he learned from day one. He was a smart kid. I just had a great time with him.

Years later, he left and went out to Palo Alto when his dad coached Stanford. We had heard from his friends that he was throwing with Elway. John Elway was at Stanford at that time. Every day he was out there throwing balls with Elway. I'm going, "Oh my gosh, what better person to learn from than the best?" When he did come back to Michigan, he goes, "I'm going to be the starting quarterback at Michigan someday."

Before he came back to Michigan, I moved up to the high school and started coaching there. We had quite a few of the

Michigan coaches' sons on the football team. These coaches would let us come into the indoor facility to practice and watch their practices. When Jim came back to play, he would come over and say hi, or whatever. Of course, he didn't start out as the starting quarterback. But you knew. He goes, "I'll be starting. I'll be starting."

After that, I didn't see him for a long time. The next time I saw him was when he was trying out for the Detroit **LIONS***, later in his career. Marty Mornhinweg was the head coach and they were running that West Coast Offense. Jim was a drop back. My son and I went up to the training camp, at Saginaw Valley. They had a little barrier you had to stand behind that the players ran though. Near the end, here comes Jim jogging out from the locker room. He jogs by us and I said, "Jim Harbaugh, Coach Lillie." He takes about five more steps and then he comes running back. He grabs me over the barrier and body slams me. I mean, he didn't get me on the ground, but he brought me over and my feet are flying in the air. "What are you doing here?" We came up to see you and whatever. "How long are you going to be here?" I said we were just here for the day to watch them practice. He says, "Where are you sitting?" I said right over there in the bleachers. Halfway through, a man in a golf cart drives up "Coach Lillie?" I said, "Yeah, over here." He says, "Jim wants to invite you and your son to have lunch with him and the Lions." We got to go in with the Lions that day for lunch. We finished eating in about a half hour. Then Jim sat there for two hours with us. That was the last time I talked to him. I haven't seen him since he came back. But I've got his Tappan Junior High jersey and his letter that we gave out to the athletes with the Tappan "T." I've got a plate with "Harbaugh" on it, from when he was playing at Tappan. I'm going to go down to the football office one day and have Jay Harbaugh

---

*Wayne Fontes is the winningest and the losingest coach in Detroit **LIONS** history.

come take his old jersey, put it on, and then cover it up with a Michigan jacket. Then during the meeting, take his Michigan jacket off and have Jim's old Tappan Junior High football jersey on. He would probably get a chuckle out of that.

The only difference between Jim and John was the forwardness of Jim, compared to the more reserved John. But I'm not saying John was any less competitive than Jim. It's just that he didn't show it or talk it. He just went out and did it. The Super Bowl a couple of years ago was great. We were going down. We're going to visit friends for a month in Florida. We're coming near Orlando and I get a phone call. I answer it. It's *The Baltimore Sun*, and they wanted to ask me questions about John and Jim in the game. I talked to them for about an hour. We get down to this island off the Gulf Coast of Florida where our friends live. I'm sitting on the deck drinking a beer, watching the sunset. I get a phone call from the NFL Network. They start talking to me about it. They said, "We're going to be in Ann Arbor to interview you and do a little thing with you." I said, "I'll tell you what. I'm sitting on the porch in Florida, drinking a beer and watching the sunset. I don't think I'm going to be there." They asked me a couple more questions. Then, of course, they come up with that question: "Who are you rooting for?" I said, "I'm not rooting for either. I hope it's a good game. All I know is that whoever wins, I'm going to wear that color shirt for the next year. If John wins, I'm wearing purple. If Jim wins, I'm wearing red." I don't really like red, because our biggest rivals wore red. I wore purple for a whole year—a nice purple golf shirt when I went golfing.

I have not been surprised at all by how good of a coach Jim has been. Here's a little one from ninth grade. We're in that equipment room talking, which a lot of the kids would come and do. Jim goes, "I don't like this four-four defense that you're running." I said, "Well, ninth grade teams don't pass a lot, so if I put four linemen up there, we stop the run. If I've got linebackers, you guys can clean up the rest of it. Four linebackers." He said, "Oh, man. That's not the way. You've got to run a five-two, like Michigan." I said, "Well, I'll tell you what. I'm not going to do it, but the coach at one of the high schools runs a four-four and he invited me there and gave me his playbook. I've got all the drills drawn up. We can do that if you want. Why don't you have your dad send me something?" He said, "I can do that." The next day he comes in. He says, "I got something for you, coach." And he pulls out a wadded piece of paper from his pocket. Here is this elaborate sketch of a five-two defense scribbled on the paper. He said, "Here you go." "Okay, Jim. Thanks a lot. That'll help a lot." I had about 40 pages of this other guy's playbook describing every position and move. But Jim was always trying. He was always trying to gain an advantage. He was always working hard.

At the end of practice, we'd always run this hill up from our practice field. We would run up. Then one day the coaches decided to do something different. Let's have everybody run 10, and then only the top two get to run more. The other coach said that will be cool. We do it, and the kids go okay, everybody run 10 now. Whoever finishes first or second gets to run again. We had about three different groups of what would have been about six kids. They're all looking at each other, going, "Why in the heck would we want to be one-two?" A couple of fast ones just jog up the hill and touch it, so they don't get to run. A couple of linemen get it down there, and there are the five or six of them and we go, "Okay, now only the top three get to run the next one." Pretty soon it was Jim like he is now, competing all of the time. If you win, you get to do more. If you lose, you get to sit there and watch, though you should be out there competing.

Jack Harbaugh was no problem at all. He never interfered. All of the Michigan coaches at that time—they had Jerry Hanlon, the line coach, Jack was the defensive back coach and Gary Moeller was coach then—were just top of the line people.

We won the state title two years in that time, so we had pretty good teams.

I thought Jim would come back to Michigan to coach. When my son and I had lunch when Jim was with the Lions I said, "Jim, would you ever want to coach at Michigan?" He goes, "Yeah." He said, "If I coach, that would be one of the top places I'd like to coach." You've been to all of these different places around the country, what is your favorite? He said, "Well, I really like—and my family likes—San Diego." Jim has got a wonderful family, and all of them are doing well, a tribute to Jim and his wife.

IF YOU'RE LUCKY ENOUGH TO BE JIM HARBAUGH'S FRIEND, YOU'RE LUCKY ENOUGH

MIKE REINHOLD

Muskegon's Mike Reinhold might have had the worst luck of any Michigan player in history. He broke his leg in six places, ruptured his Achilles tendon twice and lost a kidney. The linebacker and nose guard still lives in Muskegon. After retiring from Kraft, Reinhold is contemplating a writing career.

I came in with Jim back in 1982 as a freshman. Right away he stuck out. He was working out all of the time. We were trying to figure out our classes, but he was always in shorts and a T-shirt, always wanting to work out. We hit it off pretty well, right out of the gate. What I liked about him was that he was competitive. He knew what he wanted. He was a little different than the other freshmen who came in. He had already been there. He had already worked as a ball boy with Bo. He had the lay of the land, so he stuck out a little bit.

We had our first freshman meeting with Bo. Jim shows up 10 minutes late. We're all sitting in there, and Bo is up at the podium. Jim just saunters in and walks past the podium. We're like, "Holy smokes." Coach Schembechler went crazy. He threw the podium on the ground, told Jim he would never play a down in his career at Michigan and that he was going to call his dad. We're just 18-year old freshmen, and we're looking at each other back there like, "Do we really need this?" I mean, it was crazy. We're looking and we had no idea we were getting into this. At that point, we went on "Bo Time." Bo had us turn our watches ahead 10 minutes and all of our clocks at home ahead 10 minutes. At that point forward, we were on "Bo Time" and nobody was ever late again. Jim set the tone pretty good. Jim, of all people, should have known better than to ever be late for a meeting. That's what was funny about it. There are a lot of guys who have told that story, just from that freshman class. You had to have been there. It was something else. We started off with fireworks. Jim came back and sat down with all of us, and he just looked stunned. I don't think he thought he was late. But we were all there. He knew right away, though, when the podium hit the ground. He walked right past Bo, like he didn't even see him. You could see Jim's face was red, and he was very embarrassed. We were just all pretty stunned. That was our first real introduction to Bo. Right away we had one of the guys that was never going to play a down out of our class, and the dad was going to be called. It actually ended up being a fun story for everybody. I know Coach Schembechler would tell that story from time to time, too. I had never heard of Harbaugh before that day.

We spent two years in the dorms together. Actually, I was about two doors down from Jim. Then we got an opportunity to go out on our own and get a house or an apartment, and you got an opportunity to choose who you lived with. Jim and I and two other guys got together, and we lived out our five-year careers together.

Jim has got to win. He and I were playing together in a team racquetball championship match. He broke five racquets. I broke a few, also. We were in the Intramural Building, and the match went back and forth. It went five games. The last two points, best of five. Throughout that five-game series, he had to go back up to the desk and get racquet, after racquet, after racquet. He didn't want to lose that match. Actually, I beat him by two in the last game and Jim wouldn't talk to me for a week.

He went through five racquets. They weren't going to give us another one. The guy at the front desk said, "No, that's it. I'm not giving any more racquets to you guys."

We worked together almost every summer. You know how you play that triangle football game? You take a piece of paper and fold it into a triangle, and that represents the football. Then you put your index fingers up and your thumbs together for the goalposts. Your opponent does the same thing. Then you use your middle finger to push the triangle football through the goalpost. You flick it through there. We're sitting down on the deck on a break. It was our second summer working together. We go back and forth, back and forth, back and forth. It's all tied up. It comes down to him having to make a field goal to win it all. It goes right over the top of my right finger, so right away I'm saying, "No good, it's off to the right." He totally disagrees. It got into a heated argument. Pretty soon the table is on the ground. He throws a chair against the wall and starts swinging at me. We're best friends. He starts swinging at me. I finally had to put him in a bear hug. That's Jim. He wasn't going to lose. He wouldn't quit until he won. He took it to a different level. I loved being around him, and the guys loved being around him, because he was a winner and a leader. He couldn't have been a better fit for our team at that time.

When I shattered my femur against Minnesota up in Minneapolis, I was a 225-pound linebacker. When I came back for my senior year in '85, I was 265, playing nose tackle, so when he started swinging at me, I was a big ole nose tackle. I was a lot bigger than him. I was totally shocked when he threw the table on the ground, and especially when he started swinging at me. He just kept saying, "It was good. I'm telling you, Reinhold, it was good. It was good. I saw it go over the inside part of your index finger. It was good." I'm saying, "I don't think so." He threw the table on the ground. The chair went flying. I didn't think he was going to come at me like that over a triangle football game.

I've got another story that proves that nobody at Michigan was getting paid. It's our senior year—we're going into our fifth year—and Jim's finally put together a few dollars from our summer work to buy himself his first car. I go with him to a cheap car lot. He falls in love with a slug bug, one of those little VW bugs. He had only $500 to spend, by the way. We're at the used car lot. I'm supposed to be helping him pick out this car. He likes it. He goes, "Reiny, this is the one, man." It's red. One of those Volkswagens? I had to help push it off the lot to get that thing running. He bought it. Then when he couldn't get it to continue to run that whole year, we let all of our frustrations out on that car. Before our last spring game, we turned it upside down in our front yard. I got the first swing at the windshield, because I had ruptured my Achilles tendon and everybody told me to go first. That car got completely totaled. But $500—that's what he spent on that car. He drove it when it worked. At the used car lot, I said, "Jim, you can't buy this, man." I'm running along the side of the car so that he can get it started and off the lot. He was going with that car. He was committed to that car. When Jim knows what he wants, he goes and gets it. That's just who he is—he goes after what he wants. He liked that car for some reason, and that was the car he was going to get. I ran off the lot with it. I had to jump in, in the last second, when he got it jump-started with the clutch. That's how we got off the lot. Do you know where that car is today? Probably at the old Volks home. Can you imagine? He's an All-American quarterback and is going to be drafted in the first round. That Volkswagen is what he's driving. I tell everybody, because they say, "You guys were getting this and that under the table." No, we didn't get anything. Nobody got anything. That proves the point.

Jim was very competitive and always had to win. But he had an incredible heart. He treated the walk-ons as well as he treated the seniors. We all learned a lot from that. We went to South Bend when we were fifth-year seniors. This was supposed to be a great year for him. I had come back and beat the femur, and this was supposed to be my big year, too—my fifth year. The week before we played Notre Dame in the opening game, I ruptured my Achilles. I was devastated. We go to South Bend. Bo brings me along. I've had the surgery and am on crutches. The game goes back and forth. We were ranked second and they were ranked first in the country, September '86. We ended up winning the game in the last second—a field goal. We didn't know which way it was going to go. We got back in the locker room and everybody was going crazy. It was a huge win for us in South Bend. Jim was awarded the game ball. He goes, "This game ball is going to Mike Reinhold." Everybody went crazy. I had tears. I was an emotional wreck. I was happy we won the game, but I wanted to participate. He gave me the game ball. Jim and Bo stood up there on the stage, and he did that. All the time people ask, "What's your greatest memory and your best honor?" I always tell people that one. I didn't play in that game, and I had a friend that was so...so committed and loyal and unselfish. It was his game ball. He was given the game ball and he said, "No, no, this one is going to Mike Reinhold." I rushed out of there with tears in my eyes. My sons now have that ball, along with both of my Rose Bowl rings and helmet.

I tried to come back that year. That was our fifth year. I figured I had beaten the femur, so I'd beat this ruptured Achilles, too. We went to the Rose Bowl that year. That's another Jim story. Three days before the charter plane took off to go to Pasadena, I ruptured my Achilles. We had our home visits for the Christmas break. We were able to go home for three days. I tripped over my brother Stick's bag and ruptured it again. I thought I was going to at least sneak out there and play one last play and be done with it. Then I found out two months later that I had to have a kidney removed, so I wasn't going to be able to go on, anyway.

I'm living with Jim this whole year, and I'm hurting. It was hard. He helped me through all of that. Then when I ruptured the Achilles a second time, I'm in a Muskegon hospital. No one would have had any idea I had done that. I called Jim up and I explained the situation to him, and he goes, "Well, Reiny, how are you going to get out to the Rose Bowl?" My mom and dad and my brother had tickets to go to the game. I said, "I don't know." He said, "How about we do this?" The players knew my brother really well, because I helped him get some summer work when he was going through med school. All of the team knew him really well and really liked him. He goes, "Why don't you send Stick down here? We'll get him in a warm-up suit and we'll smuggle him onto the plane. You take his plane ticket and get your butt out there in time at least to watch the game." I'm delirious as I'm listening to all of this. I'm going, "Yeah, okay. Okay." Well, they did that. My brother went down and actually missed the player's charter, but got smuggled onto the injured players/alumni charter...as me! They got him a warm-up uniform and snuck him onto the plane. Jim coordinated this whole thing. All of the injured players got around my brother and got him on the plane. He gets out to the Rose Bowl, and he's in a room with one of the players. Some of the players were asking him, "What the hell are you doing here?" Then everybody found out that I had ruptured my Achilles again. Bo called the room, because I guess another guy that was not supposed to have made the trip for disciplinary reasons got on the plane. My brother answered the phone. Bo goes, "Who is this?" "Greg Reinhold, the man they call Stick." Bo didn't know that I had re-ruptured my Achilles until my brother told him about it. Bo couldn't have been sweeter. He asked him if he needed tickets. He told him to keep staying right there in the room. My brother had the time of his life out there. He is staying at the Rose Bowl hotel with the team. I'm back in Muskegon on an operating table. I'll owe Jim for the rest of my life for doing that. All he cared about is that I got out there. That was pretty cool. Nobody said anything afterward. Then six months later, my defensive line coach came up and said, "What in the hell were you guys thinking?" It wasn't my plan. I didn't tell him who planned it. But it worked, though. I thought it was pretty cool that they felt good enough about me to do that. Jim did it. I had a brutal fifth year health-wise, but he certainly helped me get through it. My brother is a year older than me, and he went to Michigan State. But he's a huge Michigan fanatic. He lived high on the hog out there. He said he was the social coordinator for the team. He had all the parties and the bars set up. Oh, man, the stories that came out of that. I'm in Muskegon and he's out there partying in Pasadena in the Rose Bowl hotel—in my spot. If anybody asked how he had that warm-up suit on, he told everybody he was a receiver—and all of the guys backed him up. "He's a receiver. He don't look like much, but he can fly!"

We worked a couple of times in the summer at the football building. We had to paint the inside of the football office and weight room. Well, it's Schembechler Hall now. But back then it was just a building, nothing fancy. We were supposed to paint the walls throughout the building. That was our job for two summers. When we were painting the building inside, everybody had rollers. Jim, Erik Campbell and I. Bo used to come up with good nicknames for a lot of players. His nickname for Erik Campbell was Soup Campbell, so that's what we called him. Anyway, about halfway through, Jim and I put our heads together on this. It wasn't going very good with just rollers in our hands. We went into the broom closet and unscrewed the broom handles from the mops and put the rollers on the ends. Then we got a couple of chairs out in the hallway and sat in those while we painted what was in front of us. Then about five minutes in we'd say, "Okay, shift left." Everybody would take their chair and shift left. We'd do the next phase of the wall. Then Bo walked in. We were in the middle of one or our moves, where we all in unison moved—pick up your chair and move at the same time, to the left, just like the Radio City Rockettes. "Oh," he said, "Are you s------- me?" He saw us three there, sitting in chairs with broom handles and rollers taped to the ends of them, just relaxing and painting the wall. We said, "This is the most efficient way to do it, Coach." We weren't getting very far with just the hand rollers. We were going all over the place.

With the roller on a broomstick, we could sit there and go up and down, up and down. Then move the chair down. We didn't have to really get too physical, so we saved ourselves for the workout afterward. We had a lot of fun, though. You can imagine the conversations we had while doing that.

We did some lawn work, too, for a farmer. It was just Jim and me on the seats. Then we worked in the Stadium, painting all of the seats another summer. I don't remember what we were getting paid. It wasn't a lot, maybe $8 an hour. We wanted that job because it was close to where we were going to work out. We needed to be close to that. Then in the Stadium when we took our breaks, we ran the steps. Everything that Jim and I did together was geared toward what we were going to get out of this besides just punching a ticket. It put us where we could compete and lift weights during our breaks and do the things that we wanted to do to get ready for football season. You're painting that many seats, you look around and—yeah, the first question you have is where the heck do we begin? We started in the middle. We got very little direction. We had to figure it out ourselves. We had the stencils for the seat numbers, and we had to figure out which ones needed it and which ones didn't. That took all summer. We got a good tan out of it. We did as many as we possibly could. We had to pick and choose which ones needed it the worst. That was a lot of fun. We had a lot of fun that summer. We didn't screw up too much. I'm sure we painted outside the lines a few times, and it wasn't a perfect job. I don't even know if anybody came in afterward and looked at it. We were just told to do the ones that we felt needed it. We were just doing the numbers. What was beneficial to both of us is we got to run the steps. It was really key for me, because I was coming back from that femur injury. I had a metal rod in my leg, 21 inches long. It was good for me. I had to get my strength back up in that leg before they could take the rod out and let me come back and play. There were never any other people around. That place was like a ghost town when we were in there painting. You'd see one or two stragglers come in.

That wasn't everybody's favorite workout, running the stadium steps. It was a long way up from the bottom. It was a perfect summer job for us. We loved it. A lot of guys did security things off the campus, but it was Jim's idea. He wanted to be where he could get a paycheck, a tan, and a workout the quickest way possible.

We had bumper pool in the house that we lived in. When anybody got beat (there were a lot of competitors in that house), the pool stick would go right through drywall. We ended up having to pay for that at the end. That was our stress release room, the bumper pool room. Anybody that lost, the stick went into the ceiling, the wall. Words were said. Nobody wanted to lose. A former player was naive enough to rent his house to us. He should have known better. It was a great house. We had myself and Jerry Quaerna, a lineman, Brad Cochran, Paul Jokisch and Paul Schmerge, the tight end. We had a great group of guys there. It was a lot of fun. Everybody competed hard and we played hard. Bill Dufek, a super guy, was the person who owned the house, of the Dufek family. There were three of them that played at Michigan. We were at 1002 Packard Street. Jim will just laugh and smile if you bring up 1002 Packard to him. It was pretty legendary on campus. Then we moved right down the road our fifth year, to 812 Packard, after a couple of other guys graduated. I don't know why we made that move, maybe it was cheaper. But we all moved together down there. We had been at 1002 for a couple of years, and it was so well known. Everybody knew 1002 Packard. Bill owned both of the houses. I don't know who made that decision.

Jim stood up for me at my wedding. We got married in Scottsdale. My first child was born in Tucson. Years later, we got a divorce. I tell you, Jim came through there, too. I was down and out, going through something like that with kids. He helped me get through that tremendously. He didn't have to do what he did. I told him, "I'm committed to you until the day I die." He did some things for me that most people wouldn't do.

That has a lot to do with why his players love him so much—as his teammates did. I hope someday to repay him for all he did for me during the most difficult time in my life.

He's got a tremendous heart. The characteristics that Bo displayed were similar. You wanted to die for him. You would have run through brick walls. Jim is able to get that out of his players as a coach as well. You have to live what you're doing to get that out of your players. Bo was Michigan. He loved what he did for a living more than anybody I ever met. That's Jim's approach to the whole thing. They know he works. He's going to sleep in his office. If you've got a guy like that, that's committed as a coach, the players are going to want to do anything they can to not let him down. Jim is going to get every single ounce of talent out of that football team—every single ounce of it. He will develop those kids and recruit kids that are good people for the program.

Jim loves his dad. Jim's dad is his idol. He had a picture of Jack above his bed, where we lived. We all knew what Jim was going to do in life. He was going to play in the pros and then he was going to coach. His dad had a lot to do with this. Jim will figure out a way to get it done. I knew if his dad wanted him back in Ann Arbor, he was going back to Ann Arbor. It is that simple. That's his sounding board. That's the most important person in his life. That's who he respects, and that's what he is going to do. He never steered him wrong.

Jim's a trip. He's a lot of fun. You don't quite ever know where he's coming from. His eyes are going around, and he's so intense. But he's a lot of fun away from the game. He lets his hair down and has a good time. Jim knows when to work and when not to. He has continued that balance. He tries to balance himself away from the game. He's learned to be able to balance it better. Jim is going to win. He almost doesn't give himself an out. He doesn't give himself a chance to even think about losing anything. He is so in your face that he doesn't give himself the chance to lose. It has got to come out the other end.

The way you are brought up and your family has a lot to do with being driven. Then your peers, as you go through middle school and high school. If you're on a good, winning football team you're a leader on that team and you take a lot of pride in that, it becomes part of you. It's like when I broke the leg and shattered it so bad they said I would never play again. Never walk right again. All of that stuff. I said, "I'm gonna play! I am playing!" The guys around you respect that. Jim broke his arm and did the same thing. They didn't think he would be able to throw right again, and he was able to come back from that injury. But not everybody wants to do that. They don't care as much. Maybe we cared too much. Maybe there is a point where you care too much.

Jim was hard to live with when he broke that arm. He was pretty miserable about the whole thing. We would have to listen to it. He knew what he wanted to do, and he went and did it. I was coming back from the femur that same year, so we did a lot together. He had his broken arm in '84 against Michigan State. I had shattered my leg in '83, so I was coming back at the same time he was. We were together through that, and it was good for both of us. When you're hurt and living with other healthy players, that's hard. They close the door and you're left behind. It's like Mitch Albom said, "It's like watching a family picnic through a window." I was in a Minnesota hospital for 40-some days over Thanksgiving when I broke my leg in six places against the Gophers. They were putting the metal rods in my legs. I watched football. I didn't think I wanted to play again. I saw the hits differently. I dropped down to 185 pounds. I was there for 40 days after the game. Over Thanksgiving, Michigan alumni who lived in Minnesota came and brought turkey to me. My leg blew up to three times the normal size. It was a horrible injury. They put a rod through my shin, through my femur, through my thigh—a 21-inch rod from my hip to my knee. All that had to come out before I was even considered to have an opportunity to play again. Then Bo moved me to nose tackle from linebacker. Billy Harris and I played back and forth that senior year, that first year I came back. We rotated at nose tackle. By the time I got to the Fiesta Bowl, I had finally figured out the position. The lights came on, as they say. I had put weight on in order to play it well enough. I had my best game in that Fiesta Bowl. I had really looked forward to that fifth year. It didn't work out.

Jim did a lot better with the girls than I did. We both did pretty good. Jim wasn't always about the most beautiful girl or anything like that. He really got to know people before he made those commitments. He actually had a girlfriend for the most part throughout our years together in Ann Arbor. They broke up after we graduated. He was pretty committed to the same girl for the most part throughout that time. We were as close to her as he was. Not in every sense. They were supposed to go to their prom—a sorority dance. I had Jim down at Rick's drinking beer and playing that golf game with the rollerball where you take your thumbs and roll it. We were in a really tight game. We were into it. He didn't want to go. I said, "You're going to be late." He wanted to play until somebody won. Two hours later we showed up at the house, and she's there with her dress on and the whole works. That was a bad night, not a good night for Jim. He had a lot of talking to do after that. Blamed it all on me, of course.

As a joke, we installed a time clock with punch in/out cards and everything outside Jim's bedroom for all the girls that would follow us home, just to get near him. Unfortunately for us, it lasted all of three days as his girlfriend found it and made us take it down.

Jim never got into trouble, disciplinary-wise, with the university. We were in Bo's office a few times, however. One night in the dorm, this was when we were freshmen and sophomores, somebody punched out the window screen at the dorm. The paddy wagon would show up at the Quad. They had two graduate assistant coaches who would show up in a van. We called it the paddy wagon, coming to pick guys up for discipline stuff.

They drag five of us down. It's my freshman year and I had just broken my leg all to hell, and I'm on crutches. I get dragged into the mess. There are five of us standing there in front of Bo. Andy Moeller, thank god, was with us. Andy, Jim, me, Jokisch and Schmerge. Bo is pounding on his desk, "I want to know who punched the screen out of the dorm window. I want to know right now." We had all committed to silence on the way there. Nobody is saying anything. Bo jumps across the desk and he glares at Harbaugh. Bo points his finger at Harbaugh and says, "You will never play another down here or ever play another down of football anywhere. I will have your a--." He called down to the equipment manager, Jon Falk, and told him to turn our locker room locks upside down. We were no longer a part of the team. All five of us. Then he starts berating Harbaugh. "I'm calling your dad." Harbaugh could not survive if he disappointed his dad or was kept from playing football. Harbaugh immediately blurted out the name of the culprit. We all fell on the ground. We had vowed that no one would say anything. Bo looks at me. I'm on crutches. "What the hell did you have to do with it?" "Nothing, not a thing. I'm on crutches. I don't even know why I'm in here." When they turn the lock upside down, that means you couldn't get into the locker anymore. You turn it backward and upside down. All we heard was "turn the locks upside down."

After all of our home games, Jackie, Jim's mom, and my mom would help clean up the house. We had pizza boxes in the corner, and her and my mom seemed to be the housecleaners. Jack was there when he could be due to his own coaching responsibilities, but I saw him often.

Jim was always real tight with his money. He never pulled out a dollar. He had his money hidden in his sock until everybody else ran out of money. Then all of a sudden, he'd have a beer in his hand. "Where did you get that?" I had this little jingle. I answered the phone one time, and I said, "Hell-O, you have reached Harbaugh Enterprises, where tight is right. We accept all forms of currency, including Carte Blanche, Diners Club, American Express, Visa, Mastercard, cashier's checks and money orders. Now...how may *you* help us?" It was Jack calling. He let me go through the entire jingle and then said in a very authoritarian voice, "Reinhold...Jack Harbaugh." I completely froze and just hung up the phone...click! He called back a bit later and Q, our roomie Jerry Quaerna, answered the phone this time. I'm sure Jack doesn't remember that call, but the whole house was in tears. Jim was always tight with his money. That's why I'm sure he's got multi-gazillions. He's always been good with his money, but in college it was tight. Then he'd pull $20 out of his sock, all of a sudden when everybody else ran out.

I definitely thought Jim would make it in the NFL. He went in the first round. He had to deal with Jim McMahon, first of all. But we felt he would do really well, and he did. He hung on for 14 years in the NFL. That's an incredible career. We were we were all sitting out on the front porch when Leigh Steinberg, a well-known agent, showed up. We were all dipping tobacco. Evidently Leigh Steinberg did his homework. He walked up with a spit cup in his hand. I said, "That's your guy right there, Harbs." That was his agent.

When Jim was in the pros, we didn't go to the games and hang out with him very much. He was in Chicago and I was in Arizona. Then I ended up in Texas for a long time. I did get an opportunity when the Bears came out to play the **COWBOYS***. I was married at that time and had two kids. I will never forget, he took us inside Cowboys Stadium and we went out to dinner at a restaurant in the Stadium. I'll never forget what he said. When we got up to leave he said, "Reiny, all I want is what you've got." We were looking out on the Cowboys Stadium. We

*The Dallas Cowboys cheerleaders get $182 a game. For more than 40 years, they got only $15 a game. Until 1967, the ***COWBOYS** cheerleaders were known as the Cowbelles.

were seated by a window that overlooked the Stadium, and he was playing the next day. I walked away completely stunned. I was happily married, with kids. He was single at that point in his life, and he wanted to be married. When you're on that level where he is, you don't know why people like you. You don't know why a woman likes you. Why are my friends, my friends? Do they like me for who I am or for what I'm doing? Because I'm an athlete? I make money? What do they want me for? He had a big struggle with that, to find somebody that liked Jim for being just Jim—and not Jim the football player. That's what he saw with me, that I had transitioned and found somebody that liked me for just who I was. I was pretty stunned by it. I've remembered it all of these years. He's got what I had now, and I'm very happy for him. He seems to be very happy. But he went through that divorce period, too. He struggled through that. That happens to many of us.

One of the guys we lived with was Jerry Quaerna. We just called him Q. He was number 75 and was a fifth-year senior, too. He actually blew his knee out three days after I ruptured my Achilles. We were all living together. Jim is the superstar of the team, and me and Q were both going to be starters. I was a defensive lineman and Jerry was an offensive lineman. We had quite a year. It was fun. Before we went to camp, for two-a-day camp, we would break away and go to Q's hometown in Wisconsin. His uncle had a tavern in Janesville, where he had Q's Eighth Annual Beer Run, Ninth Annual Beer Run, Tenth Annual Beer Run. We went to two or three of them in a row, and we let loose before we got into two-a-day camp. Jim was with us every time. There's a picture that I'm looking at right now in my office that's blown up. It's Q's Tavern in Wisconsin for our beer runs before camp every year. There are about eight of us in the picture. Jim and I are in the front. I've got an arm on Jim's shoulder. Jim didn't drink very much. I've got a shot glass in my right hand and a beer in my left hand. Q is in the back, holding up a beer. It's a beautiful picture, incredible picture. This stayed within our roommates. There are five of us that actually played that were in this picture. But Q, years later—to Jim's chagrin—blew the picture up for everybody. Jim has got a copy of this, a blown up picture just like the one I've got. I don't know what he did with it. He probably burned it. But it's on my wall. Jerry Q sent the CIA over to my house about four years ago. What is the CIA doing here? They were interviewing me because Q was getting ready to hopefully get into Homeland Security. He got the job.

John Harbaugh would come up from Oxford, Ohio, and hang out for the weekend with us. John was a year ahead of us at Miami of Ohio. Those were some fun times. John was a lot more serious than Jim. Jim had a lot more fun. He was more freewheeling. That's probably hard to understand, seeing Jim on the sideline. John always seemed to be more—I don't know if I want to say controlled —diplomatic would maybe be a good word. John was always more diplomatic. John knew the Minicks. One of them works for Jim now, Jim Minick. They grew up as kids together in Ann Arbor. John would come up and he'd get an opportunity to spend some time with us, but he would also spend time with the Minicks, too.

What hurt me the most was what I had to put in to come back from that femur. I shouldn't have ever been on the field. They didn't think I would walk right again. I had to put my soul into that comeback. Then to have the game that I had at the Fiesta Bowl, and then have the camp—I had a great spring ball, tremendous camp. Then a week before we go to South Bend, I rupture the Achilles. Then the Rose Bowl thing. Two days before the plane. Two months later, the kidney is being removed. Everything collapsed. I was pretty lucky, because if I had gotten hit wrong on the field, I would have died instantly. That kidney was so blown up. They had to put a chest tube in my back, and when they drained the kidney, it was a liter and a half of poisonous urine they drained out of there. Some of the weight that I had gained that I was so proud of—my new gut—was that kidney.

If I hadn't gotten hurt, a lot of people felt I could have played in the NFL. After the Fiesta Bowl game, I had a lot of Cardinals coaches and players wanting to talk to me. I really had a good football game out there. I had a lot going for me, going into that fifth year. As a matter of fact, they had written an article in the *Detroit Free Press* that named Jim and me as the team leaders going into that fifth year. They had his picture and my picture together. For me to have to get hurt like that was pretty discouraging. My biggest regret is not coaching for his dad. His dad offered me an opportunity to come down to Western Kentucky. It didn't work out for me, time-wise. Jack and I were on the radio a couple of years ago, and he brought that up. I wish I had done that. I didn't know Jim was going to be back there coaching. I had no idea that he was going to be doing that voluntarily, helping his dad down there. If I had been in a position to go to Western Kentucky when Jack offered it to me, I might be an NFL coach today. You never know. Things could have certainly worked out differently. But I wouldn't have had my kids. I love my kids. I've got two boys and a girl, and they are fabulous kids. Jim knows how I struggled and have struggled. It was very difficult for me. We didn't have people to talk to, like counselors and all of that stuff, back then. Everybody thought you were so tough that you just moved right on. But those were devastating injuries. It took time. I'm in a lot better place now and am doing really well.

I think we had the best college experience anyone could have ever had, great memories. Personally, I never cared or thought that much about moving onto the NFL. That was not my dream or focus. Michigan was. I'll be True Blue 'til the day I die!

A TIGER'S TALE

RON COLANGELO

New York native Ron Colangelo has been the Detroit Tigers Vice President of Communications for seven years. Before that, he served stints with the New York Jets, Florida Panthers and Florida Marlins. He attended Arizona State University before graduating from William Paterson University.

I had never met Coach Harbaugh before. I found out he was going to throw out a first pitch. When a celebrity throws a first pitch, we want to engage with the media. I wasn't really sure how much media Jim would want to do. He said, "I'm all yours. Whatever you want me to do, I'm here to make Tigers fans happy." That surprised me, because I'm always very cognizant to be respectful of their time, of their hectic pace of always being in the public eye and the media. If he had said that he didn't want to, I would have completely understood and respected that. We took him into the interview room where he was fantastic in talking about his days as a Tigers fan growing up and how this was really a unique experience for him. He was genuinely excited about it. He brought his glove. The glove was given to him by the Oakland A's when he coached first base for them during spring training. A's Manager Bob Melvin was his neighbor when Jim lived in the Bay Area. He loves to catch foul balls. He says he's nailed 20 so far. During the game itself, he and his wife and Jon Falk, the well-known retired U-M equipment manager, sat in Clint Hurdle's seats in the first row by the dugout. He sat there so he could try to snag another foul ball with his glove. Hurdle, managing the visiting Pirates that day, is from Big Rapids, Mich. When Harbaugh was a senior at Michigan in '86, he finished third in the Heisman Trophy voting. The winner two years before was Doug Flutie from Boston College. Ironically, Flutie loves to catch foul balls with his glove, also. Flutie's seats at **FENWAY PARK*** are just beyond first base, about six rows from the field. In 2012, Flutie caught foul balls four games in a row.

Our players were very surprised by how hard Harbaugh threw for a 51-year-old. A few years ago, when Nolan Ryan was almost 60, he threw out a first pitch before a Japanese League game that was clocked at 85 miles per hour.

The media saw a different side to Coach Harbaugh. He was very genuine, so down-to-earth and excited. He got a chance to talk about something that has been a childhood passion. Usually, he's sitting there and he's getting grilled about his Xs and Os and this guy and that guy. Here, he was in a whole different realm and was able to just be himself with baseball. I took him to the dugout, and he met Manager Brad Ausmus. They talked a little shop. I took him into the clubhouse, and when Miguel Cabrera saw him, his eyes got wide open. He was very receptive, respectful. Coach Harbaugh was surprised that Cabrera knew who he was. The veteran players certainly treated him with a lot of respect. Ian Kinsler, one of our star players, shook his hand and said, "I'd play for you any day of the week. I'd run through a wall for you." Kinsler is known as a gamer. He's a great athlete, and he's a guy who is not afraid to make a play and get dirty. Kinsler leads by example, and he told Harbaugh that. Coach Harbaugh said, "Wow, I really appreciate you saying that." That was cool, that I got to hear that exchange.

When we went out to the dugout, I asked, "Would you mind going on our FOX Sports pregame show?" I went through the

---

***FENWAY PARK** has the smallest foul territory of any Major League Baseball stadium and the shortest fence in the big leagues. The Pesky Pole down the right field line is only 302 feet from home plate. In 1974 at Fenway Park, Willie Horton of the Detroit Tigers killed a pigeon with a line drive.

whole format with him, and he was fine with doing everything. Afterward, he asked, "Is there a place where I could warm up?" I said, "Absolutely, let's do this right."

Do you remember when President Bush threw the first pitch after 9/11 prior to the Yankees-Diamondbacks game? President Bush made it a point of wanting to warm up. He warmed up underneath Yankee Stadium. He legitimately warmed up so he could throw a good pitch, which he did. I got one of our coaches and Bryan Holaday, our backup catcher. We went into the batting cages underneath Comerica Park, and he started loosening up. That ball was popping the catcher's mitt. He had some cheese on it. Some guys were there taking some batting practice. It was pretty close to game time. Some players still go in there close to game time to take a few swings. Cabrera and Victor Martinez were in there. They were all making comments and gestures like, "He can bring it." He had good movement on the ball, which shocked the players. That was really cool. You could see he had thrown a baseball before.

We gave Jim a Tigers jersey with his name on the back and the number 4, his number at Michigan. But he wanted to wear Mark Fidrych's number 20. Fidrych and Gates Brown were two of his favorite players when he was growing up. He asked me to hold some of his valuables—wallet, watch, whatever. I said, "Give me your phone. What's your password? Let me take pictures and video for you." Harbaugh is big into social media. I said, "The pictures and video will be on your phone and you'll have them forever." He was all for it, so I was taking pictures of him when he didn't know it, and I captured a lot of his throwing in the batting cage on video. I was right behind the catcher, behind the screen. That's a unique piece of video for him to have.

He chatted with some of the guys in the dugout again and went out and threw a pretty good pitch. He wanted to know if we clocked it. Basically, he was a kid. I found him to be very nice and very genuine. I said, "Are you generally this accommodating on a game day?" He just gave me a look like, oh, no. As far as celebrities go, they don't come much better to work with than Jim Harbaugh. That's the fun part of the job, getting to meet people like Jim.

When he was introduced on the P.A., there was a huge ovation and then applause for his first pitch. He went out there and you could tell he was all business. No surprise there. Whenever he steps foot on a field, he's all business. Generally, the first pitch bounces near the plate. Usually, we have the person stand at the bottom of the mound and not on the rubber. Jim was adamant about pitching from the rubber. He toed the slab and took a full windup and fired one to Brad Ausmus. It was very entertaining.

We had Richard Branson of Virgin Airlines throw out a first pitch one time. He was in town for a business conference, and his representatives asked if he could come out and do something unique. I said, "Well, has he ever thrown a first pitch?" They said, "No, he's never been to a Major League Baseball game." He threw a first pitch, and it was a lot of fun to be around him. The questions he was asking were really entertaining. This guy is worth like $10 billion, and I'm explaining to him how we would cover the field if it rained. Then he's asking if we ever play through the rain and do people stay around for the game? He asked a lot of good questions. He was very inquisitive. We got him to warm up a bit, too. He had never before put on a baseball glove. He wasn't bad. He's in great shape, for his age. He's an outdoors guy. He's a very good athlete. But the mechanics of throwing a baseball aren't always something that comes naturally for someone. He asked, "So where do I throw it?" I said, "Here's what you do. Overcompensate and throw for the chest. Aim that high. Whatever you do, do not bounce it. They don't care how famous you are, they will boo you if you bounce it." He said, "Okay. High." He threw it in the air all the way.

We've had actors, singers, other athletes. We've had Richard Gere. He impressed me. He's a big Yankees fan, but he stopped and bought a Tigers cap off a street vendor on his walk from the hotel. He said, "I want to be respectful. You're hosting us here, and I can't walk in with a Yankees cap." Baseball brings out—the old cliché—it brings out the kid in celebrities, and they're excited. If it's a first pitch, they're nervous about screwing it up. We've had Eminem. We've had Jay-Z. They didn't throw first pitches, but we had them here. They interacted with our players. Our players like meeting them, and our manager does, too. I can tell you this from my years of experience of being around various MLB teams in Detroit, Boston and St. Louis— baseball is actually a religion. There is a different passion. There is a different type of fanaticism, compared to, say, Yankees fans. I've got a treasure chest of history with the Tigers, and I love that part of it.

Jim Harbaugh has brought a real excitement to the whole region. He's the right guy for the Michigan job. He is the guy. Of all of the people on this planet, he's the right guy if you think about it. There's no doubt he's going to win.

As far as first pitches go, the most intense, the most prepared and most determined to succeed? Bingo. Harbaugh.

BIG JON, BIG BAD JON

JON FALK

There are few bigger legends around the Michigan locker room than Jon Falk. Following a 40-year run as Michigan's equipment manager, Falk retired before the 2014 season and wrote a fascinating book, 40 Years in the Big House. *A native of Oxford, Ohio, he was recruited by Bo Schembechler from Miami (Ohio) University in 1974.*

I went to Miami of Ohio when Bo Schembechler was the head coach there. I was working in the equipment room when the head equipment manager passed away in 1968. I was a student, going to school in the morning and taking care of all the equipment in the afternoon. Bo called me into his office one day and said, "Boy, we're going to California and you're the only one I can trust down there, because there is nobody else that knows anything about this equipment. Now, have you ever been to California before?" I said, "No, sir. I never have. I used to go to the Cincinnati stockyards quite a few times." He said, "That's good. You'll fit right in, in **SAN FRANCISCO***. You'll be just fine there." That was my first trip to San Francisco. Bo left, and I graduated. I got hired as equipment manager at Miami in '71. Then in '74, Bo called me to come to Michigan.

One of my duties as equipment manager is turning the locks upside down on the locker if a player is off the team.

****SAN FRANCISCO** Giants ace pitcher Madison Bumgarner dated a girl in high school with the same name—Madison Bumgarner—at South Caldwell (N.C.) High School. Bumgarner is the only ever big leaguer with the first name Madison.*

Whenever I turned a man's lock upside down, that meant he was done at Michigan for awhile, until Bo decided he could come back. Not a lot of people know this, but Jimmy was kicked off the team for awhile. Jimmy did the foreword for my book. The first story is Jimmy talking about being kicked off the team. He wrote, "As a registered sophomore at the University of Michigan in 1984, I was prepared to become the starting quarterback the next season. A ruckus broke out between some of my teammates in the dorm where we were housed. The commotion drew some attention. Unfortunately, some of the details slipped out to Bo Schembechler. Bo was amazing; he seemed like he heard about every little misstep taken by anyone on his team. I can still hear his voice today, 'Harbaugh,' he hissed, 'You're off the team.' And just like that, I was suspended from the team. The experience was something unnerving, to say the least. As spring break drew closer, Big Jon and I drove down to Dayton to see his mother and grandmother who lived there, and then from there we drove over to see Jon's best friend, Bobby Knight. On the drive home, we had some stops and we shared a few things. Jon suggested that things would work out to be fine. Slipped in to see Bo, to say, 'Hey, Bo, this young man has learned his lesson. Don't you think it's time to bring him back?' Bo snapped, 'Bo brings a player back when he thinks it's the right time.' So a few days later, Bo brought me back. I never missed a practice. I have learned a lot from both of these men and a long-time friendship resulted."

The thing is, I grew up with these kids. When I came to Michigan in 1974, I was 23 years old. I lived over at the golf course. The wives of the coaches would have me over to their house, a different coach's wife every night, to have dinner. It ended up that Jackie Harbaugh made some of the best Italian food. I used to go over to the Harbaughs and I got to be real close with John and Jimmy, and Joani. They were in grade school in those days. I knew them really well. Jimmy was always hanging around the locker room. He was like a gym rat. He hung around the locker room all of the time. He loved Rick Leach.

He just had a love fest on Rick Leach. I would always tease him. I'd walk into the locker room and say, "Jimmy, get out of here. Get out of here, Jimmy." He'd be running all around the locker room all of the time.

How did Jimmy come here to play? I went in to see Bo one day. I said, "Bo, I understand that Jimmy Harbaugh went down to Miami of Ohio. He's being recruited by Miami of Ohio." Bo says, "Let me tell you something, Falk. Jim Harbaugh is coming to Michigan. He doesn't know it yet, but he's coming to Michigan." Then, when signing day came, Bo called me in and he says, "Falk, get ready. Jimmy Harbaugh is coming. He's going to be the quarterback at Michigan." I said, "You mean that little kid that used to run around the locker room all of the time?" He said, "It's the same one."

Jimmy ends up coming to Michigan. Bo and I used to go over the numbers every May. Bo would assign the numbers to the players that he wanted to have certain numbers. He didn't want to change a number. After we assigned the numbers, that was it. He always said to me, "Whenever anybody comes up to you, and they want their number changed, you just say, 'This is your number. See you later.'"

Jim tells the story that when he gets on campus, he walks in to see me. He said, "I want number 10." I said, "You're number 4." He said, "Yeah, but I wore 10 in high school and I wore 11 in high school. I know I can't get 11 because it's retired. But I want number 10." I said again, "You're number 4." Later, Jim said, "I went down to talk to Bo. After I talked to Bo, that was the last time I asked about my number. And I was number 4."

During the summer, I would have players work in the building for me. They would paint the rooms and straighten up the chairs. We would get the building ready during the summer for football season the next year. Well, I picked Jimmy to be my supervisor. He was my supervisor of the other three football players. Jamie Morris was one of them. Jimmy would come in to see me every morning, and I would lay out the tasks that needed to be done that day. Jimmy was my best man. One day I told the guys, "Listen, Harbaugh and I have got to go someplace. You guys paint this hall. When I get back, I'd like to have this hallway painted so we can get to the locker room next."

When Jimmy and I got back, they had gotten the wrong paint and the football hall was painted another color than what it was supposed to be. I looked at Jimmy and said, "Jimmy, what are we going to do here?" He said, "It's the workers' fault." I said, "Jimmy, it's our fault. We're in charge. We've got to do this. We've got to straighten this out." The paint was a real dark-colored brown, and we wanted more of a light cream color, so that the walls were bright when you walked in. This brown really made the building dark. Bo never liked to have dark colors. He liked bright colors, so that when you walked down the hall you feel awake and alert, because of the bright colors.

I said, "Bo is coming down here in a few minutes and I promise you the fur is going to fly. Let's start covering this wall up right now." So we all got together and started covering the wall up. Of course, Bo walks in. "Falk, what's going on here? How come the hallway is a different color than what it should be?" I said, "Bo, we are really lucky today. We didn't get to the locker room yet, so we're fine." Bo just looked at me and laughed, and he said, "I want that building painted right." We went ahead. We got all of the walls and everything painted correctly. At the first team meeting, Bo always introduced the workers from the summer. He introduced Jimmy and Jamie and a couple of the other guys there. It might have been Erik Campbell, too. He said, "Men, I want you to thank these four men right here for the work that they've done this summer. They did a great job here in this football building." I'm just sitting back in the corner, laughing.

A few years ago, my wife and I were in Marietta, Ga., and stopped at a restaurant. I walked in, and they had some signs from a restaurant called "Bimbos" that was here in Ann Arbor quite a few years ago. I said to the waitress, "Where did that sign come from?" She said, "The owner's father used to have a restaurant in Ann Arbor, Mich." I said, "Is that right?" Well, just then this guy walks over. His name is Paul Chutich. He comes over to me and he says, "I know you. You're Jon Falk." I said, "Yes." He said, "I was a little boy with Jimmy Harbaugh, and he and I used to run around the locker room after games gathering gloves and wristbands out of the locker room and you would always come in and chase us and run us out." He said, "I remember you." We just laughed at that. I looked at him and I said, "You know what? I remember you now."

In '84 against Michigan State, Jimmy broke his arm. We struggled the rest of that season. We finished the season, but we didn't have a good year. It was the winter of 1985. Jimmy used to come down to the equipment room and he'd say, "Big Jon, now that I got my arm broke nobody wants to talk to me anymore." He said, "I don't even feel a part of the team." I said, "Jimmy, you've got to understand one thing. The train is still rolling down the track. You're just not on the train anymore. That's the way it is. You come in here any time you want, and you and I will sit and talk." So he used to come in quite a bit and visit with me. He was still part of the team. He had somebody to talk to and somebody to share his feelings with. That's the way my job has been here at Michigan. I have always been a guy who shares feelings with all of the players. It's easier for me to deal with it than it is for a coach. I embraced that, and I enjoyed that.

In early 1985, Jim's junior year, I'm driving down I-94. It's about 40 below. Cold. It started to snow. Twice I thought about turning around and going back, but I didn't. I kept driving. All of a sudden, I see a guy thumbing on the side of the road, and I thought, wow, that guy has a hat that is just like Bo's hat. I went a little further and I said, "Wait a minute. That's Bo's car." I pulled off to the side of the road. I walk back, and there is Bo, standing along I-94 heading to Detroit. His nose is red. His cheeks are red. He is shaking like a leaf. He looks at me and he goes, "I was never so happy to see your ugly face." I looked at Bo and I said, "Now, Bo, you better treat me nice. My car is running and it's still warm." I put him in the car. We're driving away and Bo is sitting there. His hands are cold, he's rubbing them. He finally goes, "I want you to know something, Falk. I have been standing on this road for 45 minutes. Not one person stopped. As a matter of fact, three state troopers went by me and they didn't stop." I said, "Well, Bo, you've got to remember one thing: you were 6-6 last season." Bo looked at me and he says, "Why don't you just shut up and get me to the airport. Have my car in the driveway tomorrow morning, running." I said, "I've got plans." Bo says, "Your plans just changed." I dropped Bo off at the airport, and I went back. I called one of my buddies who owns a wrecking place here in town, Brewer's Towing. They got the car towed for me and got it to the repair shop. They repaired it. I went and got it the next morning, and I put it into Bo's driveway before he got back.

In 1986, Bo was going to break the record for most wins at the University of Michigan as the head football coach. The record was 166, and he had 165. We were getting ready to play Minnesota here at Michigan. We were undefeated. No one had really touched us all year. Jimmy came in. He was captain of the team. He said, "Jon, we want to get something special for Bo, and I've collected $500 for this plaque to give to Bo after the Minnesota game." I said, "Okay, Jimmy. We can do that." I went out and bought this really nice plaque. I put "Michigan vs. Minnesota" and the date. "166 wins. Bo Schembechler, winningest coach in the history of Michigan football. Captain James Harbaugh." I had it all. We go out there against Minnesota and we got beat 20-17. After the game, I walk over to Jimmy. He looks at me. He didn't say much. Then a couple of days later at the Monday press conference he says, "I guarantee you that we're going to beat Ohio State this week." They said, "Guarantee?" He says, "I guarantee we are going to beat Ohio State next week."

I saw Bo later that day and said, "Hey, Bo, did you hear about what Jimmy said today?" He said, "Yes." I said, "He guaranteed that we're going to beat Ohio State." He said, "Well, you know what Jon? First of all, he didn't say we were going to lose. That's my boy. That's the way my boy plays football."

Friday, we're driving down to Columbus in the equipment truck. At that time, I didn't have the big semi that had "Michigan" across the side, so nobody knew who we were. We were driving into Columbus, Ohio. When you're from Michigan, that might be the best way to get into Columbus incognito so people don't know who you are. We're heading down this hill in Columbus, and the brakes go out on the truck. We're heading toward the street to get to the stadium. As we're going down this hill, we're pumping the brakes and nothing is happening. There is a problem. We're getting ready to go to Lane Avenue and I see a big semi crossing the street in front of us. All I'm saying is, "Semi, please get into the intersection and then we've got a chance to hit the side of you." Our truck hits the side of the semi and pulls it to the right a little bit. We were okay, and the semi got through. We had to call the Columbus police department. I had my Michigan gear on, and I'm out there talking to the guy. The policeman looks at me and he goes, "What you got in that truck, buddy?" I said, "Well, sir, I've got University of Michigan football gear. We're heading over to Ohio Stadium right now." He goes, "Is Jim Harbaugh's #@$&% on that truck? I said, "Yes sir, it is." He says, "Well, we're going to have to quarantine this truck for the next 48 hours." I looked at him and I said, "Sir, are you kidding?" He looked at me and he shook his fist a little bit and hit my ribs and laughed. We were able to get to the game.

I told Jimmy the whole week before the Ohio State game, I said, "Jimmy, listen, people think the Ohio State-Michigan game is big. But right now, I've just had to redo a $500 plaque that is now up to $600 that we have got to give Bo. We have got to win this game for Bo and the $600 plaque that we've got the money into." He said, "Don't worry, Big Jon. I'll take care of it." When we took the field against Ohio State, I never saw a player get booed, harassed and just treated like the devil like Jimmy Harbaugh that day. We fell behind 14-3, and we came back to beat them, 26-24. Jimmy Harbaugh is a great leader, and he was able to hold onto that team and bring them back.

I tell people the difference between the two Harbaugh boys is John Harbaugh is the type of guy who will go and out-work you, but he'll never say a word to you. He will go out, and he will beat you. He will outwork you and beat you. Jimmy Harbaugh is the type of guy that he'll look you in the eye and he'll tell you, "I'm going to beat you." And then he'll outwork you, and then he'll beat you. That's the difference between the two guys. Jimmy wants you to know that he's going to beat you. Jimmy Harbaugh is like a stallion. The one thing I've learned about great athletes is all great athletes are like stallions. They know they're good, they know they've got talent. The last thing you want to do with a stallion is break him down. Because once you break him down, he becomes a circus ride for kids at the fair. You want to let that stallion run and jump and kick his heels and bellow. When people know that he walks on the field and walks into that field, every horse in there—every per-son there—knows, "I run this place. This is my field." That's the way Jimmy Harbaugh is. He's a stallion, through and through. I love the kid. He treats me great here. I've told him I'll do any-thing I can do to help him and Michigan football. Jimmy is really grateful for that, and I am too, because that's the way I was raised.

I've got 17 Big Ten championship rings, and people always ask me which ring is my best ring. I always tell them my best ring is going to be my next ring. Tom Brady loved that. Every time I walked into the locker room he said, "Hey, Big Jon, which one is your best ring?" I said, "My best ring is my next ring, Tommy." When Brady won his second Super Bowl ring some press guy says, "Hey, Tom, you've won two world championships now.

Which one is your best one?" Tommy said, "You know what? We've got an equipment guy back in Michigan by the name of Big Jon with 17 Big Ten championship rings. I always asked him which ring was his best ring and he always said, 'My best ring is going to be my next ring.' That's pretty much the way I feel."

Jack Harbaugh was here. He came up from Iowa in '73. I met him in '74. They lived over at the golf course for a time, but they weren't living there when I came in '74. The golf course clubhouse had little rooms upstairs, where they had little cubicles with beds. I'm not going to say it was the best place in the world, but that's where people stayed when they first got here. Then an apartment opened up downstairs. Bo got me that apartment downstairs. It had a kitchen, a living room with a **TV***, a bathroom and a bedroom. That's where I lived. Jimmy and his family moved out, and they got a house. The whole Harbaugh family lived over at the golf course before I got there. Jim tells a story that when he lived there, the golf course had a driving range where you drove golf balls into a net. He and John would go down there every night and play and hit golf balls into that net. Jim plays golf all the time.

When I first knew Jim, he was a gym rat. He was everywhere. He loved athletics. He was a little kid that had a lot of confidence in himself. He was fun to be around. We used to laugh at him all of the time. We would walk onto the practice field. There would be Jimmy out there, sitting on the field waiting for football practice to start. Sometimes he'd get in the way of a drill or something and Bo would go, "Will you get that kid out of that drill? Get that kid out of that drill." Bo loved Jimmy

---

*In 1994, Terry Bradshaw and Jim Harbaugh were in an episode of the **TV** series *The Adventures of Brisco County, Jr.* Bradshaw played a colonel and Harbaugh was one of his men, Mason "Cowboy" Dixon.... In 1996, Harbaugh appeared as himself in *Saved by the Bell: The New Class*.

Harbaugh. He loved him. Now, was he hard on him? Yes. He was hard on him.

When Jim was young, he'd come into the equipment room. He'd come into the locker room. He would horse around, and all the players would tease him. He was just a guy that wanted to be around the locker room all of the time. It was fun. He was a fun pest to have around. We used to tease him and joke with him, run him out of the locker room. "Get out of here, Harbaugh. You little so-and-so, get out of here. Go home."

You could see his leadership begin to develop big in 1985. We had a decent club then, but we lost to Iowa in Iowa City on a late field goal. We were ranked No. 2 and they were No. 1. We went on to play Nebraska in the Fiesta Bowl. They had a great team that year. We were down 14-3 at the half. We just couldn't move the ball. Jimmy Harbaugh went around to all of those players at the half and talked to them about getting back in the game. He said, "I'm going to play my best game this half, and I want you guys to play your best game, too." We came back the second half with a different attitude. We came back and beat them, 27-23. The players looked up to Jimmy. That's what leadership is.

I'll be honest with you, he had some of the same qualities that Tom Brady's got—lots of similarities with Tommy Brady. Both of them love to play the game. Both of them have a work ethic that is unbelievable. They're the first ones in, and they're the last ones to leave. They get along well with the players. The players respected them and looked up to them. That's what I always noticed about Tom Brady and Jimmy Harbaugh. Every one of those players looked up to them. They looked to them for the leadership. They looked to them to lead them where they wanted the team to go. Both of them are great team guys. That's the biggest similarity.

Bo used to read something called "The Penalty of Leadership," that was written back in 1915 by the Cadillac Motor

Company. He would read it to the team every year. It started out, "In every field of human endeavour, he that is first must perpetually live in the white light of publicity. Whether the leadership be vested in a man or in a manufactured project, emulation and envy are ever at work...If his work be mediocre, he will be left severely alone—if he achieves a masterpiece, it will set a million tongues a-wagging." And you know what? That's true. Take a look at what Jim has done at San Diego, Stanford and San Francisco. Is there anybody out there that can match what's happened there?

I knew that Harbaugh was a determined guy. Don't you think he learned an awful lot from Mike Ditka? I saw Mike Ditka a few years ago, down in Chicago. He's not afraid to tell you what he thinks. He said, "That Harbaugh was one of the toughest kids that I ever coached. He may have been one of the hardest kids I ever coached, but he was one of the toughest kids I ever coached."

I'm not surprised by any success that Jimmy Harbaugh has. That's the type of guy he is. You knew when he left Michigan he was moving on to success. You just didn't know how big or how far he was going to go—to be able to come back to the University of Michigan to coach the University of Michigan football team. What a complete cycle a man could have, to be able to have the legend of his dad, and his dad coaching here. Of course, John grew up here, too. The memories that Jack Harbaugh must have, his family to turning out like they have. Isn't that great?

There are so many different deals out there, you never know how things are going to go. But I had hoped that Harbaugh was going to take the job the first time in Michigan. But it didn't work out that way. Now, this second time—sometimes things turn out to be the way they should be. Just like Bo not beating Minnesota to break the record for most wins at Michigan—he had to break it against Ohio State. Maybe, sometimes the timing just works out. Maybe it's time for Jimmy Harbaugh to come back and help bring Michigan football back to the forefront.

A HARD WAY TO MAKE AN EASY LIVING

LEIGH STEINBERG

Leigh Steinberg was the real-life inspiration for the sports agent in the film Jerry Maguire. *Steinberg, 66, has represented more than 300 professional athletes during his 41-year career. A graduate of Cal-Berkeley, Steinberg lives in Newport Beach, Calif. He was Jim Harbaugh's first agent.*

In 1987, Jim was a big star at Michigan. He and I conversed about representation. Our practice has always been based on role models, players who are willing to retrace their roots to the high school, collegiate and professional community and make an impact—so we look for brighter, more socially aware players. Quarterbacks have always been my specialty. I've had 60 first-round draft picks in the NFL, and eight of them were the first overall pick in the whole draft. One time I had 22 NFL quarterbacks—Troy Aikman, Warren Moon, Steve Young, Drew Bledsloe, Jake Plummer, Mark Brunell and on and on.

Jim fit what was I was looking for perfectly. Handsome. Really bright. Great family, great parents—Jack and Jackie. He was a prototypical model for what we looked for, which is, he played the key position, which meant that his profile would be higher. He was telegenic, he was funny. As a matter of fact, the later Jim Harbaugh of the San Francisco era, I just don't recognize, from the years I've spent with him. Jim had a hilarious sense of humor. He had the ability to laugh at himself. He had perspective. He was a fiery competitor on the field. I saw a much looser, warmer Jim Harbaugh. But of course, that's my role.

When I went back to meet with him in '87, I flew into the Detroit airport, went to Ann Arbor, and I kept calling his number. No one answered. I knocked on his door. I kept knocking and knocking. All of a sudden, the door creaks open, like it's a crypt keeper. Jim is dressed in a sheet, and he's perspiring. This little creaky voice says, "Yeah? Who's there?" I said, "Jim, it's Leigh." He said, "I'm really sick. I don't feel well." I said, "I understand, but I've come all the way here thinking we could meet." He rallied, as he always did. It turned out he was in the early stage of chicken pox. We sat, and he was very impressive, extremely bright, very ambitious. It was a fit from the start. Jim and I had a series of talks. He was very cautious. I spent time with his family, back and forth. Those were days when people felt a real pressure to make agent decisions. Today, because the agents pay for training in January, they decide very quickly. But back then, players would take a leisurely amount of time prior to the draft.

He got drafted in the first round before he asked me to represent him. He goes up on draft day to Chicago, to do the traditional draft day interviews. He has chicken pox. I asked one of the reporters how he did, and he said, "Gosh, he'd be really handsome if he did something about his complexion." That was Jim, always up to the challenge. Some people would have said, "I can't come. I'm too sick. I look too unsightly." But Jim has a rough and ready aspect to him. He might recognize a challenge, but he'll just go ahead and do it. That comes a lot from being the son of a coach and the brother of a coach. He was bought up with great fundamental values.

Now we go into the negotiation process. Today, you have slotting, so players sign more rapidly. Back then, in 1987 (the year he signed), you might remember that was the year of the strike. Five of the players in the first round didn't even sign until after the strike was over. It tended to be holdout time, for most of the first rounders. We started negotiating with Ted Phillips of the Bears. This was Ted's first first-round contract.

The negotiations got long and prolonged. At one point, I had an associate helping me. I negotiated until about 11:00 at night. Then Jeff Moorad, who later became my partner, took over. I said, "You've got to take this now. I've got to go home." I went home. I came back about 7:00 or so the next morning and they're still talking.

I knew that Mike Ditka was a ticking time bomb. The key to a quarterback having any chance to make it with Ditka is being there on time and taking the snaps from the start. I knew we really didn't have the option to have Jim late. At some point, Ditka was going to explode and that would then impact the beginning of their relationship. Ditka had no room for agents, no room for contracts. His players were already there and so in we go. He could be pretty explosive.

Training camp opened, and I said, "Jim, look, we've just got to drive up there." A player is not allowed in training camp without a signed contact, so he can't even be physically present. Nonetheless, I said, "We don't have time to waste here. Let's just go up there. We'll put you in a hotel. I'll try to finish it with Ted." I met Jim in Chicago, where he already had an apartment. We drove up to Platteville, Wisconsin. Now, this is before all of the terrorists, guns and craziness. I said, "Let's do something funny." I said, "Let's dress up like we're '30s Chicago gangsters, and we'll invade Ted's office with plastic guns that look like machine guns." Today you wouldn't do something like that, because of all of the horrible things that have happened with guns. But then it was an easier time. We drove up. As we're going through Dubuque, Iowa, there was a tornado warning. "I hope this is not symbolic." We kept driving, and we finally got up to Platteville. Jim and I drove to the practice facility. We burst into Ted's office and pelted him with water guns. In a way it broke the ice, okay? So instead of this being a tense situation, it got more relaxed. Jim left. I finished the contract. He didn't miss any training camp, except the first few hours. He didn't miss any time on the field. That started him in Chicago.

Chicago is the most passionate pro football town in America. Notwithstanding the success of the Bulls, the Chicago Bears are the No. 1 passion. Jim had come from Michigan, so it all was a marriage made in heaven. Then there was Ditka. Had it been somebody else than Jim Harbaugh, the first-round quarterback in that situation would have self-destructed. Ditka was so verbal and screamed at Jim every time he made an error. But Jim, because he was a coach's son and had grown up in Bo's system, could handle that without it being personalized. In other words, he didn't internalize Ditka's loud yelling as some fundamental rejection of him. I saw that quality in him, which was an amazing quality, particularly, when you're sitting in front of passionate fans and a coach that is highly verbal and critical. Yet, he did fine. He was very popular in the city. At that point, he had a girlfriend, but Jim was a matinee idol—women swooned over him. Every time we'd go out in Chicago, there would be a heavy rush that would happen in the restaurant or bar, or wherever. We would be festooned. Women would hand him their phone numbers. Women were just lined up to try to meet him. Men, too. He has always been a man's man.

Jim Harbaugh was very interested in a variety of other topics. He was interested in politics and culture and a whole bunch of things. Our discussions went far beyond the reach of simply football. We talked about social issues and politics and sociology and movies. He loved movies, music, all sorts of things. He had a very eclectic group of interests. On the field, he was all football and passing, and all the rest of it.

Jim had a propensity and had the quality that separates great quarterbacks from average ones. In critical situations, faced with adversity—you've thrown a couple of interceptions, the crowd is booing and the game looks out of hand. The offensive linemen are looking back and wondering what substance the quarterback is high on. In that situation, Jim had the ability to compartmentalize and adopt a quiet mind and elevate his level of play to a high level. For example, there was one game against the New York Jets. It was *Monday Night Football*. The game either went to overtime or it came down to the end—every play was critical. Jim was always at his best in adversity, when the game was on the line. If you're looking for a franchise quarterback, you look for someone you can build a team around for 10 or 12 years. Someone that you can win because of rather than with, and someone who ultimately has the capacity to elevate his level of play at critical times and take the team on his back. Jim could do that.

He led a series of comebacks over the years and played for teams that had mixed success, but it wasn't really his fault. He had a great time in Chicago. He had a tremendous amount of friendships. You talked with him after a game, and the things that would bother somebody else didn't really bother him internally. He could, again, compartmentalize and get rid of every other thought in his head except success. The Bears didn't have a totally stunning cast of characters around him. They didn't have great receivers. In many ways, they were still a running team. We hadn't seen the complete advent of the modern passing game yet.

He was much in demand for endorsements. He was much in demand for speaking. Even when the team wasn't doing well, he remained a popular figure, because he was perpetually optimistic and upbeat. In competition, he turned into an alpha male, like the proverbial junkyard dog who would never give up, would never stop trying. Again, those were qualities that came from his upbringing and experience.

Jim kept a set of pretty eclectic friends. One of his friends was the assistant to retired Ronald Reagan when he was in Century City. He had a bunch of friends who were not in football. One of his best friends, Dave Feldman, was in broadcasting and now is on Comcast. He knew people in politics. He knew people in media. He knew people everywhere outside of football.

To this day, he is still the only player that called in the Jim Rome show during the Smackoff. Jim Rome has a very popular national radio show. The whole goal of the Smackoff segment is to call in when you have a strong opinion and can express it in a colorful way. At the end of the year, they would have a final Smackoff competition. The callers would call in to see who, in three minutes, could do the most interesting, well spoken take on sports. Jim actually called in and participated in the Smackoff. He had all sorts of interests, and he had a good enough mind that I know he would have been very successful in business. He would have been great in broadcast. He was very high spirited. His teammates loved him at the Bears. They loved him at the Colts and loved him at San Diego.

This imagery that occurred later, of him as a sort of mad scientist who was alienated from people and who didn't have any people skills—I didn't see that. The Jim Harbaugh I knew totally understood how to relate to a coach, totally understood how to relate to teammates, understood it was a team game and had very strong relationships with teammates and other people. He was considered highly approachable. He was considered the one player on the team you could just always rely on. He was never going to quit, and he was never going to stop trying to get better.

He went to Indianapolis, where he got the nickname "Captain Comeback," because he led them in the playoffs in a whole series of drives that essentially could have gone either way— but he made them go well. Did he have the strongest passing arm in the NFL? Probably not, but he was really smart and he had good control of the game. He could pass well, and he had mobility. He had the ability to run, escape from the pocket and all the rest of it. When things looked dire, he was the speck of brightness. He had great leadership qualities. He was willing to give up his body, he was willing to do anything to make the team more successful. That period went well. Then he ended up at San Diego. At that point, he was more a backup QB, and he wanted to coach. Experts say that stars have problems coaching, because big stars can do things so effortlessly that they have little tolerance, in most cases, for the barriers and foibles of players that they coach. They get frustrated because they, as players, could do what they're asking their current players to do—and in a way, they just don't understand that sometimes people are not as talented or worse, far worse, they won't make the maximum effort. For Jim Harbaugh, you would have thought that someone who had that high level of intelligence and could master a playbook effortlessly—could he coach people that couldn't? Could he coach people of lesser talent? Would he have the patience? Now, he would always be fiery. I knew he'd be a great coach, because he had grown up in the game. He had a mastery of the inherent understanding of how football is played. He understood passing offense in a quarterback situation. Plus, he'd grown up in that hard-knuckled Mike Ditka run, run game, so he had an appreciation for running the football, that you had to control the line of scrimmage. You have to insert your will by running and grinding down the other team and then by innovation.

He was willing to coach at the University of San Diego, which was not a highly touted major college program. He was very successful. When he went to Stanford, that was a perfect fit. Jim was in high school while his father was coaching John Elway at Stanford. He could relate to players who were intellectually bright, but—like him—had a sheer drive to succeed and were willing to play physical football. All football is physical, but the point is, there are programs that are more finesse than physical. Jim's concept from Michigan and the Chicago Bears was ram it down their throats and be physically active on defense. I knew that would be a major success, because Jim Harbaugh walking into a parent's front room would be, for most parents, like a dream come true. Here is this movie star handsome, extremely bright, extremely enthusiastic person telling a parent that he will take care of their son. He would be really hard to compete with. And he was offering a scholarship to Stanford for a world-class education that leads to networking. Stanford is a very tight network. Michigan is a tight network. Stanford does what some of the public schools don't do, which is that the alums mentor the students and help them in their careers. He had all that going and a great offensive tradition. I knew he would be a major success.

Then he goes to the 49ers. He executes one of the fastest turnarounds imaginable. The 49ers had shifted then, so it's not Eddie DeBartolo and Carmen Policy, as it was for many years. Those two ran the highest quality organization in football. Players loved to go there. Eddie DeBartolo lavished love and **FINANCIAL*** riches on the players. They had superb coaching. Carmen Policy was a wizard as a general manager. But DeBartolo got in trouble in Louisiana with the bribe on the gambling deal, and the trade-off was that he had to give up what he really loved, the 49ers. He flipped that with his sister, who was running the shopping center empire. He took that, and she ended up owning the team. She is married to former physician, John York, and he became the owner. Now his son started to aspire power. In other words, the 49ers are/were DeBartolo. He took the players to Las Vegas at the end of the year, gave them gambling chips. When they went to the Super Bowl, they had two airplanes, all first class. Not only did they take the players, he took the families. He housed their families. Everything they did was first class. When Jim got there, it was a different atmosphere. They had Trent Baalke as general manager. From their standpoint, they felt that Jim pushed them really hard and was never satisfied with the facilities, with the rules, with the whatever. Jim's standpoint was everything that he was pushing for

---

*****Sports Illustrated** reports that 78 percent of NFL players are bankrupt or in serious **FINANCIAL** stress within two years of retirement . . . 60 percent of all NBA players are broke within five years of retirement.

was in the best interest of the players and the success of the team. He got there, and they had extraordinary success and he ended up playoff, playoff, Super Bowl, and all the rest. His last year, they suffered terrible defensive injuries. They lost more players than was imaginable. They didn't do so well on the field. Then the front office felt like he was pushing them, and it wasn't comfortable. Then they essentially made moves without him.

That is not the Jim Harbaugh I knew. It's also not the Jim Harbaugh I represented. I didn't do his coach contract. The Jim Harbaugh I knew would come to me and say, "Here is the problem." We'd talk it out. He was pragmatic in understanding how to get things done. He has every option in the world. If you can discount what the 49ers saw as his unmanageability, which I never saw, then every team in the league would want him as a coach. He has not failed at anything he has ever done. He has always created a big turnaround. He made a tough choice to elevate Colin Kaepernick over Alex Smith, and it worked. Kaepernick fell back last year. Kaepernick reminded Jim Harbaugh of himself—rough and ready, pulling plays out of some bodily orifice. He really flourished when Jim put him in charge.

SOMETIMES GOD JUST HANDS YA ONE

WILLIE TAGGART

Willie Taggart is the head football coach at the University of South Florida. He replaced Tommie Frazier as quarterback at the perennial Florida prep power-house Manatee High in Bradenton, Fla. Frazier quarterbacked one of the greatest college teams ever at Nebraska.

I'll tell you what, the Harbaugh family is the best. They are the best. They helped mold and shape the life of Willie Taggart. In the spring of '94, my senior year in high school, I came home from track practice. My sister told me that a guy by the name of Jim Harbaugh called and wanted to talk to me. He was at Western Kentucky University. Jim Harbaugh. The only Jim Harbaugh I know plays for the Chicago Bears, so it can't be that Jim Harbaugh.

At the time, my family didn't have long distance, so I had to go to a pay phone and call collect. Back then you could. I went to a pay phone and called and said, "Can I speak to Jim Harbaugh?" He was like, "Speaking." I said, "This is Willie Taggart from Manatee High School returning your phone call." We started talking. Then he asked me if I knew who he was. I said, "The only Jim Harbaugh I know plays for the Chicago Bears." He was like, "That's me." I was like, "Yeah, right." He said, "No, I'm serious. This is me. I'm helping my dad. He's the head coach here at Western Kentucky." Then Jim put his dad on the phone, who explained.

To be honest with you, I still thought it was a joke. I remember it like it was yesterday. Jim said, "I'm coming to your school on Tuesday—around lunchtime—to meet you." I went to school the next day and told my high school coach what had happened, and I had him check to see if that was legit. He came back and said, "Well, his dad does coach at Western Kentucky." Sure enough, that Tuesday at lunchtime, I was eating lunch in the lunchroom and who comes around the corner? It's Jim Harbaugh and another coach.

It was actually a pretty cool day for me. My best friend played on my team, and he was known as "Mr. Football," so he was the big man on campus. But that day, I was. Jim came in, and everyone was looking. I had told everyone what had happened. So I was hoping that he would show up. Sure enough, he did. We went into the field house, and we were talking ball. By the time we came out of the field house, there were about 25, 30 or 40 people outside with their Michigan and Chicago Bears hats, wanting autographs. I'm standing there next to Jim Harbaugh. I thought I was a big man. From that day on, it just has been great. He hit it off with my family. He's been a great mentor, a great role model for me, to be honest with you, ever since that day. I tell everyone, ever since that day, my life has been going nowhere but up.

I really got into coaching because of Jim and his dad, and his brother. Just the way they treated me, the way they guided me, the way they mentored me—to help me see and help me get where it was I was trying to get to, and to see how to get it. My whole perspective on life and what I can do changed when I got around them and what they showed me. That's when I decided that I wanted to coach myself. Like what they did to me, I could do it to a lot of other people. Jim and I became the best of friends. That was the first time for me personally that someone outside of my family really cared about me as a person, not what I can do as an athlete, but as a person. Jim always called and checked on me, even when I got to Western Kentucky. He would still check on me and see how I was doing—see how I was doing in school, just making sure I was doing what I was supposed to do. That was big time.

He was the best man at my wedding. I was in his wedding. I would give my right arm for Jim Harbaugh, Jack Harbaugh, the whole Harbaugh family. I'm in debt to that family, and they mean the world to me.

All the former players that I played with, that we coached—all of them feel the same way I do about Jack. At the time, they probably didn't like him. But as they got older, they appreciated everything he taught them, because they're using it in their life and with their families. That's what is great to see and great to hear, that Coach Harbaugh—I'm talking Jack—touched a lot of people's lives and changed a lot of people. That's what coaching is all about. I try to emulate both of those guys all of the time. I want to be like them.

I wouldn't call myself a "hotshot," but I took care of business. I played behind Tommie Frazier in high school. He was a senior and I was a sophomore. I was his backup. Then I started one game my sophomore year, the first time a sophomore ever started for our high school. We won that game. Tommie Frazier didn't like that too well. He said, "You better like it now, because I'll be back next week." I learned I had to go out and take care of business. We ended up winning a state championship my junior year. I don't know if I was a hotshot or not, but I was one of those guys that helped the team win.

I was recruited by many schools. I had a chance to go to Nebraska. I didn't want to. Every year somebody from Manatee High School was going to Nebraska. Every single year. Every year. Growing up, my ideal school was Florida State. I wanted to go there and play for them. But as I got older, and really, once I met Jim, that changed everything, my whole perspective on things. My entire life I always depended upon my mom and dad to help me. I figured I couldn't go away to school somewhere where nobody was going to help me. I wasn't ready to do it by myself. Then getting to know Jim—and we became close—and it was like that friend I needed. Jim and

Jack, they cared. They were going to punish me when I needed to be punished, but they were going to love me when I needed to be loved. They were going to help me grow. It was easily one of the best decisions I ever made in my life.

I had never heard of Western Kentucky. Never, ever, ever. That's the beauty of it all. I keep going back and saying how I'm in debt to the Harbaugh family. They came down to Palmetto, Fla., and recruited me to go to Western. I met my wife in school. Beautiful kid. It just couldn't have been any better than what it has been.

When Jim came to my school that day, he started talking about Western; he talked about what they were going to do. He did a lot of talking about him and who he was—not just the football player, but Jim Harbaugh the person and what he was about. He explained what his dad was trying to get accomplished there at Western. Then going up and meeting his dad, it just felt right. It felt genuine. A lot of my recruiting—the way that I recruit to this day—is how Jim Harbaugh recruited me. Everything was just real and how it was supposed to be. That's the beauty of Jim Harbaugh—you don't get any untruths from him. Everything about Jim Harbaugh is real, and you appreciate that. That's why the players appreciate playing for him, because they know they're going to get it real and not...uncut.

They flew me up. They had a recruiting budget—it wasn't that big. But they flew us up. Bowling Green, Ky., was great. I had a ball. The players were nice. It was cold. I wasn't used to that. The players were cool, and the coaches were cool. I just felt at home. I was one of those guys that I didn't need all of that limelight and adulation. I just wanted to be somewhere where I could be comfortable and be successful. I knew the only way to do that was to be around good people.

Jim came down sometimes. We used to love that. We ran the option at Western Kentucky, and when Jim came down, especially in the springtime, all of the players enjoyed that, because they knew we were going to throw the ball a lot more. When he came down in the spring, we changed our offense to the "high pro set," and we were throwing the ball big time. One time, an offensive lineman got knocked back and rolled into my knee, and I tore my medial meniscus and that was it for the high pro. We got back to running football after that.

The best tip Jim ever gave me was, "Fear no man, no circumstances, no other program." Be true to who you are. You don't have to change for anyone.

Jim came to a couple of games. He was at a couple of games throughout the year during the off week. We played Indiana State in Terre Haute, and he drove over from Indianapolis. He went to Marshall when we played there. Usually when he had an off week, he'd come down to our game.

Jim's coaching style was not as much hands on, because he wasn't there long. But when he was there, he wanted to see a pass play. So, he'd go in the staff meeting and draw up a pass play, and Coach Harbaugh—his dad—would let him run a couple of plays and we'd go out and try to get it accomplished.

Playing for Jack Harbaugh was awesome. He would make you want to run through a wall—run through anything—when he spoke to you. He had no problem getting you ready for a game. You get one of those speeches, you're ready to go. You better not dare give less than 100 percent. He'd talk to you, and he'd get so excited and motivated that he would accidentally spit on you while he was talking, especially if you were sitting up front. He would spit on you because he's tall and he's so passionate. One day, one of the guys tried to wipe it off, and he was like, "Don't wipe it off! I know I spit on you!"

I'll tell you a great Jack Harbaugh story. I thought it was one of his best coaching jobs, at least for me. It was my senior year. You'll get a kick out of this. We played the University of South Florida—where I'm working now. My senior year, we played South Florida down here in Tampa. I grew up about 45 minutes from here. I had a family reunion at the game. Everybody was there. My high school coach brought his team. Just everybody was there. It was the first time I played in the state of Florida since high school. It was a big game for me. South Florida was undefeated at the time. They had a really good defense. That first quarter, I was just playing bad. I wasn't playing myself. We ran the option one time. I went to pitch the ball to the back, and it was tipped and was an interception. USF goes on to score. Now we're down 17-0. They intercepted the ball and as I'm getting off the ground, I look over and I see Coach Harbaugh walking down the sideline. I'm like, uh-oh, he's going to chew me out in front of all of my friends. They were sitting right behind the bench. This is not good. I thought I was slick. I tried to go around our players to get to the bench. He cut through the players and met me. He stood there. Oh, boy. He is getting ready to give it to me. He looked at me and he looked me in the eye and said, "I'm not mad at you. You're back home in front of your family and your friends and you're just not playing like you normally play. But you're a great player and you'll lead us to victory today. It's gonna be the greatest game of your life!" All the weight just came off my shoulders. Wow. I was expecting the worst, and he went totally opposite of what I expected. That next series, I just took off. I had my best game ever. We came back and won the game. I threw for three touchdowns, rushed for 205 yards and had the game-winning touchdown. It was all because he went the total opposite of what I expected. I thought that was a big-time coaching move by him. It really made me loosen up and play better. That was pretty cool. After that game, I was in hog heaven. Everybody was around. My mom actually brought over a nice red velvet cake for me. I had it on the plane, and everybody wanted a piece. No! It was great. We stayed an extra night down here when we came down. That was fun. That was really fun.

My first year at Western Kentucky, we were 2-8. Then the second year, we were 7-4. The third year, we went 10-2 and went to the AA playoffs for the first time. Things just got better.

It got better because of Jim—not only did he recruit me, but he recruited a lot of other talented kids from down here each year. He recruited a lot of kids. I'll tell you what, the year that we won the national championship at Western, we probably had about 15 kids on that team that Jim Harbaugh recruited personally. Do you remember the XFL, when they had that kid, "He Hate Me" Rod Smart? "He Hate Me." That was one of Jim Harbaugh's guys. He's living in North Carolina now and he's actually doing films, trying to do movies and act.

Jim and I became close throughout the years. Our relationship just grew. Any opportunity I could get around him I would go, just to be around him. He was life changing for me. Ever since I met him, my life has been going nowhere but up. You talk about best friends? He became my best friend and I wanted him to be in my wedding. Sure enough, he was in it. It was one heck of a wedding, too. It was fun. He made it fun and he made it funny. He had me at ease. I wasn't nervous or anything. He was fun. Even during the wedding, when my wife opened the door and you can hear this "whew." I look back and I see the bride and her father coming down the aisle, and Jim was standing next to me, like, "You're sure you want to do this? I've got a car running outside right now." He made it really lighthearted and made it easy for me. It was pretty cool.

I was not surprised at all when Jim Harbaugh went into coaching. His first coaching job was with the Raiders. I was an intern for the Raiders at the same time. It was awesome, one of the best experiences I've had in my coaching career. That was my first internship, and it was his first coaching job.

I'll tell you a quick story. It's pretty cool. I was at the NFL Combine with Jim and John. They invited me up there with them. I was coaching at Western at the time. John was introducing me to everyone. He introduced me to a couple of GMs and coaches, really trying to help me get an internship. I knew Jim had an interview with Al Davis that same day. We were walking around, and while I'm with these guys, I'm hearing all of these

Al Davis stories. They really had me scared of Al Davis. You just hear all of the stories of how he is as a person. All of these stories. Then at the Combine, Al Davis and his GM were sitting there, and nobody was within 20 feet around them. You're seeing all of this, and you're like, geez, I don't ever want to be around this guy. We're walking, and the Harbaughs started talking to someone. I said, "Guys, I'll be right back. I'm going to the rest-room." I went in the bathroom and Al Davis is in there with a lot of coaches. I'm in there. I'm like, wow, here is an owner of an NFL team. This is *the* Al Davis. You hear all these stories. I used the restroom and by the time I finished, it was just me and Al Davis in the bathroom. I'm saying to myself, should I say something to him or should I just let it be? I'm scared he's going to go off and do something weird. I don't know where I got it from, but I just thought, you know what? Heck with it. I went over and introduced myself. "Hi, Mr. Davis. How you doing? I'm Willie Taggart and I'm a coach at Western Kentucky University. I just wanted to introduce myself to you." He was like, "I know where that is. Jack Harbaugh is the coach there. Do you know his son, Jimmy? I'm going to interview Jimmy in a little bit." That's cool. After that, he asked me, "Have you ever coached in the NFL before?" My heart dropped. Whoa. I said, "No, sir. But I am looking to try to get an internship." By that time, I had met probably three or four GMs and some coaches. They all knew I wanted an internship and I was trying to get one. I had interviews lined up with the Panthers and with the Raiders. I got the one with the Raiders because of Al Davis. In the restroom. It worked out for him to know I wanted to get an internship. "I'm sure I can help you with that," he said. I gave him my card. Then I saw him put my card in his wallet, where the dollar bills go. I thought, "He's going to see that again." I felt good about that. Sure enough, I got an internship. When I came out of the bathroom, I saw Jim and John. I said, "You guys won't believe what just happened to me." I told them the story and Jim was like, "Damn, Willie, you're about to get the job I'm trying to get." He laughed.

Jim was assistant coach and I was with the coaching staff. I was working with the quarterbacks with Coach Marc Trestman at the time. Jim was quality control. Boy, they worked Jim a lot at that point. You could tell that Jim had so much knowledge. In a staff meeting, Jim was speaking up and really challenging the coaches even though he was an unpaid assistant. They'd ask him a question and he'd respond, holding no punches. We had some conflict going on in there, a good conflict, back and forth. I tell you what, between Coach Bill Callahan and Jim, when they talked about the two-minute drill, I learned so much about the two-minute offense just from that conversation they had. It was really interesting, and it was a point that I had never thought about before. Wow, these guys were something else. It was awesome. You watch all of the other coaches...it was like him and Bill, really, with all the discussion—this was big time. Jim opened a lot of eyes of a lot of people that day in that room. But you knew he was going to be a great coach.

He is a great coach. He's a leader of men. He's a great leader of men. That entire family is. The apple doesn't fall too far from the tree.

I'm never surprised with Jim Harbaugh. You never bet against him, either. He's going to win. He's such a believer. He went out to the University of San Diego and he did a good job. He actually wanted me to come there with him, but I couldn't from a financial standpoint. San Diego. I just couldn't make that. As soon as he got the job with Stanford, he brought me along with him. He was in for some other jobs, and I knew I was going to go with him, but once he got that, he brought me with him. I was out there at Stanford with him the first three years. That was awesome. I learned a lot of football, really learned how to run a football program. We were able to turn that program around because of Jim. He just changed everybody's attitude and the way they thought of Stanford. You always heard people say it's hard to win at Stanford because of the academic standards. You can't get the great athletes in there because of the admissions. Not one time did you ever hear Jim make an excuse for that. He made sure that everybody in that office and that building didn't make an excuse for it. Jim was like, "That's a bunch of malarkey. There are players out there who can get into Stanford, but they're going to Florida, they're going to USC, they're going to those schools when they should be coming here. We've got to find those guys and get them here." He was adamant about it. He held all of us accountable to do it. Not going to make any excuses, because there are guys out there that should be here. Not only did we get out, but Jim was out recruiting all over.

I am a pretty good recruiter, but it doesn't get any better than Jim Harbaugh. He is just a genuine person. He is just a genuine, good person. You meet him, and he just makes you feel like you've known him forever. He is unbelievable. When we were at Stanford, we were going on a home visit and Jim looked in the refrigerator. He looked in the kid's refrigerator and saw that it had whole milk instead of skim milk, and he told the kid's dad, "That's my kind of guy—a whole milk guy." You have got to be kidding me! You're in the house looking in the fridge? It was just so different, where the kid is looking like, wow! Jim was just Jim. He doesn't try to be anything else. He'll wrestle around with the dog. He'll spend the night at the kid's house. He'll do it all. Jim goes above and beyond. He is so good at thinking outside the box. Sometimes Jim will come up with an idea, and a normal person would just be like, "Come on, Coach. That's not...you can't do that." Jim will always say, "You know I'm right." Sure enough, he is. It always works.

Our first year at Stanford, they were coming off of a 1-11 season. It was springtime and that's when he made the comment, "We bow down to no man and no program." That was relating to USC. The media made it bigger than what it was between Jim and Pete Carroll. They tried to make it sound like Jim was going back on his word. He immediately said again, "We bow down to no man and no program here at Stanford."

The next day, it was big, bold print in the paper. USC had all of these All-Americans that year on their team.

That was the turning point of Stanford football. That statement was back in the spring of that first year. That was the turning point because before everyone was afraid of USC and didn't think Stanford could do this and do that. Jim was totally the opposite. He believed, and he got everybody else to believe. It was amazing in that game, because we had lost our star quarterback the Sunday before we played them. We still won that game at USC. It was all just on the belief of the head coach, and he got everybody to believe. It was the turning point. It was truly one of the biggest upsets in the history of college football.

Another good one is that spring we played softball against our players—coaching staff versus the players. We beat the players. Now Coach is going to let you know when he beats you. He lets you know. The players didn't like it. They were hot. They were mad. "You guys lost the game." They were like, "Play us in basketball." They wanted to **DUNK*** on us and everything. They think, okay, you got older guys and we can just go and dunk and run around. If you know Jim like I know Jim, are you going to challenge him? Boy, he's going to take you up on that. We'd be walking on the field and they kept saying, "Play us in basketball, play us in basketball." Jim said, "Okay, we'll play you in basketball. But not only will we play you in basketball, we're going to play you at the halftime of the Stanford-Cal basketball game." Here we go. The staff is saying, "C'mon, Coach! Not then. We're too old for that." We said okay, thinking that by that time, he'll forget about it. The Stanford-Cal game was on a Thursday. That Wednesday evening, Coach Harbaugh went down to the basketball coach and got a couple of plays. The

---

*The shortest winner of the NBA Slam **DUNK** Contest was Spud Webb, at 5-foot-7. Dwight Howard, at 6-foot-11, was the tallest to win the Slam Dunk.

staff was on the court practicing those plays. We were actually practicing basketball plays for that game the next day. At half-time, we went out and played the players. We ended up tied. It was fun, but that was typical Jim Harbaugh. You never challenge him. Boy, he is all for that.

Jim doesn't forget anything. That is one thing about him, he doesn't forget anything. You don't want to get on his bad side, because once you get on that, you're staying over there. He is all for getting after you.

Once I graduated from Western, I coached there. That's when we won the national championship, in '02. Then Jack Harbaugh retired. I was the offensive coordinator in '02. I learned a lot more football, just being with Jack. He was always that guy—at least for me—that you wanted to always impress and never let down. First as a player and then as a coach. That really helped me become a better coach, because I wanted to please him so much. I made sure I was on top of my game, and my guys knew exactly what they were doing. Just being around him, I learned a lot of football, and understanding the game of football and understanding how to lead people. He is so great at doing that with everyone, and being demanding. I tell you what, you see Jack Harbaugh, and then working with Jim, it's funny. When I went to work with Jim at Stanford and we're sitting in team meetings and you hear Jim talking, I'm saying to myself, he sounds just like his dad. It's all over again. This is crazy. I called Jack once to tell him, "This is ridiculous. It's like listening to you sitting up there." His tone—just the way he does it. Then when—God bless the dead—when Bo Schembechler passed and you started hearing Bo speak, that's Jack all over again. It was just so crazy, the effect that Bo Schembechler had on both of them, Jack and Jim. Then I watched myself, on how Jim and Jack have been a big influence on me. It's amazing, just how it all works. When you get around a good person, a good coach, you can really influence people.

Jim told Bo stories. When we were at Stanford, he talked about him. A lot of the things he did, he learned from Bo. When you watched Stanford or you watched Western Kentucky, you saw a lot of Michigan in both of those schools.

John Harbaugh is highly competitive. Different—but not different—from Jim and his dad. John is more like his mom. When I say that, though, Jackie, she'll get after you, too. That's why they're all great, because of Jackie. We talk about Jack all of the time, but Jackie is the head coach. She is going to tell you like she sees it, tell you hard. But she's really smart and really caring. That's what you get when you see John. He's very smart, but demanding. They all are enthusiastic. But they're all good with people. That's one of the qualities they have that most people don't have. They do great with people.

Someone made an analogy, and I thought it was perfect: Jim is one of those guys that is going to run through the wall, and John is one of those guys who will find a way around the wall. But they're both going to get to the other side. I thought that was perfect.

I'm in debt to the Harbaugh family. I would die for the Harbaugh family. To put it all in a nutshell, they mean everything. I look at my life and the way it has gone, they have been a big part of that. I think about my wife and my kids all of the time. If I never would have met Jim, it probably wouldn't have been that way. Not the way that it is. I owe everything to him. They call and need something? They know I'm all over it. I know the same thing. To this day, I don't make any professional decisions without consulting with them. I know they're going to steer me the right way. When everything gets tough or I need some advice or I just need someone to talk to, I call one of them. Whenever I get off the phone with any one of them, I just feel like I can go and accomplish anything I want to accomplish. That's the effect they have on people. They're just great people, man. We need more Harbaughs in this world.

I wasn't surprised about Jim going back to Michigan. He's going to do a great job. Jim has done a great job wherever he's been. And, again, it's because he's such a leader of men and so strong in his conviction and what he wants to do. It's hard for you to be around him if you're not that way, too. He has put together a phenomenal staff that is going to understand Michigan and what Michigan is all about. He lived it. I don't think Michigan is that far away. He's going to take them over the top. Especially with the way he recruits, he's going to get the players in there, and he's going to demand excellence from them. The players are going to want it. At the end of the day, they're going to want to play for him. They're not going to want to let him down. That's one of the qualities that Jim Harbaugh has—he's going to train you, he's going to be on you and he's going to get you going. But at the end of the day, you're not going to want to let Jim Harbaugh down. That's why he's had success wherever he's been. He's a great leader of men.

Just look at Jim's track record, not only with the players, but the program. Everything Jim Harbaugh touches turns to gold. In Oakland, they went to the Super Bowl. He went to San Diego, and he turned that program around. He went to Stanford—look at what they're doing now. Then with the 49ers, you see what they did. Everything that guy touches turns to gold.

The Harbaughs are the best. There is nothing I wouldn't do for them. I try to emulate all those guys in the way I coach and the way I am as a husband and as a father. To me, that's how you should be. I want to be the father and the husband that they are. It started with Jack and the way that he is. He's always around, and you see how his kids are. Then being around John and Jim, with their kids. And their sister, Joani. We're leaving Joani out, but she's awesome, too. Their family is great. I tell everybody that Jim is my role model. I just think he is the best.

SOONER LATER

CLAY MILLER

Clay Miller was born in Columbus, Ohio, and grew up in Norman, Okla. Yet, he passed on the opportunity to play football at Ohio State University and the University of Oklahoma. He chose Michigan. The offensive lineman was an All-Big Ten selection in 1985 and an Academic All-American. He earned a law degree from Northwestern and attended Harvard Business School.

When I grew up in Norman in the late '70s, let's put it this way...the stoplights would start to flash at midnight. Everything would go yellow. There was no hard stoplight after midnight. It was a small town, and it was surrounded by farmland. Nowadays, it's a suburb of Oklahoma City. But in those days, Norman was a very sleepy college town that woke up six or seven Saturdays every fall for the OU games. That was *the* event. Football was everything. I played my high school games on the same field as OU, at Owen Field, Oklahoma Memorial Stadium. We used to have 25,000-30,000 fans for a high school football game.

Barry Switzer was entertaining. The question was always when was the bottom going to fall out of the place? That was my take. Ann Arbor has always been a little more sophisticated. I don't mean that in a derogatory sense toward Norman. Ann Arbor is a university town with a worldwide view. Even today, Norman is a wonderful place to live and a great college town, but it doesn't have nearly the 30,000-foot view of the world that you get in Ann Arbor. It's a different academic institution.

I went to Michigan because it was the best combination of football and academics that I could find. I looked at Stanford. Stanford had great academics and not such great football back then. I looked at the Ivy League schools. They also had great academics and not such great football. But Michigan had the combination of the two that you just couldn't touch.

Bo Schembechler sat in your living room and told you, "I want you to be at Michigan. I want you to be a Michigan man." It was special. It was a time and a place. I'm grateful that I had the opportunity to play at Michigan with the history and the tradition. We had success, and had the opportunity to play for a guy like Bo. What more could you ever ask for as a kid? There are other places that maybe give it a run, but there is no place that I could ever imagine I'd have had a better college career.

We opened the '84 season against Miami of Florida, the defending national champion. They came into our house and we beat them, 22-14. We were off on a roll. But it was a M.A.S.H. unit the rest of the year, punctuated by Jim Harbaugh's injury. He broke his arm. We were playing Michigan State and there was a fumble. The ball bounced to the side and I saw Jim jump in to try to recover it. He stuck out his arm and somebody from Michigan State put a helmet right on his upper arm. I heard it crack when they hit it.

That was really unfortunate, because we didn't have any-body behind him. We had a couple of freshman kids who were way in over their heads. We had almost everybody back the next year, and we finished No. 2 in the country. We shouldn't have lost the one game we lost, 12-10, in the rain at **IOWA***. No. 1 vs. No. 2. They didn't even score a touchdown. They had four field goals. We had a chance for an interception in the fourth quarter that would have put it away. It was wet, and the ball

*George Raveling, former **IOWA** basketball coach, has the original copy of Martin Luther King, Jr.'s "I Have A Dream" speech from 1963 and it's worth $25 million.

bounced out of one of our player's hands. The hardest part is being an offensive lineman and watching that, because you can't do anything about it.

The '86 season was great, too. We won the Big Ten, even though we lost to Minnesota. Our only other loss was to Arizona State in the Rose Bowl. Jim was great the entire season. I still remember our game at Ohio State. We were ahead by three points late in the fourth quarter, heading into the north end zone. Jim let go of a long bomb to John Kolesar. I still remember watching the ball go out over my head, and seeing Kolesar catch it about 30 yards downfield, and run into the end zone for a touchdown that put it away.

Jim was all business in the huddle. When he was just starting out, he had a little bit of an ego. We'd give him a "lookout" block to keep him honest. In a game, he was laser focused. We were all laser focused. It was something else to be 21-years-old in front of that kind of a crowd with that kind of a stage.

My experiences at Michigan put me on such a great path. So many of us enjoyed success. A lot of that is what we learned from the program, from Bo. It isn't about you. It isn't about the ego. It's about doing things the right way all of the time. It's about working hard, outworking the other guy. It doesn't always happen overnight, but if you keep working hard and you keep doing the right things, eventually success will come to you.

Go into Schembechler Hall and look up on the wall where they honor the Academic All-Americans. I don't know how many Michigan players have won that award, but two-thirds of those guys played for Bo. That tells you the kind of guys he recruited. Jim was serious about school. He worked hard. If Bo hadn't been a football coach, he could have been the CEO of a Fortune 500 company. The same is true for Jim. He has a presence. He has an ability to focus. He has discipline. He has a work ethic. Those things are critical to success. You look at a lot of us who have been fortunate enough to do well, it's the same background. It's the same drill.

We've always had the infrastructure at Michigan. We've always had the tradition. Recently, we just didn't have the right key to the lock. I can't tell you how thrilled I am to have Jim back. Jim is a competitor. The guy would cheat the devil in order to win. He would do whatever it took. He'd get hit hard and you'd know he was hurting, but he wouldn't even show it. He'd just get up and keep at it. He learned a lot, and he taught everybody else a lot at the same time. I have a tremendous amount of respect for Jim and was just thrilled that he was my quarterback. I got to keep his jersey clean for a little while.

Chapter 2

SWEET HOME
ANN ARBOR:

GRADE 5 RM. 5A
Sr. Diane Pitera
Alton, Erica
Belanger, Tim
Blackman, Debbie
Brown, Dave
Carder, Jeff
Decker, Chris
Farrell, Loretta

Fister, William
Fushrer, Milton
Gillman, Denise
Harbaugh, Jim
Hiraga, John
Ibarra, John
Mathea, Dawn
Martin, Tom

McCalla, Joe
Moset, Jill
Nielsen, Julie
Nobile, Vanessa
Nordman, Eric
O'Connor, Mike
O'Sullivan, Ann
Peters, Aaron

Pollock, Robert
Rizzardi, Yvonne
Selenis, Paul
Shields, Mike
Spring, Paula
Sullivan, Jean
Wade, Joe
Walters, Roy

THE BIG TEN,
THE BIG HOUSE,
THE BIG TIME

A ROOMIE WITH A VIEW

JERRY QUAERNA

"Q," as Jerry Quaerna is known, grew up in Janesville and Fort Atkinson, Wisconsin. He was recruited by all the Big Ten schools, but once he walked in The Big House, it was all over for the other schools. Q lives in Lake Geneva, Wisconsin, and commutes to Lincoln, Nebraska, where he is a vital cog working for the Department of Homeland Security.

I was recruited to play football at Michigan. When I went there, Jim was my roommate. Jim and I were paired up as freshmen. We didn't know each other. Then we lived together as fifth-year seniors. I got to see Jim before he was a big star and after he was big time.

I had a long trip over from Wisconsin. I got unpacked, and I was sleeping on my bed in the dorm when Jim showed up with Jim Minick. He grew up with Minick in Ann Arbor. Minick spent 26 years in the Marines and is now Jim's right-hand man on his Michigan staff. I woke up and introduced myself to these guys. What was the first thing Jim did? This was back in the day. This was '82. We had LPs. I was into music, and I had about 20 LPs and my turntable. Those were going to go out the window in three or four years, but I had a nice collection of vinyl there. After Jim shook my hand, he went straight to my vinyl collection, and he critiqued it. I'm not kidding you. I had good stuff. I had the Doors, I had Jimi Hendrix. I had plenty of Beatles. I'm a big Beatles fan. Jethro Tull. I had *Hot Rocks* from the Stones. I loved that album. I had Black Sabbath. I had some great independent records. I had some Priest.

Jim is going through my records, and he's saying, "Yep, no, yep, no. Doors, no. Beatles, nope. Jethro Tull, no." When he's done critiquing my collection, he goes, "You don't have any Who." I don't have any Who, but I like the Who enough. Then he had a reference to Tom Petty, because he was a big Tom Petty and the Heartbreakers fan. I had a full critique of my album collection within about three minutes of meeting Jim. Within a week or two, Jim and I had a very heated argument over who would be a better front man. He was a big Who fan, and he was a big Roger Daltrey fan. I loved Led Zeppelin. I'm thinking of course Robert Plant is a better singer than Roger Daltrey, and Jim is taking the opposite side of that debate. The thing you've got to understand is when it's on and it's go time and you're defending your position—it's on. I'm sure this resonates down the road with some of his coaching staffs and all. It's an all out heated conversation. There wasn't any "let's just agree to disagree." We had a heated battle over Daltrey versus Plant. I won that debate. But even today, I'm taking Robert Plant over Roger Daltrey, and I like Daltrey.

When Jim walked into the dorm room that first time, I was sleeping—taking a nap before our first big meeting with Bo. Of course, what happened at that meeting is legendary, because Minick dropped off Jim late. He was about 10 minutes late to our very first freshman meeting. Jim didn't just get his butt chewed, he was disemboweled in front of the whole freshman class. Seriously, it was just a butt chewing. That evening, Jim and I were back at the room. I was trying to console the guy somewhat over this complete disemboweling in front of the freshman class. Jim had a wooden closet next to his bed. He was pounding on this closet and dropping some choice expletives. Here I was, four hours into Michigan football, thinking, what did I get myself into? That was Day One.

Jack Harbaugh was in Kalamazoo when I was a freshman with Jim, so I didn't see him much. He'd show up on occasion, but he was busy with his own team at Western Michigan. He didn't gravitate toward Ann Arbor except on the rare occasion.

Flash forward to December of that first year. There's another story that I want you to know. It's far out. But it was one of the worst episodes of me putting my foot in my mouth, just a major, big-time gaffe. It's seared into my skull. We had just finished with Rose Bowl practices, and we were going to fly out to California on Christmas Day. But we had the 23rd and 24th for vacation time. Everybody got to go home. I was too far away, and the people that were too far away could stay at a hotel. That would have been fine. But Jim offered to have me go home to Kalamazoo and spend Christmas with his family for two days. Yeah, I don't want to be stuck in a hotel. Sure, I'll go home with you 90 miles to Kalamazoo.

So we got there, and I met the Harbaugh family. Very hospitable. Very tight. I got to meet John for the first time. John is different from Jim. John is a little more laid-back. He's more of a diplomat. Jim is more fiery. We were having a big debate in the basement. Jack was there, John was there, I was there, Jim was there. What were we discussing? We were discussing if the game were on the line, do you want to be behind and have the ball or do you want to be ahead and be on defense? We're getting into this knockdown, drag out thing. I knew what position I was going to take. Jim phrased it, in the heat of the moment. He said, "Here's the situation. It's the biggest game. It's the Super Bowl. Do you want the ball and be behind to win the game? Or do you want your defense out there with the lead?" I said, of course, I wanted the defense. Defense wins championships. I gave him that whole spin. John agreed with me. He wanted the lead, and he wanted the defense out on the field. Jim was doing cartwheels, because he took the opposite side of that debate. He said, "I want the ball." Now remember, he phrased this one, "The game is on the line, and it's the Super Bowl." We were going back and forth, and it was heated. Jack was sitting right there, but he wasn't chiming in. He was just sitting back and enjoying it. He was soaking it up. Here was when it went really ugly for me. I was ready to just throw it out and sink Jim's ship. We were debating fiercely. I said, "All right, Jim." Jim's guy was John Elway. He loved John Elway. Elway wound up finishing second in the Heisman Trophy voting his senior year. That would have been the year Jim and I were freshmen—1982.

Jim talked about Elway quite a bit. Jim was a big Joe Montana fan, too, and he had a picture of Joe Montana on the wall. He also had...was it Joe Montana's girlfriend or Dwight Clark's girlfriend? It was Dwight Clark's girlfriend, Shawn Weatherly, Miss Universe. Very aesthetically pleasing.

Anyway, Elway put up some pretty good numbers. Jim watched John Elway play at Stanford when Jim was playing at Palo Alto High. I was going for the knockout blow. I said, "Okay, Jim, what just happened with your boy Elway, perhaps the greatest college quarterback who has ever played the game? Why didn't he go to any bowl games? It wasn't because they weren't scoring points. It was because they weren't stopping people." I was thinking, okay, that was a point for me. The place got real quiet. Deathly quiet. Jim and John both looked at me, stared at me and said, "Damn, that's just cold, Q." Okay, I just won the debate. What's so cold about that? Unbeknownst to me, Jack was the defensive coordinator for Stanford for Elway's sophomore and junior years. Here I was, being taken care of really well by this family, and I just threw my foot in my mouth big time. I'll never forget that moment in my entire life. I had the debate won, and the next thing you know, those guys are looking at me and the conversation just ended. On a dime.

Flash forward years later. I was watching Jim and John coach against each other in the Super Bowl, and I was thinking, okay, I remember this. That was the context of that conversation that went horribly wrong for me. I watched the game, and

it looked like it was on the verge of a blowout. The **RAVENS*** were going to win big. Then the power went out at the Superdome.

When play resumed, Jim's 49ers started creeping back. I was thinking, holy cow. That was what transpired. Jim's team was coming from behind, and they had the ball with an opportunity to win at the end of the game. That discussion just came full circle. It was just astonishing to me. But I assure you, it happened. I will never forget it. Perhaps John and Jim and Jack don't remember the time the Big Cheese stuck that size-16 right in his mouth to finish off that debate. It was really weird. I don't know if they remember that. They were so busy and so accomplished, maybe it wasn't that big of a deal. But for me, it seared into my skull. Here I was, being hosted by a marvelous family, and I just had that huge gaffe. I will never forget it until I hit the grave.

Here's another story. It was the time the "paddy wagon" showed up. I had a good vantage point. Somebody got carried away at a donut shop, late at night, after bar time. There were some punches thrown. Bo found out immediately and had these guys rounded up. I sat up on the fifth floor and saw the paddy wagon show up. It was assistant coaches, and they rounded up these guys and took them down to Bo. I wasn't part of the meeting. Luckily, I wasn't hanging out with them that night.

Jim and I were not exactly fashionistas. We were more ham-and-eggers. But our fashion senses clashed on occasion. If there is an argument that is ensuing, it's on. There was one conversation we were having about the shorts we were wearing. I had a sweet pair of green shorts with white stripes. They were a dark green. I just loved them and wore them a lot. They were indestructible. They were the perfect shorts for me. Jim had these goofy-looking red plaid shorts that went down below his knees. I don't know how to describe them, but I wouldn't have worn those things if you paid me. Jim and I were going

*The Baltimore **RAVENS** once were the Cleveland Browns; the Baltimore Orioles once were the St. Louis Browns.

back and forth about who had the sweetest shorts. Nobody was winning that conversation, but it just kept going on. Flash forward to some of what I was reading from Jim's wife about the khaki pants. I'm saying to myself, I understand your side of the argument, with these khaki pants. But you're not going to win, so don't bother going there. That's what I'm telling myself, because I'm just flashing back to when we were clashing in our fashion senses. Obviously, neither one of us was the Tim Gunn of the day. I could identify with her frustrations, because I was there.

Those shorts were like golfing, purple plaid/reddish plaid Capri pants. He was telling me they were so sweet. I was wearing my green shorts and told him, "I wouldn't trade mine for a 100 pairs of yours. Those things look horrible on you." Neither one of us won.

One thing about living with Jim was what you see, that's reality. What you see on the sideline, that's reality. It's not an act. I was more of a guy of let's just leave it on the field, let's go back to the dorm and lick our wounds and get ready for the next day. But a lot of times, it was almost like we were shark fetuses sharing a womb in the South Quad for a year. It was just like that. You had to be on, and every opinion was contested.

One time Mike Reinhold—Reiny—and I came back from a freshman philosophy class, a philosophy of religion class. We had to write a paper on the pros and cons—the strong suits and the weak points—of the atheist perspective. Reiny and I were in the dorm. Jim was doing his thing. He wasn't part of that class. Reiny and I were ripping on point A, point B, point C, point D. Then for the other side of the equation, we had point A, B, C and D. Well, Jim joined the conversation. He was so displeased with the pro-atheist side that he had a conniption. He barged right in on the conversation and laid down the law according to Jim. "There was a God, and the atheists are wrong. They're wrong because of X, Y and Z." He wasn't even part of the class, and here he was, getting into a heated discussion about atheism. He just jumped right in and called them out and said that it ain't happening.

Jim was pretty darned mad with that whole atheist debate. There was smoke coming out of his ears. He wanted nothing to do with hearing the "pros" of an atheist. Reiny and I were looking at each other, like, oh, wow. He was pretty hot. And he was only a freshman.

Another time he was mad even worse than the atheist episode. Jim went home after our sophomore year and stayed at home for about six weeks. He was going to come back in a day or two, but didn't. Reiny and I threw down a huge party at 1002 Packard. Jim didn't show up until the next day or the day after that. He found out that we had this butt-kicking party down at 1002 before he got back from Kalamazoo. Jim was white-hot livid after that one, just white-hot. It got ugly. We were driving to Rick's American Café. Reiny and I were in the backseat, and John and Jim were in the front. John had dropped Jim off. We were going to party at Rick's for $2 pitcher night. Jim could not let it go, the fact that Reiny and I had thrown this party prior to his arrival. It got so bad that I had the impulse to just pop Jim right there. It was that ugly. I probably should have popped him, just to settle him down. I should have given him a shiner. It was that bad. That's probably the maddest I've ever seen him. It was a great party, though.

I didn't see John that much. He was busy playing at Miami, and then he started coaching. Our paths crossed and I tell you what, I love that guy. He's one of the best guys I've ever met in my life. I just love his demeanor, his mannerism. Very professional. Very diplomatic. In fact, the State Department would be lucky to have that guy. Yes, he's got a fight to him. Of course, he's got fight to him, but that guy would make a fantastic diplomat, just fantastic.

I have one story about women and Jim that you can print. I've got a lot of them, but I've got one that you can print. Jim had a girlfriend when we were fifth-year seniors. Her name was Linda, but we called her Lindy. She was marvelous. Well, Jim and Lindy would play a lot of chess games to pass the time, and Jim had a little plastic cardboard box chess set that he kept in his room. I had a marble chess set that I purchased down in Tijuana when we were down there for the Holiday Bowl. I brought it back on the plane. It was big and had hand-carved pieces. I've still got it. I had that chess set out at all times. Reiny and I were sharing the biggest room in the house. We had a marvelous couch there. We always had this chess set in front of this marvelous couch. There were a lot of chess games being played. None of us were Bobby Fischer. We weren't Boris Spassky, either. But it was fun. There was one time when Lindy came to see me after getting annihilated by Jim for the millionth straight time. She pleaded with me, "Q, will you play Jim in chess? You can beat him. He's getting too cocky." I said, "Yeah, okay, Lindy. Send him in. I'll b---- slap him for you. Jim sat down. The thing you have to understand about my hand-carved chess set is that if you weren't really familiar with it, the bishops and pawns had very similar shapes. The bishops were just a little bit taller. It was easy to not distinguish between the two, unless you were experienced with the set. What I did was— as soon as I could—move my bishops up into the second rank, so that they looked like pawns. The first time I struck with those bishops, he said, "Are you serious? You can't move a pawn like that." I said, "That's a bishop." "Are you serious? You're going to take that?" I said, "Hell, yes, I am." We proceeded, and it was beautiful. This is a girl story that's G-rated for you. All of a sudden, the game was going south for Jim, because I was striking from my second row with my bishops and taking his knights. He was getting all heated. "You can't do that! That's a pawn!" I said, "That's a bishop." I won those games, a couple of them. Lindy was thrilled. But I have to say—to be honest—there was a little home-cooking going on, a little home court advantage.

Let me tell you a story about that couch. I had the best couch ever to get into Ann Arbor. My buddy in Fort Atkinson, his parents had this couch that must have been nine feet long. It was super comfortable. It might have been the only thing that got me through two-a-days, because if you were on that couch and wanted to get comfortable, you were out. It was perhaps the best couch I've ever been on in my life. Well, Jim and the other roomies were going to get rid of it. I said, "Are you kidding?" It had '70s colors. It had oranges, yellows, browns and stripes. They wanted to get rid of it just for style. I said, "This is a very substantive couch." Everybody loved this couch. Well, I didn't have a place to put it after our sophomore year, so I asked Jim, who was renting a house with Reiny. I said, "Hey, I need a place to stash my couch." He said, "Bring it in. Hell, yeah. We'll even help you." We moved the couch in there, and it was there all summer.

In the fall, it was time for me to get my couch out of that house, because I wasn't living with them as a junior. They kept telling me in the locker room, "Oh, no. You're never getting that couch back. No, it's perfect right where it is." What I had to do was wait and creep in there when I knew the door was open, but when I knew those guys were doing something football-related. I had to move it out on the sly. I got my couch out of there. I left a big chasm in the living room when it was all said and done. I don't think they were too thrilled when they got home.

Jim was a bright student. He didn't have any issues. He was solid. He was very good. He took a lot of classes with Lindy. He went out with her for a few years. If I'm not mistaken, she ended up becoming a lawyer.

Jim was very disappointed once. We were freshmen. I got a call. I answered the phone and said, "Hello." A voice I didn't recognize said, "Is Jim there?" I said he wasn't there right now, could I take a message. "Tell him Gil Brandt called." That's the head scout for the Dallas Cowboys, one of the best scouts going back in the day. Jim got back, and I gave him the good news. We were just freshmen. We were nobodies. I said, "Jim, you're not going to believe this. Gil Brandt called a little while ago." He said, "You're kidding." "No, he called, man." Jim was doing cartwheels. He was jacked up. His dad called a couple of hours later, and said, "Sorry to disappoint you. That was your uncle." He had an uncle who was a football coach somewhere out in Pittsburgh or somewhere. His name was Jerry. I could be mistaken. But it was his uncle, playing a joke on him through me. Jim was looking at me like I was part of the scam. Who am I to say? Gil Brandt called, you know? He was looking at me like I was an idiot.

When you're a freshman and you're not going to play, you end up on the meat squad. I was on the meat squad. Reiny was on the meat squad. Most of us ended up on what we called the Demo Squad—the demonstration squad, the scout team. We ran the plays of the opposing teams against the first-team players. We all got creamed by the first-teamers, time after time. Well, all of the back-up quarterbacks, except Jim, were doing demo work. There were only a handful of freshmen who avoided that kind of abuse. Jim was watching our first-team offense most of the time. It was very rare to see him down getting his brains blown out behind a bunch of freshmen linemen trying to play against the first-teamers. That might have been a good indicator right there that Jim was a little bit different. He was being spared the carnage, shall we say.

When Jim finally was able to start, as a junior, he got his arm broken against Michigan State halfway through the season. After that, we had some trouble moving the ball and ended up 6-6. I don't know how to describe it, but the behavior of the coaches going through that, coaches who were not used to a 6-6 season versus some seasons when we had some really great success. It was interesting to watch the whole dynamic go down. Then they made some tweaks, and Jim came back. We finished second in the country the following year. It was a famine to feast operation there.

Have you ever read Steven Pressfield? Before you die, read *Gates of Fire* by Steven Pressfield. Marvelous book. He's a historical fiction writer, and he invents a mundane character and puts that character in front of a lot of heavy hitters. I didn't know Jim or anybody when I showed up in Ann Arbor, and Jim was my roommate. Now I'm watching him have all the success that he's had. I've seen some of these big figures, big towering figures in football, like Bo, and like Jim. I've seen John and all of them. Sometimes I think I'm one of those mundane characters in a Pressfield novel, when I see all of the success that these guys have had. It has been cool, humbling. Jim and I lived together as first-year freshmen and again as fifth-year seniors, so I got to see the before and after.

After the loss to Arizona State in the '87 Rose Bowl, let me share a discussion where I swayed Jim's opinion. One of our receivers went on a TV sports show. He was asked, "Why did you guys lose to Arizona State?" Typical stuff comes out—grass versus turf, heat, climate, being so far away from home—the standard B.S. that you hear. I spoke up as a bunch of the guys were going back and forth. I said, "Guys, I can tell you why we lost to Arizona State. Arizona State had a great team, and they had one of the best offensive lines that this game has ever seen. That interior five was fantastic. However, a big reason we lost— and a big reason why under Bo we did not have a lot of success in bowl games—was because we scrimmaged too much." When you are in the season, in an 11- and 12-game season, you're insulated from constant banging.

Our practices were usually pretty brutal when we hit, and our hitting days were Tuesday and Wednesday. If we had a game on Saturday, we got to rest on Sunday. We're running around in shorts and jerseys on Mondays. When we hit on Tuesday and Wednesday, it was on, and it was far more hitting than you would see in a game. Then we'd rest Thursday and Friday. We'd have two days of rest before the game on Saturday. Well, let me tell you what happened at the Rose Bowl. We had four straight days—four straight days!—of pads. Bo was not going to allow anybody to outwork him. That could have been his Achilles heel in those bowl games. I assure you that in all of those bowl games, he was never outworked. However, I don't think his teams played with legs. If they won, they were winning on heart. They did not have fresh legs. Leading up to the Rose Bowl that year, we had four straight hitting days. We'd heard that we weren't going to hit the following day so that we could have three days of rest before the game. There was at least one coach who prevailed upon Bo to scrimmage more. His point was, "The reason that we've had so much futility out there on grass is because our timing is off. We're coming from turf, and we're going to grass, and it screws up our splits. We have to tighten it up a little bit, and our timing is always off. That's why we lose." I wanted us to go three days without hitting so that we could be somewhat fresh for that game. We didn't know if we were going to hit until we showed up for practice. Sure enough, we got our pads on, and we just kicked the crap out of each other again. What happened was we had five straight days of all out hitting, with the standard 48 hours of rest before the bowl game.

When I woke up that day, January 1st, I felt like an old man. I thought, holy crap, I'm sore. Anyway, I woke up that Rose Bowl day, and I was sore from head to toe. A lot of that had to do with going five incredibly hard practices with the standard two days of rest. I have a swimmer's background, and swimmers taper for the Big Dance. Bo's teams never tapered. He never, ever tapered. The two days of rest were always there, but it wasn't sufficient for the team to be playing with fresh legs. We had that debate up in the house with the guys, and they all looked at me and said, "You know what, Q? You're right. We don't taper, and we never tapered."

That's one of the problems you get with omnipotence. When you get somebody who is omnipotent, like Bo—and he was omnipotent—and you get surrounded with a bunch of people who are inclined to say "yes" and not use some critical thinking skills, there was nobody there to say, "Hey, Bo, time out. We've done too much. We need to let these guys rest for the game." It didn't happen. There was not a guy like that there.

We could have made it a better game. Or actually could have won. Don't get me wrong, Arizona State was a great team, and their quarterback, Jeff Van Raaphorst, had a great day. He was zipping in some passes that were right on our defenders' fingertips and just getting through. There was one over one of our cornerbacks, down in the end zone. I thought it was going to be a pick-six—and it fluttered right through our guy's fingertips, right into the receiver's hands for a touchdown. Here I am, jacked up, thinking, oh, wow, we've got a pick-six. Then, bam, there's a touchdown the other way. With legs, those plays might have—they could have—gone differently. Van Raaphorst had a fantastic game, and that offensive line could have played in the pros, all of them together. You could have plugged those guys into the pros, and they would have done an adequate job.

The relationship between Bo and Jim was pretty special. Did you ever hear what Reiny and Harbaugh did to Shemy's Nerf football? Shemy was Bo's son, just a little rugrat running around the complex, and he felt pretty comfortable in there. Reiny and Harbaugh stole the Nerf football. Shemy always had his football with him. They took some white athletic tape, and they crawled on top of our lockers in the freshmen locker room—we had a freshmen locker room and then there was the varsity locker room. There were a bunch of pipes on the ceiling, and Reiny and Harbaugh took the athletic tape and they taped his Nerf football to the tallest pipe that they could find. It was probably 12 or 13 feet off the ground. The poor kid couldn't get it, so he ran down and got his old man, dragged his old man down to the freshmen locker room, and there is the Nerf football taped to a pipe near the ceiling. What did Bo do? He shook his head and did a 180. I'm sure he went and told one of the trainers to make sure they got the ball down. There was no butt chewing, no nothing.

Bo and Jim had similar personalities. If you had an opinion that differed from either one of those two, you had better be ready to defend it with vigor. Even if you did, most likely, if it differed from their opinion, you were wrong. Or so it would seem. There wasn't a whole lot of "let's agree to disagree" going on back then.

Jim bought a lot of time when he wanted to throw the ball. He was shifty when he got outside of the pocket, deceptively so. There was a game where he just went off. It was against Illinois, his fifth year. He put 69 points on the board. It was just a barrage of nice pass after nice pass. We were getting gassed running up and down the field after those big bombs. It was something. That particular game stands out because we didn't typically see the passing game. We looked like Miami of Florida there—for a game—putting up 69 with all kinds of big passes. It was fun.

I felt horrible for Jim, watching him with the Bears, getting beat by the **PACKERS***. He was getting creamed, and he kept getting up. I was just marveling at his resilience. I listened to sports talk radio the next day, after Jim got his brains beat out. A guy called in and said, "Yeah, well, if Jim wasn't getting his brains blown out, he could have led his receiver a little bit better than he did on that one pass." Are you kidding me? He was lucky he was alive. The media and fans couldn't see that Jim was being helped up from the ground after every play, and then he'd get even more abused on the next play. I suppose the one time the line held, Jim wasn't spot-on accurate with some pass. Give me a break.

*In the early days, the Green Bay **PACKERS** played in a facility called City Park. City Park had two men's rooms, no ladies' room.

I was at Michigan on a recruiting trip in January, and I had never seen a football game at The Big House. There was an assistant coach who was taking me around—Jerry Meter, a very nice guy. He was the defensive line coach. It's Meter and I, and we're going into the corner end zone away from the tunnel. He just walked me in. The Big House is not imposing from the outside—at least it wasn't at the time. It's different now, because of the new construction, so it looks imposing with the new press box and all the other boxes. But at the time, as you walked in, it didn't look like a gigantic structure. It's deceiving, because it's dug into a hill. Then you walk in, and you see this massive expanse of seats. It is just perfect. I looked at that, and I had ridiculous warm fuzzies. I just thought that was perfection. This was in January. It was windy and cold. I'm from Wisconsin, so it was no big deal. I was looking at this stadium, and I just fell in love with it. I said, "Yeah, man, this looks like perfection." The size. The scale. It's a fantastic place. You just have to experience it.

Jim is going to do well as Michigan's head coach. I've got an email chain with Reiny and another buddy, Rick Peterson, who we went to school with. Two weeks before the announcement from Jim, there was vigorous conjecture going on in the email chain among the three of us. I wrote, "You know what guys? I think he's coming." They were like, "Why do you think he's coming?" I wrote, "The thing that stands out is that Jim is smart enough to know—and he's diplomatic enough to know—that his name is bandied about for this gig. If he isn't interested, he'd have backed off immediately, just out of courtesy to Jim Hackett and his search committee. He'd say, 'I'm going to stay in the NFL' or, 'I'm going to go to x, y or z college.' He's said nothing. His silence speaks volumes to me. He hasn't said no. He hasn't discounted the option." It would have been a lousy situation for him to have gone and left Hackett dangling for two or three weeks, if he knew all along that he wasn't going to go. I interpreted his silence as he's coming, guys.

You put some other perspective in there. Jim loved Stanford, because he was out there when he was in high school. He coached there. Jim's team for the NFL was the 49ers. He coached there. What's the next rung in that ladder? Don't think for a moment that coaching at Michigan is a step down, because it's one of the best gigs going out there, period. Coaching at Michigan is as big as any NFL gig you're going to name, in my opinion. This completes his equation. It would be nice to see him coach at Michigan for a good 15 years. It's going to be fantastic.

I sent Jim an invitation to my daughter's graduation party in June, and he sent her a very nice graduation card. She was thrilled. He put his cell phone number in there, but I cut that off, because with these girls and social media, the last thing I needed was for her to post a picture of this graduation card from Jim with that cell phone number all over cyberspace. She was thrilled to get his card.

Jim Harbaugh has brought a lot of laughter and fun into my life, even when I was ready to kill him. He needs to improve his taste for fashion and music, though.

JIM HARBAUGH WAS A HUMAN RED BULL

JAMIE MORRIS

Jamie Morris is the career receptions leader for running backs at Michigan. He set U-M records for most yards rushing in a season (1,703) and for a career (4,392).

It was weird. I first met Jim out on the field. We were in a huddle. He shook my hand and introduced himself, "Jim Harbaugh." I said, "Jamie Morris." Then we ran plays. Bo wanted to put together the guys he was going to play together. He made the whole offense go over to the sidelines, and he called the names of players he wanted to see together. He called Harbaugh, and then he called the fullback. Then he called my name. Just listening to Jim in the huddle, it was incredible. He took a very commanding role. It was like, "Hey, this is my huddle." He took over. Then, as we grew together my sophomore and junior years, his junior and senior years, you could see him become the coach on the field. He knew what every person was supposed to do, and he could tell you what every person was supposed to do.

If you screwed up, he got into you. He lit into wide receivers. He lit into everyone who screwed up. He would let you know if you did something wrong. But I'm going to just say this, nine times out of 10, if you had Jim Harbaugh on your team, you knew you were going to win that game.

You could just see his determination. He always wanted a long drive. There was a helmet decal we could get if we could do a drive over 80 yards. Real men didn't throw the ball. You know how Bo Schembechler was: "We're just going to ram it down their throat. We're going to run it down their throat." That was the mandate at the time. It was Jim Harbaugh who pushed that. He'd say, "All right, let's have a 12-play drive. Let's have a 12-play drive!" As a running back, you're like, "Wow!"

You loved that attitude. You loved everything about it. You loved his fire. We had the same fire, but everybody would show their emotions. He would show his emotions. He wore his heart on his sleeve as a player, and you can see he wears it as a coach, too.

I was hopeful that Jim would take the Michigan job once it was clear that Brady Hoke wasn't going to be here. First of all, pride came into it, because that's the guy I played with. That's my quarterback. Of course you want that guy—you want him. He's been successful everywhere he's been, so you want him to come back, come home again. The program was down. You want him to take the program back to that level.

The quarterbacks I played with in the pros—Doug Williams and Mark Rypien—were dropback passers. Jimmy is a dropback quarterback, but he could run, too. He could take off and run when things broke down. Most quarterbacks knew if it wasn't there—eat the ball, throw the ball away. Jimmy is not going to waste a down. He was a great passer. He had a great arm.

There was a time when Jim got mad at a practice. Bo would get mad, and he would say, "Son of a b----. Son of a b----." Jim was so mad that he started swearing. Bo yelled at him, "Harbaugh, I'll do the cussing here, not you." I've seen him really angry when we lost a game we were supposed to win. We lost to **MINNESOTA*** in his senior year, in '86. As Bo would say, we

*Bruce Smith, the 1941 Heisman Trophy winner from **MINNESOTA**, was nominated for sainthood by a Father Cantwell, and his application is still on file at the Vatican.

were thinking ahead, thinking about the Ohio State game. We didn't have our heads in the game, and we lost that game. I could sense that Jim Harbaugh was upset, too.

After we beat Ohio State in '86, we had a game against the University of Hawaii. We took the athletic campus with us to Hawaii for a week. It was crazy. Bo was saying, "This is not a holiday trip. This is not a bowl trip, gentlemen. We are going there to play football." I'll never forget that, because the NCAA—as dumb as they are nowadays, they were even dumber back then. You couldn't have a stopover, so we took a flight from Detroit to Honolulu. We had to fly direct there. Then we got off the plane and everybody went to the hotel except for the players. They took us straight to the stadium, and Bo made us run two miles in the stadium to get us tired. "You guys don't want to go out tonight, do you?" he said.

I've got to tell you that Michigan fans are expecting a lot in 2015. They are really expecting. Oh my god, the euphoria. This is a spoiled fan base, and they are expecting a 10-win season, but they would be content with a seven- or eight-game winning season, too. They're thinking Jim Harbaugh is going to come in here and fix everything—make guys run faster, jump higher, play better football. It's the athletes that we bring in. I can see the difference in the athletes and the recruits that Jimmy is bringing in and is recruiting, as opposed to the years before. You can see the difference.

Between you, me and the fencepost, when Jim Harbaugh goes out and signs a fifth-year senior, that tells you something. They just don't bring in a fifth-year senior transfer from Iowa (Jake Rudock) and expect him to sit the bench and just be here, right? This fan base is starving for a winning coach. As I said, this team will improve. By how much? I give it two or three more wins. They won five games last year, so if they win two or three more games, they're 8-4, 8-5.

Eight-and-four is not a bad year. It's a **BOWL GAME***. It takes you down to Florida.

Jim is between a rock and a hard place. He's got Lansing to the north of him, and he's got Columbus to the south of him—and both of those schools aren't afraid to go over that line every now and then. I'm not even worried about Brian Kelly. We don't play Notre Dame—as Bo would say, "The hell with Notre Dame."

Jim was the guy that was a bridge between players—offense and defense, black players and white players. He tried to get along with all of the players.

*The longest running **BOWL GAME** no longer played is the Bluebonnet Bowl, which called it quits after 29 years.

WHERE THE PAST IS PRESENT

JERRY HANLON

Jerry Hanlon was Jim Harbaugh's quarterback coach at Michigan. Hanlon was the only assistant to coach on the Michigan staff during all of Bo Schembechler's 21 years in The Big House. Hanlon retired from coaching and still lives in Ann Arbor. He said, "I still live in the same house I moved into in 1969. I couldn't afford to move in and now I can't afford to move out."

At the time I didn't think it was a privilege, but I did have the privilege of coaching Jimmy. Everybody asks me what he's like. I say, "Well, he was the hardest and the easiest kid I ever coached." By that, I mean that in one sense he was a thorough listener. He would do what you told him. He was very, very dedicated to everything we were trying to do. He was a great teammate. But in the other sense, he was so competitive and so wanting to do everything himself and do it right, that he got almost obnoxious with that attitude. So he was a study in contrasts. But I certainly have grown to really have a great relationship with him.

Jack Harbaugh coached here, and Jim was raised on the Michigan football field. He and Johnny, you had to kick them out of your drills so they didn't hurt some of your players. They were always around. They were always trying to get involved. He had a better idea of what Michigan was like. He started out here in Ann Arbor at Pioneer High School. When Jack went to California, Jim ended up playing at Palo Alto High School. We thought that if we could get him back here and just show him what we had, not from a standpoint of facilities or things like that, but the opportunities that were going to be here, that we might have a good shot at him. Jack, of course, was in our corner, too. We had a kid here, Stevie Smith, and Steve Smith was one of the best athletes we ever had at Michigan. He was a very talented quarterback. He was going to be a senior when Jim came in as a freshman. It was the idea that Jim was going to come in and watch his freshman year and then be able to take over after Steve graduated. We didn't really have a great deal of depth at that position at the time. The fact that he was going to have an opportunity to come in and contribute early was also a factor in his coming to Michigan.

Steve Smith played senior year. I could talk for hours about him. He was really a great athlete. We had success with him. Certainly, he was a different type of quarterback than Jimmy Harbaugh was going to be. Steve could throw the ball, but he was very quick, was a very good runner. We could run with the option if we wanted to, whereas Jim was a little bit more of a pure drop back, handoff quarterback—although I did make him run the option. But, anyway, Jim was going to be a different type of quarterback, and we knew that primarily we were going to have to change our offensive strategy when Jimmy became the quarterback. That was a challenge for us, but it was also a challenge for him to allow us to do it.

A number of things made Harbaugh good. Genes, No. 1. He came from very good parents, I'll guarantee you that. Jack and Jackie raised him the right way. Jim had not just athletic genes, but he had the intelligence and the attitude that allows you to be a great athlete. That was No. 1. Jimmy was the most competitive athlete—or at least one of the most competitive athletes—that I've ever coached. That competitiveness really drove him to try to be the best he could, but he had a little problem with it. He wanted everybody to be just as competitive as he was, and that just wasn't possible for kids. Jimmy and I had a little problem—not a problem, but a situation. I, of course, knew him from the time he was a kid, knew his mom and dad and aunts and uncles and everybody. I was close with their family. As he became my quarterback during the pre-season, his competitiveness started to show. He would throw a ball down the field, and it would be 15 yards over the receiver's head. The receiver would run toward it and know he couldn't get it. He'd stop and come back and get ready for another play. Jimmy would go over and start hollering, "I don't know why you stopped. You should have kept running. You should have dove for the ball," because that's what Jimmy would have done. He would have ran and dove on the ground, even though he couldn't have caught it. He was going to make an effort. But he would holler at some of our receivers and people who were running the routes, and they didn't particularly take too well to that. One day, I called him into the office and I said, "Listen, who's the quarterback on this team?" He said, "I am, Coach." I said, "Who's the coach on this team?" He looked at me and said, "You are." I said, "Okay, then you quarterback, and I'll coach. Now do you understand that?" He looked at me and just said, "Yes, I understand it." He got up and walked out. From that time on, we talked football. Everything I said about football, he listened. He paid attention. He didn't miss a beat. But as far as any social talk, like how's the family, how's Mom and Dad, or how's Ann, my wife, we had none of that. It was all business and nothing else.

Along about the seventh or eighth game of the season, we were going to play Purdue. I'm sitting in my office and the door opened. Jim came in, closed the door, sat down, and said, "Coach, I don't like this." I said, "What are you talking about?" He said, "You know what I mean. I don't like this. We're not talking like we should, like we used to. Now I understand what you were trying to say. I understand what you were talking about. But I don't want to be like this." From that day on, we developed a really close relationship that has existed right up until today. I followed his progress after he left Michigan. I'd go over to preseason practice in Chicago. Mike Ditka would hit me in the rear end with a golf cart and say, "Get in here." We'd ride around and watch practice. I went a couple of times when Jim was in Chicago.

I don't know what makes one kid competitive and another kid ultracompetitive. If I knew that, I'd be able to go out and put it all into one kid, every kid. It comes from his upbringing. Jim and his brother, Johnny, were reared together and competed against each other in everything that they did. They always were trying to outdo each other, and it carried right over into the coaching profession. Johnny's a little bit more laid back, and Jim's a little bit more outgoing. That's just something that's part of your gene makeup, I guess. I'm not a professional doctor, but that has some part in it. You can develop it. I don't know how far you can get them to go, but you can make kids competitive. You can challenge them and reward them. That's part of what you're trying to do as a coach. You challenge them and make them competitive. When they do something good, you reward them, pat them on the back. That's the idea of what coaching is all about. I had to pat Jimmy on the back. I didn't have to make him competitive, that's for sure.

I thought Bo Schembechler was going to shoot me a number of times. I was in the press box calling plays, and he would be on the phone on the field. Anything that Jim did wrong, Bo blamed on me. Being the quarterback coach, I got blamed for it. Jimmy not only was competitive, but he would take chances on the field. He would go back to throw a pass, and if it wasn't open, he'd start to run around. He'd scramble to the right, and he'd scramble to the left, and then he'd be running backward. On the phone, I was hearing, "Hanlon, can't you teach that kid anything? My god, look where he is, oh, my god." Then, "Oh, whadda great play! Wow, whadda touchdown!" I had to put up with that with Jim because he would innovate when he'd get in a bad situation. It worked most of the time because he was smart enough to know to get rid of the ball when he should and to make a play when he could. He had a little bit more latitude to do that back there than you might want with some kids, because he was really an intelligent football player. He knew what we were trying to do.

That was one of the things that made him a favorite of mine. He fit into what we were trying to do so well, because of him being an intelligent player. I always wanted to run an offense that the defense tells you you're supposed to run. In other words, you don't go to the line of scrimmage and guess. You look at the defense, and it tells you what you want to do. He had a lot of latitude at the line of scrimmage to call the plays we should run and how we should block it or where we should throw a pass and all those things. It was built into our offense, and it took a lot of time and effort to learn that and then execute it. Jimmy certainly gave me the latitude to do the things that I wanted to do as a quarterback coach, because he could pick up on them and use them, and we became a very, very effective offense because of that.

Jim Harbaugh dips tobacco. I tried to get him out of the habit. I told him a long time ago to get rid of that stuff. I said, "Next thing you know, you're going to kiss your wife or your kids, and you won't have a lower lip. Now what do you think about that?"

Fifteen years ago, I got a call from Jack, and he said, "Jerry, what are you doing the second week in January?" I said, "Jack, I don't know what I'm doing tomorrow, let alone the second week in January." He said, "Listen, keep it open." I said, "Why?" Jimmy was at that time coaching at the University of San Diego. He said, "Jimmy's going to coach an all-star game in **LAS VEGAS***, and he wants you to be his offensive line coach." I said, "I'm not working for that little you know what." He said, "No, he wants you to see how he's developed as a

---

*In 2007, Michigan became the first Top-5 team to drop out of the Top-25 after just a single loss, when Appalachian State beat the Wolverines, 34-32. Appalachian State was the first FCS team to defeat a ranked FBS team. **LAS VEGAS** casinos had no line on the game.

coach. He really would like that." I said, "Jack, I'd love to." We went out to Las Vegas and coached a group of college seniors who weren't quite good enough to make it at the other all-star games. It was East versus West. The pros put it on and paid for it. The scouts tested them and watched them practice. We coached them to play the game. I was Jimmy's offensive line coach, and we had a great time. I enjoyed it. We had fun. We made out our practice schedules and did all the other things. It was probably halfway through the first quarter, a little bit maybe into the second quarter, and Jim came to me and said, "What do you think?" My line wasn't doing very well. I said, "Will you quit throwing the ball all over the ballpark and line up and run it?" He turned, looked at me and he said, "My god, some things never change." So we did. We started buckling up. From then, we beat the heck out of the other team. That was enjoyable. Jack was the head coach of the other team, and we beat him.

Jack knew better than to try to tell me what to do when Jim was at Michigan. Jack was so tied up in his own little coaching bailiwicks that he couldn't get back for many of the games. He did get to a couple of bowl games. Jack didn't see Jim play very much at Michigan, but Jackie used to come to the games every once in a while. I told her it was just to get away from Jack, it wasn't to see Jim. I coached with Jack at Michigan. Jack was really a good football coach. He had a great rapport with kids. Kids loved to play for him. The biggest thing was, I told him he didn't know anything about football, because I went to Miami of Ohio, and Jack went to Bowling Green. We were great rivals, Bowling Green and Miami. I told him he went to a school that didn't know anything about football and never gave anybody an education.

Back in those days, it was different than it is today. We didn't make all these million dollars and thousands and thousands of dollars. We were lucky to have enough money to keep the food on the table with our families. Our idea of a big celebration was to go to each other's house after a football victory and have everybody bring something to eat, a couple of beers. That's how we celebrated. We would go to different houses, and Jack and Jackie, of course, were on that list. You'd go there, and we always had a great time. We went to each other's houses, and that's how we became so close. We became not just close as coaches, but our families got to know each other a whole lot better that way. The wives met and commiserated and said how bad they had it and how good the coaches had it. Jack and I used to argue about the **CLEVELAND INDIANS***, too. That's for sure. I grew up near Cincinnati, so I was a big Reds fan.

*In 1958, Vic Power of the **CLEVELAND INDIANS** was the last player to steal home twice in one game, which he did against the Detroit Tigers. Power had only one other steal the entire year.

Graduation Day

Jim and John Harbaugh...Either the uniform
was too tight or Jim had to go to the bathroom.

Joani, John, Jim.

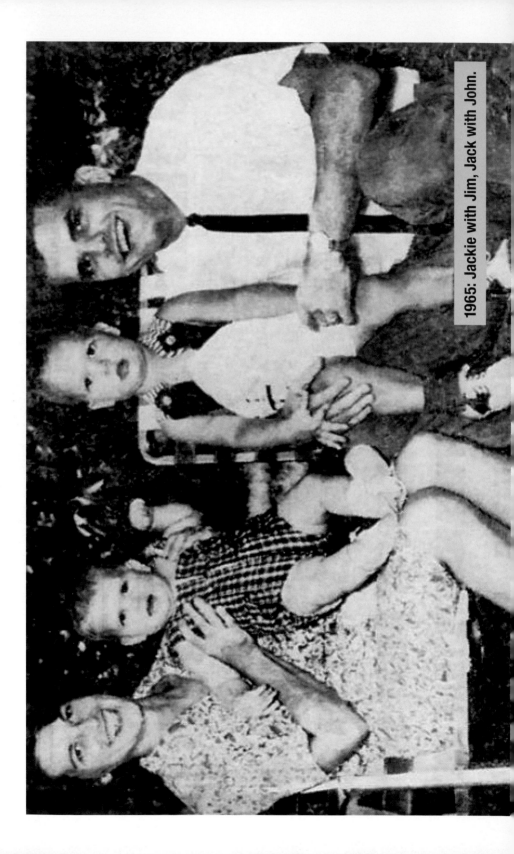

1965: Jackie with Jim, Jack with John.

Michigan Stadium mid-70s: John, Jim, Joani, Jack and Jackie.

First day of practice, freshman year:
Jerry Quaerna, Coach Alex Agase, Mike Reinhold,Jim Harbaugh

Janesville, Wisconsin, 1986: Drinking Gatorade, getting ready for Bo's fall practices.
From left, front: Jim Harbaugh, Mike Reinhold (NT), Marty Rice, Eddie Quaerna.
Back: Rick Frazer (OT- glasses), Joe Quaerna, Dieter Heren (OLB), Jerry Quaerna (OT), Rod Charles.

Mike Reinhold wedding, 1991, Scottsdale, Arizona...
From left: Jim Harbaugh, Rick Peterson, Dr. Greg "Stick" Reinhold, Mike Reinhold,
All-American Brad Cochran, Jerry "Q" Quaerna and Bob Hegbloom.

49ers office at 1a.m., September 10, 2012: After flying back from a Green Bay victory, Jim Harbaugh shows "Bo's Blue Book of Life's Lessons." (Photo courtesy of Todd Anson)

MICHIGAN
WOLVERINES

JIM HARBAUGH

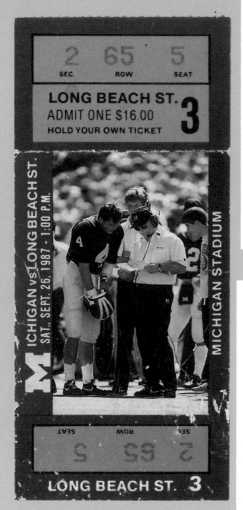

MICHIGAN vs LONG BEACH ST.
SAT. SEPT. 26, 1987 - 1:00 P.M.

MICHIGAN STADIUM

2 65 5
SEC. ROW SEAT

LONG BEACH ST.
ADMIT ONE $16.00
HOLD YOUR OWN TICKET
3

LONG BEACH ST. 3

JIM HARBAUGH
Quarterback 1983-86

Acknowledged to be the best throwing quarterback in Michigan history; four year letterman and three year starter; Big Ten Player-of-the-Year and All-American as a senior; third in balloting for the Heisman Trophy; the first Big Ten quarterback to lead the nation in passing efficiency for a single season; 5,449 yards and 31 touchdowns passing for his career; threw for 2,729 yards on 180-277 (65%) as a senior and 1,976 yards on 145-227 (63.9%) as a junior; 18 TD passes as a junior; first Wolverine quarterback to throw for more than 300 yards in a game; led the Wolverines to a #2 national ranking after beating Nebraska 27-23 in the 1986 Fiesta Bowl; averaged over 200 yards per game passing as a senior; All-time Michigan leader for career pass completions (387), career pass yardage (5,449), single season pass yardage (2,729), single season pass completions (180), single season total offense (2,847), and single season TD passes (18); drafted in the first round of the NFL draft by the Chicago Bears.

UNIVERSITY OF MICHIGAN
Card 7 of 22

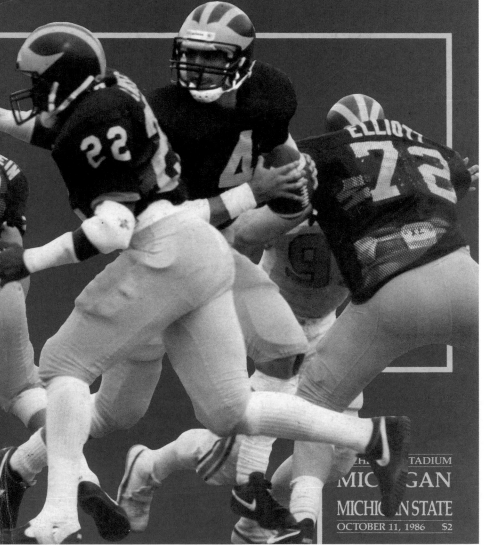

MICHIGAN

THE STADIUM
MICHIGAN
MICHIGAN STATE
OCTOBER 11, 1986 $2

INVESTIGATING THE NCAA INVESTIGATORS
JERRY FALWELL'S TEAM • GAMES & GUNS IN SEOUL

SPORT

SEPTEMBER 1986/$2   CANADA $2.50

COLLEGE FOOTBALL PREVIEW
LOOK WHO'S NO. 1

MICHIGAN,
WITH
QB JIM
HARBAUGH,
IS THE
LEADER
OF THE
PACK.

MICHIGAN STADIUM
MICHIGAN
vs
ILLINOIS
NOVEMBER 1, 1986 $2

MICHIGAN

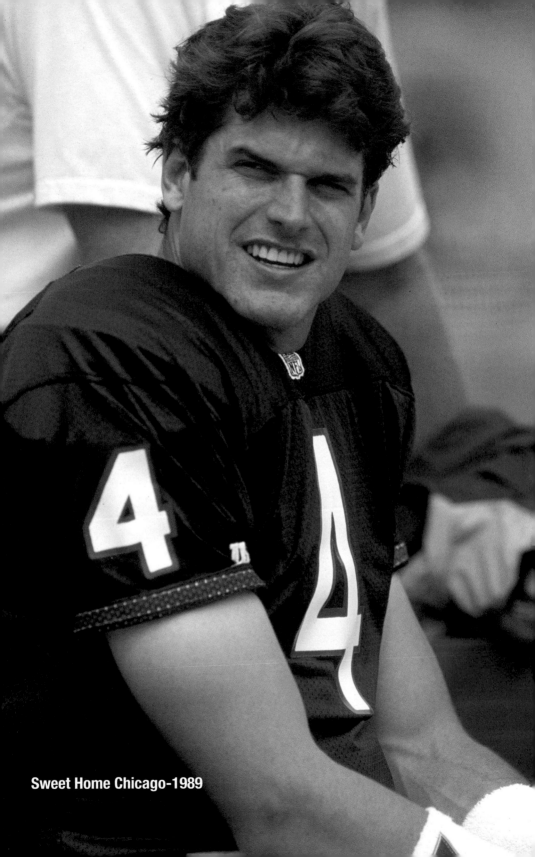
Sweet Home Chicago-1989

SEPTEMBER 14, 1992 •$2.95

Sports Illustrated

nfl '92
KICKS OFF

Good News Bears

Jim Harbaugh passes Chicago to a last-second win over Detroit

0 724454 6
37
10096

THE DAYS ARE LONG, THE YEARS ARE SHORT

JOHN KOLESAR

John Kolesar made two of the most famous catches in Michigan football history. The first one was a 77-yarder from Jim Harbaugh when he was a true freshman, against Ohio State. Even though he was from the Cleveland area—and still lives there—and Ohio State coveted him, he followed his father's footsteps by playing for the Wolverines. Kolesar has been in the Internet security business for 20 years, protecting the world from hackers for Fox Technologies.

I can't believe it's been almost 30 years. I was joking with my wife. We've been together, 16, 17 years now, married. The days are long, the years are fast. We have four kids: a senior, a freshman, a sixth grader, and a second grader, age seven. We had them a little later. We're going to be busy for awhile.

When I first met Jim, I was a wet-behind-the-ears freshman. In the Michigan program, if you're a freshman, you're seen and not heard. The senior leadership and the way Bo ran those teams was pretty spelled out. I worked hard and did what I could. I was able to play as a freshman, which didn't happen as often in those days as it does now. Bo threw only on third-and-forever. My freshman year, I averaged 28 yards on 12 catches.

What happened in our relationship was the trust factor after the '85 Illinois game. We had only one loss against Iowa. We go to Illinois, and tied 3-3. As much as I could, as a freshman, I'd go back to the huddle and tell Jimmy, "Hey, man,

I'm open. I've got man-to-man coverage on me every play. I'm wide open." He didn't throw it to me that entire game. We watched the film the next day. Bo let Jim know that I was open! Jim probably figured, hey, this kid can run some routes. He got open. He was wide open. Why am I not throwing it to him?

For the '85 game against Ohio State, it was a late start day game that turned into a night game at Michigan Stadium. It was real cold, a little drizzly. I was shaking and shivering in the huddle. It was that cold out on the field. Ohio State had just scored. Cris Carter made a great leaping catch in the end zone. A quick momentum switch their way. It was seven or eight minutes into the fourth quarter. CBS had all the shots right on the line of scrimmage. That's why there isn't good video on that play. Jim called the play. Typically, when we called plays back then, they were a combination running/pass audibles. It would sound something like, "2324, roll 366." What that means is, 2324 is a running play, left or right, and then roll 366 is the pass. Jim would look at the defensive front. He would look at the coverage, and then he would select a play based on what he saw. Does he go left? Does he go right with the run, or does he think he can throw the pass? The pass was a "6-route" that I was running. The "6-route" was a post run in our scheme. Typically, the way he read it was, I was the first read, and then he went across left to right to the tight end, to the split end and to the back. Oftentimes, I'm just getting into my route, and he's already looked me off because I'm not into my route enough and he can't read the coverage. So he's going off to his second read. In that case, in that play, they had the corner blitz, the strong safety blitz. He read that. He saw the corner sit on me. He has to trust that I'm going to take this over the top, which I did, and he lofted it out to me. That was the trust from that Illinois game, from the Purdue game. He knew I had some speed. William White, who later played in the NFL, was a tremendous defensive back for Ohio State. He thought I was going to do an "out" route. Earlier in the game, we had another drive where we had two third downs-and-long. Jimmy had thrown two "out" routes to me for first downs. White was sitting on the route, thinking that I was going to do an "out" route so he could break on it. But we just went over the top of him, and it was a perfect call at a perfect time and a perfect pass and a perfect night, the way we came back and shut the door on Ohio State's comeback. Jim threw a perfect pass.

When I saw that ball coming toward me, it's like any receiver seeing a ball coming in the air, trying to catch a brown ball against a dark blue sky in the middle of the night with a little bit of rain coming at you. All sorts of things go through your mind. The most important things are just the fundamentals—keep running, keep your eye on the ball and get your hands out there. First and foremost, catch that football. I was wearing contacts, and as I was looking back and running, the wind caught in my eye and the contact got folded up. I was basically one-eyed, trying to look at this ball. I actually lost it a little bit, because I'm blinking as I'm running. But all that goes back to how you catch a football and those little drills you do in your bed at night, throwing the ball up in the air and catching it, throwing the ball up in the air and catching it. You know where that ball's going to land, even if you lose sight of it. If the defender puts his hand in your **FACE***, you still have a good idea where that ball is going to be. Unfortunately, it was dark. There were portable lights. Everybody made a big deal about the so-called first night game at Michigan, which was in 2013 against Notre Dame. That '85 game was really the first night game. It was well after 5 o'clock in the second half and in Michigan in November, it's dark at 5 o'clock. We had portable lights, and they set them up on the corners. If you're running a post route and you're looking back at the quarterback, you're looking directly into the southeast portable lights. You had that complexity. There was a lot that could have gone wrong.

---

*The **FACE** of the New England Patriots' logo is modeled after Elvis Presley....In 1968, the Patriots played a regular season game in Birmingham, Alabama.

Fortunately, the training and the way we're taught and the repetition that we had in practice, all contribute to you performing and doing your job. My job was to catch that football, and that was the first thing that I did. After I caught it, then I just ran for the pylon. I got on my wheels and went downhill.

I had no idea that 30 years later, they'd still be talking about that play. It's like fish stories. They get bigger and bigger as they go. It was a tremendous thrill for me. Most of my life, being raised in Ohio, my dad going to Michigan, I was always a Michigan fan. Half of my school pictures, I had a Michigan shirt on. To come in as a freshman and to play against a great Ohio State team and to be in an integral play of that victory was like a dream. It takes 11 guys on the field to execute that play and at that point, we had a quarterback named Jim Harbaugh who made it happen. He led the Big Ten in passing efficiency, even though we weren't a big throwing team.

I wasn't in touch with Jim when he went to the Bears for lots of reasons. He's got his season, and we've got our season. You're in the same season. You can't go watch each other play. Even the teammates that I played with that don't go pro, we all come from different places. Life happens and all of a sudden when you come see each other again for reunions, it's just like yesterday. It's no different with my relationship with Jim. I played in the NFL with Jim Kelly and Bernie Kosar. Jim is the best quarterback I ever played with. Jim Kelly is a tremendous competitor and is in the Hall of Fame. What he's missing is what Jim Harbaugh had, that "it" factor, that confidence factor that brings the other teammates to that Promised Land. There's just something there. You knew that he had the confidence that he was going to do it.

People make fun of Jim's 1985 guarantee against Ohio State. I don't look at it that way. Maybe it was a poor choice of words, but I understand exactly where he's coming from. He was going to win that game, as simple as that. It's not cocky. It's just the way he commanded himself to do things. I'd take him in a heartbeat as a quarterback, just because of the experience that I had with him.

I didn't interact with him very much over the last 25 years, but when I sit down with him, it's just like yesterday. Jim was influenced by some of the greatest football minds in the history of the game: Bo, his Dad, Ditka and Ted Marchibroda. All that stuff is in his DNA now and that's immeasurable. That's why I'm excited for these Michigan recruits to experience that. That's why I said I'd play for him. I'd coach with him, and I'd have my kid play for him. He's all about football, the good football, too.

Jack Harbaugh and I are likeminded in many ways. He was coaching at Western. He could hardly get to many of our games, maybe one, depending on how that worked out. When I see the Harbaughs to this day, they're family to me. It's just one of those things. I see Jackie. Certainly John, the thing about John and Jim, my brother played at Miami of Ohio. John was his teammate. A couple of years ago, my brother and I were watching the Super Bowl, the Brothers' Bowl, right, when John and Jim were coaching. It was funny. Twenty-five years later, my brother played with John, and I played with Jim. They're coaching the Super Bowl, and my brother and I are just VPs of sales for a company. I said to my brother, "It's kind of the same thing. We're basically coaching. We're just in a different venue."

We had Mass before each game. Jim was there and everybody else who was Catholic. Because I was the freshman, I had to do the reading. We played Notre Dame my first game in '85. That was Gerry Faust's last season. I did the reading, and we won. Because we had won, I was considered good luck, so I did the reading for the rest of the year for the Mass as a good luck charm. That carried on to next year, the good luck charm, and we won all those games, too, until I broke my collarbone.

I see it every day when I work and do things, the people I try to hire. When I work and try to coach people, it's almost frowned upon. I've got to be careful about what I say, how I say it, when I say it to get people just to do their jobs. Just to tell them what it is to be excellent, what it is to do that. It is frustrating. When I look to hire, I try to find an athlete that played football. I try to find Marines. They're the only people left that can understand.

I've got four kids with college educations to fund. I still do it. Even if it falls on deaf ears, I can't help but do it. I can't help getting up early. I can't help to do some work. I can't help putting a full day in and then some. I can't do it any other way. I don't know how. I'm a disciple of that system, Woody Hayes, Bo, Jimmy Harbaugh. My playing field is selling, that's what I do. We all can't be head coach of Michigan. We all want to be. For whatever reason, we take our career paths and go where we need to go.

It's a special thing. The thing that Harbs created this year, who got it better than us? Nobody, and I echo that. It's an experience that lasts a lifetime. Part of it is because it's fleeting. It is because it's only four or five years. You've just got to do it.

ALL IT TAKES IS ALL YA GOT

JOHN DUERR

John Duerr's childhood was in Southern California, but he graduated from St. Alphonsus High School in Dearborn, Mich., before walking on at Michigan. Duerr lives in Auburn Hills and works for Chappell Steel Co. in Detroit.

Hardly a day goes by that somebody—a customer of mine, a friend, whoever—doesn't ask, "Well, is Harbaugh going to do it? Is he going to get that place turned around?" The answer is yes, not because he coached in the NFL or because he coached at Stanford. It's because of what he learned at Michigan. One thing I know for a fact is you're going to see effort, tenacity. You're not going to see guys mail in a block. Just like we learned from Bo, you're not going to see guys start game in and game out if they aren't performing. That has happened a little bit too much for our liking. I'm sure that Jim learned it from his dad, and all of the coaches that he was around, and his older brother, John—everything that he absorbed when he was a kid.

I was there with Jim three years, and under Bo for four. I went on to coach **HIGH SCHOOL*** football. Everything that I know about football, I learned from those guys, the same teachers that Jim had. Now, he is 1,000 times more advanced than I am, but I don't care what level you're at—you've got to be tough. You've got to bust your butt. You can't mail in a block. You can't sulk. Those are the things that Jim learned. That's why

---

*In 2012, four million **HIGH SCHOOL** students played tackle football with no fatalities. In the same year, 30 skateboarders died, eight students died in gym class, six more on the playgrounds. In 1968, there were 36 football fatalities.

Michigan football is going to be good, because they're going to do it the right way. There is no alternative.

We had seven-on-sevens in the summer of '86, and we had off-season workouts. There wasn't a lot of talking. It was just go do it. You were expected to do it. Go do it. Guys like Harbaugh and Jim Scarcelli, they held people accountable. You didn't even need the coaches around. Those guys would make sure that you were living up to the standard, and if you weren't, they were going to call you out. That was the thing that made all of these guys who played at Michigan successful in winning titles like they did.

My junior year, we played in Hawaii after the Ohio State game. Scarcelli and Harbaugh and I were at a place, and he asked these girls at the bar, "You know who that guy looks like? Who does that look like?" He says I look like Huey Lewis, so he liked to introduce me as Huey Lewis' cousin.

Jim's senior year—it would have been the '86 season— right around the time when we started camp. At that time, we voted on captains. We're at dinner in South Quad. We're at dinner with all of the guys—you just gravitate to the guys that you hang out with, whether it's your roommate or guys who play the same position as you. I always ate with the same guys, the Stites brothers, Don Lessner, Scott Harrala, Kyle Anderson, this group of walk-ons. We're sitting at our same dinner table that we sat at all of the time. Lo and behold, Harbaugh pulls up a chair to eat with us. Well, we both were captains a few days after that. We all thought that was peculiar, that he would choose that day to sit down with a bunch of walk-ons. The Stites boys called him out and he swore he was just looking for a place to sit.

When Harbaugh was coaching at San Diego, there was a guy I worked with whose grandson was a good football player. I emailed Jim and said, "Hey, I got a guy here that might be the guy you're looking for." Jim emailed back, "I need tough guys.

I need good students, tough guys." The kid ended up playing lacrosse for Penn State.

I teach my kids things Bo taught me and things I learned playing football as part of a team—the whole team concept. I preach to my kids that you have to remember that the world doesn't revolve around you. At some point, you're going to be part of a company or a team, and you're going to be responsible for a certain aspect that the whole team's success is based on you doing your job. It doesn't matter what job you have. It doesn't matter what company you work for. It doesn't matter what you do. You have a responsibility for the betterment of the team, and if you don't do your job, the team is not going to succeed. I'm glad that I got that experience around those people, in that stadium, on that campus. Michigan runs through my blood, and I try to pass it onto my kids.

I still hang out with those guys, those walk-ons that I told you about, that sat at the table where Harbaugh came. Those guys, we all still hang out. If I'm up in Ann Arbor, I'll call and we'll go to lunch. One of the guys lives in **CINCINNATI***, and when I'm down there on business, I stay at his place. The other guy is here locally and we go and hunt together. On November 15, all of us get together over by Grand Rapids and have hunt camp. I bring my son and he gets to enjoy these guys that I played football with 30 years ago. I wouldn't trade a second of what we had to do to make it. These guys mean that much to me. The experience that we went through together means that much. I love them.

The greatest play I ever saw Harbaugh make was that 77-yard TD pass to John Kolesar in '85 against Ohio State. He stood there in the pocket and took a shot right in the head as

---

*In May of 2003, David Horton, 24, a fugitive from justice, took a date to Great America Ballpark in **CINCINNATI** to watch the Reds. He and his date were shown on the Kiss Cam, his parole officer was at the game, he was arrested in his seat.

he released the ball. Kolesar was running toward the north end zone and caught that ball. That's the loudest I have ever heard Michigan Stadium. That was beautiful, man. That play was just phenomenal. What a great pass, under pressure, in a big game like that. Man.

My old teammate, Mike Reinhold, was moved from linebacker to nose guard. He said, "You know the difference between linebacker and nose guard? Nose guard is you're at a party every day that you ain't invited to." I never forgot that line. I used to tell that to every kid I had who played nose guard: "You're going to a party and you ain't invited." He was a good guy. Reiny was a good guy.

~ ~ ~ ~ ~ ~ ~ ~ ~ ~ ~ ~ ~ ~ ~ ~ ~ ~ ~

Who was the only Major League Baseball player to grace the cover of the college football edition of Sports Illustrated? Bo Jackson? No. Kirk Gibson? No. Rick Leach of Michigan? Yes.

In the 1983 Holiday Bowl, Brigham Young University quarterback Steve Young caught the winning touchdown pass in a 21-17 victory over Missouri.

DOWN AT THE CORNER OF WHAT AND IF

THOMAS WILCHER

Thomas Wilcher is a very successful head coach in football and track & field at Cass Technical High School in Detroit. He was a running back for U-M from 1982-86 and an NCAA indoor track champion in the 55-meter hurdles.

My memories of Jim are that he's a hard worker. Time on task. A straightforward guy. Always doing the right thing. We really started talking on the first day in the locker room. We had a few guys that were from the South in the locker room, too. They were white guys, Caucasian guys. Jim Harbaugh and Andy Moeller had to smooth those guys over, because for some of the guys, it was their first time interacting with blacks at that level. It was a culture shock for them. I remember Jim talking to the guys, smoothing it out, trying to create a team atmosphere.

In the huddle Jim, was, "Let's get it guys. Let's get this on. Let's go." He was like that. Straightforward. Have a breakdown? Got to get this third down. "Come on, let's get this. Let's make this play. Come on. Let's get it." He'd clench up his fist in the huddle and say, "Come on, let's get this. We've got this, guys."

The most disappointing thing I did when playing with Jim was when we played Iowa in '85. Iowa was ranked No. 1 in country, and we were ranked second. We lost the game, 12-10. Late in the game, we needed about five yards for the first down, and Jim threw the ball at me. I turned to the right, but I was really supposed to turn to the left. I turned and the ball was coming. I went across my body to try to catch it and it flicked off my hands, off my shoulder pad, and I missed it. That was probably one of my most disappointing plays. We didn't get the first down. We were driving the ball, and that stopped the drive. I don't even remember going back toward the sideline, toward everybody. I went back toward the end of the bench. I don't know if I even talked to anybody coming back home, because I was so disappointed. It was a catchable pass, but I just opened up the wrong way. The ball came to the right spot. That's what happened. That was the game. I felt terrible, but Jim refused to blame me for anything.

Later, when I was grown, I was driving down the freeway and Bo spotted me. He started blowing his horn, and he pulled me over. He just started hugging me, on the freeway. He just kept hugging me, telling me how glad he was to see me, how glad he was that I was doing all these great things in the city of Detroit, how glad he was that I was coaching. He just kept telling me, "Just keep doing it." He just kept praising me. I didn't think it was any big deal.

Whenever I saw Bo, he always talked about how proud he was of me and everything. He would talk about how we'd make special plays in practice, and he was always shocked at what I could do. He would always talk about that. I still talk to Bo's son, Shemy. Shemy talks to me like he knows everything about me. Shemy is a really good guy.

When you look at Jim Harbaugh, every place he's been, he turned everybody around. San Francisco wasn't going to the doggone Super Bowl. They got him, and guess what? He turned it around. All I'm trying to say is that sometimes people have to be ready for what you ask for, and you have to stand back and watch it. When you get ready to paint a picture, sometimes you stand back and get your thoughts—and then you start painting that picture. People try to figure out what you're doing—what are you doing, what are you doing, what are you doing? Then they step back and gaze at it. Ah, I see it. Ah, I like it. That's Jim Harbaugh.

After he took the Michigan job, it was probably a few days before Jim called me. He was real busy. We talked about family and kids, our vision. We talked about some different things I was still doing—what was my vision, my goal? What was my high school's vision? Did I have any vision for college and all of that? That's what we talked about, really.

I would love to coach in college. I would love for a coach to say, "Hey, Coach Wilcher, we'd love to have you on our **STAFF***." I'd love to do that. That takes time, though.

I know for a fact that Jim will turn it around here, because he's trying to find the tools right away. He's not trying to implement something too hard. He's trying to implement something that's going to be simple. The most important thing to do when you're trying to be successful is not implement something that's hard, but implement something that's simple for the team to grasp onto. Make sure the team can figure it out so they can go wholeheartedly into it at 120 percent, full speed ahead. You want to keep it simple.

*"You can't afford to have one bad coach on your **STAFF**."
— Jim Harbaugh

HOOPS: THERE IT IS

TONY GANT

Tony Gant is from Fremont, Ohio, home of Rob Lytle and Charles Woodson. Gant was awarded the James A. Rhodes Trophy as the most outstanding high school football player in Ohio in his senior season, beating out Bernie Kosar and Keith Byars.

I'll tell you a story about Jim's competitiveness. We were juniors, playing pickup basketball at the IM Building. It's my fourth or fifth pickup game. I'm scoring about a third of my team's points. Harbaugh walks in. He watched a couple of our games. Immediately, he wanted to cover me—just to see if he could shut me down—because he knew that I was doing all of the scoring. He had some success. I'm not going to give him all the credit. He was just right up on me. He wouldn't let me shoot the ball. He was just so determined to shut me down and keep me from scoring. That's his competitive nature.

Those very first times Jim and I met or had an interaction with each other—obviously we're freshmen, sharing the same locker room. We are going into the training room to get our legs taped, so we've got to shave our legs with a razor. I accidentally dropped the razor or shears, or whatever you want to call them, and they fell on Harbaugh's leg and actually opened up a nice little cut on his leg. I'm thinking, Oh my god, we're going to have a confrontation here with this guy and I'm going to have to fight him. He just had composure. He just looked at me and said, "How you doing? I'm Jim Harbaugh." "Hi, how you doing? I'm Tony Gant. I'm sorry about that."

I was vacillating between Michigan and Ohio State. I grew up in Ohio and loved Ohio State. I was player of the year in

Ohio my senior year. At the time, they didn't have a Mr. Football award, but the top player received a governor's trophy as the most outstanding player in the State of Ohio. Keith Byars probably got runner up, and then Bernie Kosar was third. That was our '81 season, which was our senior season. I'm pretty proud of that.

My son, Allen, is currently on the Michigan team. He's a redshirt junior and is an outside linebacker. He came in as a defensive back, and they switched him to linebacker. He just gained a lot of weight. Allen was elated when he heard about Harbaugh becoming the coach, just like I was. I've always told Allen that I wanted him to play for Bo, like I did. This is the next best thing—playing for Jim Harbaugh. He's going to get exactly what I had 30 years ago, because he's going to get tremendous coaching. I said, "Allen, I promise you, you guys are going to win." Everyone is saying we're going to have a down year and it's going to take Jim two to three years to get his team. Our cupboards are not bare—we just need some of these kids to be developed. It was a thrill to play for Michigan and then have my son out there coached by one of my good friends.

Being on the defensive side of the ball, I didn't really know how good Jim was until after we graduated. I see some of the old football games on ESPN Classic or the Big Ten Network. I've always known he was a great leader, that's without question. A lot of times, we didn't really get to see each other play. I was on the defensive side, so I was sitting down taking orders from the defensive coordinator, while he was on the field doing what he did, and vice versa. I really didn't know how great of a player he was until after we left. Then I'm looking at him against **OHIO STATE***, the guarantee game back in '86. I saw our South Carolina game on one of the reruns. Man, this guy was great. I knew he was an All-American and I bragged about him, but wow!

*The **OHIO STATE** University College of Veterinary Medicine includes a fenced dog-walking area with a fire hydrant painted in Michigan colors.

I played in the Japan Bowl after my senior season, and Vinny Testaverde was the big-name quarterback there, along with Mike Shula. I'd tell these guys from Miami, "My quarterback is better than anybody here." I was upset because Testaverde wore number 14 in the Japan Bowl. That was my number all five years at Michigan. Just because he won the Heisman Trophy, I had to revert to number 13. Jim was third in the Heisman voting. Back then, the Japan Bowl was the second-best bowl to go to. You always had the Senior Bowl and the East-West Shrine game. I played with a lot of college superstars—a lot of future NFL players—in Japan.

After my senior season, I didn't see a lot of the guys. We'd still go into the weight room quite a bit, but I don't recall seeing Jim that much, except on Pro Day. Jim didn't know how fast I was at the time. I'd broken my leg returning a punt my junior year, and I played two years after that. We had a Pro Day. I don't know who came in and timed us, maybe it was Tony Dungy, who was at Pittsburgh at the time. I came back into the training room and said, "I just ran a 4.47 and a 4.49." Jim said, "No way, get out of here." I did. Jim went up to the coaches, asking if Tony Gant really ran that fast. I looked slow to all my teammates.

Jim was a great leader on our team, from the day that he took the helm. Back in '84, we were decimated with injuries. That's the year we went 6-6. We lost at least four—and maybe five—starters off that team. I was the first to go down, with a broken leg. That was the third game of the season, against Wisconsin. Two or three games later, Jim broke his arm against Michigan State. Jim and I were at the doctor's office and, for some reason, we were holding our x-rays, waiting for our doctor—Dr. Gerald O'Connor—to come and see us. Jim put his x-ray against the light, put it on that x-ray board, and said, "Hey, Tony, this doesn't look too good does it?" "Actually, Jim, it doesn't. I broke both of the bones in my leg, but your break looks worse than mine." Obviously, Jim was extremely concerned about his broken arm, and I'm not sure it healed properly either. Mike Reinhold had his injury that same year. They had to put a pin in his hip. When I went to the hospital to get a cast changed, going from a full cast to a half cast, I could hear them hammering the pin out of Mike's leg. That was scary.

During the '84 season, we were decimated by injuries. So, we really wanted to impress the coaches in '85. We always started camp by running a mile and a half for time. We had other tests we had to do, but all of the coaches would come out and watch us run the mile and a half. The coaches were really impressed in '85, because coming across that finish line were three guys who were basically out the year before. Jim Harbaugh came in first, I came in third and Mike Reinhold came in fourth. We were just impressing the coaches that we had come back from those devastating injuries. After you have a season-ending injury, initially you are just so down in the dumps. I was devastated. I had pro aspirations. I read some of the clippings, and I knew where I stood. There was some preseason All-American talk about me back in '84. We opened up that year against Miami (Florida) and I had a tremendous game. We upset them. They were the No. 1 team in the country. Two days later, I broke my leg. It was a real bad break. I severed my nerves, so it was the nerve damage that really hurt me, not the broken bones. I was on crutches for four months and in a cast for about six, just feeling so down on myself. But I tell you what, I was crutching across campus—the middle of campus at Michigan is called The Diag—and I was feeling sorry for myself. I was going to class one day. I kid you not, I saw the blind leading the blind. I saw a blind person leading another person across campus. I was feeling sorry for myself. I had my health. My leg was going to heal. I was going to play football in another four to five months. These two people would never get their sight back. That was a reality check for me. I embraced it, took it for what it was worth. I was going to play again. Maybe I wouldn't be as good as I once was, but I learned to just enjoy the moment.

SHORT STORIES FROM LONG MEMORIES

BUMP ELLIOTT

Bump Elliott, 90, was a star running back and the head coach at Michigan. While he was the director of athletics at the University of Iowa, he hired Dan Gable, Hayden Fry and Lute Olson. Elliott served with the Marines in China during World War II.

Who is to say what problems you're going to run into, because you never know in coaching. But Jim will do just an outstanding job. He seems to me, as I look at it now, to be perfect for the job. He has the background of Michigan, and he knows the traditions and he knows the things that are important at the University. It appears to me that he is a great coach. He has had excellent success at the various schools—and pro team—he has been with since he got into the coaching business. I just think he is going to be fine. Particularly, one of the things that I really felt was always very good to have is some background of the University, because Michigan is pretty special. They have traditions, and they have had a lot of success there. To understand those traditions and understand where they're going and what they're doing is important to make it go.

You can't second guess after it's over with, but obviously it was an excellent move. Hopefully, there will be nothing but good times ahead. I have lots of confidence in Jim. He'll do a great job. I'm rooting that Jim and the Wolverines will be fine. Of course, I root for Iowa, too, you know, so it's a little bit upsetting when they have to play each other.

Jack Harbaugh is great. Jack is just a super guy. He was a great coach at Iowa under Frank Lauterbur before joining Bo's staff at Michigan in '74. The one thing I remember most is my daughter, Betsy, babysat for both John and Jim. (Said Betsy: "I remember Jimmy and John would jump up and down on the couch for hours. I can't remember anything about Joani being there. Isn't that awful? She must have been very well behaved. I must have been the world's worst babysitter!") That was a great family. We really loved them when they were here. Jack will love moving to Ann Arbor. That town is just like Iowa City, only there is a nice big city next to it—Detroit—if you want to go in. He'll love Ann Arbor. (Said Jack: "I have great respect for the Elliott family. I worked at Iowa for two years under Bump. I coached his son, Bobby, and his daughter, Betsy, **BABYSAT*** for our kids. Bump introduced me to a former teammate of his at Michigan by the name of Jack Harbaugh. What are the odds? I then went to Michigan and coached Pete Elliott's son, David, which would make a great trivia question!")

PAT DAVIS

Pat Davis was Jim Harbaugh's seventh grade math teacher at St. Francis of Assisi Catholic School in Ann Arbor.

I had Jim for seventh grade math from 1976-77. He was a great student. He was fun and very smart. We had a math program that was individualized so that you could go at your own pace. He was always up to pace or ahead of things, which made it more fun for him. He was very good hearted.

I also had his brother, John, for seventh and eighth grade math. John was a little bit shyer, but still the same, a really good-hearted kid. I never met their parents, but I could tell they both came from a great family and had a good upbringing. They were kind to the other students. They didn't get into any of the seventh and eighth grade kind of normal terrible behavior. They were really nice kids.

*When she was a teenager, Martha Stewart **BABYSAT** for Mickey Mantle's and Yogi Berra's kids.

Jim had a very shy smile on his face when he was working on things, and you could tell he was maybe in on something going on that you didn't know about. He was just good hearted about his approach toward everything

I have not seen him since the seventh grade. Of course, I watched him play for U of M and saw him occasionally in the news as his name crossed the candidates list around here. But I never personally made any contact with him. It made me feel good to see how he succeeded. As a teacher, any student you've had that goes on to succeed, you feel great about. When he came back to Ann Arbor, I was excited, but not surprised. I was hoping that he would accept it. U of M needed some help, and I'm glad that he was ready to be the man of the hour for them.

I like to tease people that I was the only math teacher I know who had taught both of the opposing coaches in the same **SUPER BOWL***.

ANDY BOROWSKI

Recruited out of St. Xavier High School in Cincinnati, Andy Borowski was a center on the U-M football teams from 1983-87. Today he is the national accounts manager at Amcor Rigid Plastics.

We always had a rule that nobody went out to a bar on a Thursday night. That was the night that we all had to be very focused. Usually, we'd have team meetings or player-only meetings. If there was any word that some player might be out at a bar, Jim would go and check to see if a player was there. That's how a lot of discipline was handed out.

---

*Danica Patrick has starred in more **SUPER BOWL** spots than any other celebrity.

All of us were accountable. If you hear Jim talk about these things today, it's accountability to one another. The camaraderie was that accountability to one another, to the guy that was next to you, to the guy that was running the ball. The camaraderie you're seeing is coming from that accountability.

Jim lived in a house on Packard Street. It was the summer before my junior year. You'd see Jim sitting on the stairs, usually with a girl, and talking to another girl on the phone. It was the craziest thing I ever saw. I thought, how the heck does he do that?

DAVE HOCHMAN

Dave Hochman was a student at Ann Arbor Pioneer High School. He would skip class to attend Bo Schembechler's weekly Monday noon meetings with the U of M Club of Ann Arbor. His teachers were unimpressed. He now lives half the year in Ann Arbor and half in the Phoenix area.

The **SUPER BOWL**** came to the Phoenix area for the first time in 1996 when Jim Harbaugh was an active player with the Colts. I met him at a party at Planet Hollywood in Phoenix. I told him I was a Michigan fan who still lived half the year in Ann Arbor. His brother-in-law, Tom Crean, was then an assistant basketball coach at Michigan State, so I asked him who he'd be rooting for in the upcoming UM-MSU basketball game. He said, "I've gotta go with State."

My second meeting with Harbaugh came a few years later when he was making an appearance at the Outback Steakhouse in Ann Arbor. He stopped by every table to chat with fans. I asked him about the 1986 Michigan-Minnesota game. Michigan was undefeated late in the year, and Bo Schembechler—in

---

The half-time show at the first **SUPER BOWL in 1967 were the bands from the University of Michigan and the University of Arizona.

his 18th year at Michigan—had a real chance at his first national championship. Bo played for a tie, but lost the game anyway. UM trailed by seven points when they scored a touchdown with a couple minutes remaining. There was no overtime back then. Unlike Tom Osborne's decision to go for two and the win in the epic National Title game with Miami, Bo chose to kick the extra point, tying the game. But Minnesota ended up kicking a last second field goal to win. After the game Harbaugh made his famous guarantee that U-M would beat Ohio State in Columbus the next week and go to the Rose Bowl. They did just that! I asked Harbaugh what he thought of Bo going for the tie and was pleasantly surprised when he responded, "I hated it."

DOUG JAMES

Bo Schembechler once told Doug James that he had "the worst body in the history of Michigan football." James wound up starting on the offensive line for three years and was co-captain of the 1984 team. Since graduating, he's been a sports announcer and executive for several radio stations and networks in his hometown of Louisville, as well as Charlotte and New York.

I was a co-captain in 1984. Jim's first start was against **MIAMI***, the defending national champion, ranked No. 1. It was my third year as a starter in the offensive line. I had a lot of game experience and played with a lot of good players, a lot of good leaders. The first time we had the ball, Jim walked into the huddle with a lot of swagger. I knew right then that even though I was the offensive team captain, in the huddle it was his team.

---

*The University of **MIAMI** (Fla.) teams are named the Hurricanes because their first football game was delayed by a hurricane.

We were driving down the field and were getting close to scoring. Jim jumped in the huddle and started yelling at the offensive line to get more excited. "C'mon, we're getting ready to score! You guys need to be pumped up!" I said, "Jim, we're in the trenches here. We don't get too excited. We just line up and play, bud." He was slapping guys on the helmet. I reeled him in a little, not to the detriment of anybody. It was obvious that even though it was his first start, he was going to take owner-ship and lead the team.

We were destined to have a good season, and then Jim broke his arm against Michigan State. He broke his humerus, his upper arm bone. It was a devastating injury. I always felt that what happened in '84, when we finished 6-6, was sort of the perfect storm. I was confident that Bo was going to turn that around, and Jim was going to be the guy to lead the offense. The next year they came back and had a successful season, winning the Fiesta Bowl and finishing second in the country.

I was on the field when Jim broke his arm. Michigan State was winning, but we had a good drive going. We ran an off-tackle play. I pulled around and blocked a linebacker. Jamie Morris got up in the hole. I think it was the strong safety who hit him and he fumbled. The ball bounced all the way into the backfield. Jim dived to recover the ball, and a guy flew in at the same time and hit him in the upper arm. I'd never seen an injury like that. I don't think it was a compound break, but you don't see guys break their upper arm bone in football. At Michigan, your expectations are next man up. The guys that were backing up Jim didn't have enough ability to do what Jim did. As it turned out, Jim was a really special player. We lost that game. It was the only time I lost to Michigan State in my five years.

Bo would always say that most of us weren't going to play in the NFL, and even if we did, we weren't going to play for very long. We needed to get a degree. We had to go to class. He used to carry our transcripts in his briefcase, in case he wanted to have a conversation with someone about how they were doing at school. I was injured in my last season and was on crutches. I was a December graduate and didn't really have a future in the NFL. Bo wanted me to consider coaching. I was a graduate assistant coach for awhile and worked for him through the summer. I sat with him in the conference room next to his office, and he had every player's transcript. He hand wrote notes on each transcript to the parents. The note might have read, "Doug's doing really well in school. You should be proud of what he's doing." Or it might have read, "Doug needs to work harder. I'll do my part to keep pushing him, but make sure that you stay on him about working hard in school." He wrote the notes, and I addressed the envelopes and put a stamp on them. Those were the kinds of things that Bo did when he ran the program. I think Jim takes a lot of that with him. That's a big part of who Jim Harbaugh is.

RICK BAY

Rick Bay was captain of the U-M wrestling team in 1964-65 and the Wolverines' head wrestling coach from 1970-74. He moved into athletic administration and was the athletic director at Oregon (1981-84), Ohio State (1984-87), Minnesota (1988-91) and San Diego State (1995-2003). He also served as chief operating officer of the New York Yankees and president of the Cleveland Indians.

From 1966-81, I coached **WRESTLING*** and worked for the alumni office at Michigan. Jack was the secondary coach for Bo, and we were good friends. We had a lot of fun together. He has a great sense of humor. I love him and Jackie to death. One funny thing I remember about Jack is—and we always laughed about it—we were on the same athletic department softball team. Bo played first base. Jack was left fielder, and I played

---

*Abe Lincoln is in the **WRESTLING** Hall of Fame.

shortstop. We had a great time playing. One game somebody hit a fly ball to left field, and Jack had trouble with it. Jack was a good athlete, but he had trouble with this particular fly ball. It seemed like he staggered and circled underneath this fly ball for 10 minutes before he finally got his bearings and made the catch falling down. It was a routine play. It should have been a routine play. I've always kidded Jack about that ever since. Jack is very knowledgeable about the Cleveland Indians. The older Harbaughs grew up in Crestline, Ohio. I did hear from him when I got the Indians job, but I didn't know that he knew baseball trivia like a genius.

Jim Harbaugh killed Ohio State in 1985 when I was the athletic director at OSU. Jim was the quarterback. It was a game, as often Ohio State-Michigan games were, that probably determined the Big Ten champion, and we were behind with a few minutes to go. Cris Carter, our wide receiver, now a Hall of Famer, made a circus catch in the end zone to put us within striking distance of Michigan. On the very next possession, Michigan was in a bit of a hole. We knew that Harbaugh was going to throw the ball. We sent a blitz, a safety blitz, and our safety didn't quite get there. Harbaugh read it perfectly and hit his wide receiver in stride for an 80-yard touchdown pass on the first play from scrimmage after Carter had put us back in the game. That killed us!

We played Michigan four times when I was AD at Ohio State. I was there four years, four football seasons. We won two, and they won two. We won the last one, which was the most dramatic because it was 1987 in Ann Arbor. The Monday before the Michigan game, I was told to fire our head coach, Earle Bruce. I resigned, because I wouldn't fire Earle. The president did. But we did go up to Michigan. That was our last game, a fired coaching staff and myself, a resigned AD. We went to Michigan five days later, Earle's last game, and we beat Michigan.

Jim's hiring has put a lot of anticipation into the probability that the Michigan-Ohio State rivalry will get new energy. Ohio State has dominated Michigan in the last eight or nine years to the point where the rivalry has lost some of its sizzle. But with Jim at Michigan and Urban Meyer at Ohio State, both controversial kinds of figures, it will generate a lot of interest. It could come close to the Woody-Bo thing or even Bo and Earle. People forget. People talk about Woody-Bo, but Earle Bruce was 5-4 against Bo in his nine years.

Overall, I think Michigan and Ohio State have a great rivalry. I still consider it the epitome of a football rivalry. It's just that it's been one-sided for several years now. But there's so much history there. Even this recent dominance by Ohio State doesn't take a lot of the luster off of it. People still get pumped up when Michigan plays Ohio State, and I still think it's the best rivalry in college football.

CHRIS ANSON

Chris Anson is a 2012 Michigan law school graduate.

Jim Harbaugh is a brilliantly intellectual coach, befitting a man with a classical education. He is super smart and extraordinarily adept at keeping himself narrowly focused on football.

JOHN BARNES

John Barnes and Jim Harbaugh were among six founding partners who created IndyCar team Panther Racing in 1997. Barnes co-owned and managed Panther Racing from its inception until the team was dissolved in 2014.

Shortly after Jim Harbaugh joined us in forming Panther Racing, we were racing at Dover International Speedway in Delaware. There was a driver on the track who ran into our driver's car. Jim was up on the spotter's table and got into a shoving match over it and hurt his shoulder. The next day he had to report to the Colts training camp. It sent a powerful message to our team. "Yes, he was invested in this."

His association with our team meant a lot to him and how we did in the races meant a lot to him. I would laugh at anybody who thinks Jim Harbaugh does anything halfway. He's totally engaged in everything that he does. Before Jim joined Panther Racing he was a racing fan. He did commercials with one of the other partners on the team, Gary Pedigo, who owned a Chevrolet dealership in town. It was Gary's idea to bring Jim onboard. Jim is a "guy's guy." All our partners were good because each of us had a role. Jim was the face of our team because of his **NFL*** status. I didn't have to worry about telling the Panther Racing story or speaking to the press. Jim was the guy.

Jim makes everybody around him better. I've never met anyone like him in my life. Whether it was a race car driver or a Fortune 100 CEO, Jim has an incredible knack for seeing things around him, analyzing it quickly and making smart decisions.

Jim was always involved, always engaged. He would help the pit crew and would give suggestions on how to make pit stops better. He wasn't a guy who would just stand around and sign autographs. He was always engaged and that's why everyone around him was always so blown away. He was a big deal, but he never acted like it. He was just a regular guy. The khaki pants and the sweatshirts, that's Jim. He wasn't there to get the attention. He was there to get the results. He wasn't afraid of coming to me and I wasn't afraid to go to him. People are people, whether you're driving a milk truck, driving an IndyCar at 230 miles per hour or throwing a football.

Jim had an organization called the Harbaugh Hill Foundation. He would give Colts tickets to inner city kids and we

*The last Alabama quarterback to win an **NFL** game was Jeff Rutledge.

would bring the kids to our racing shop for Christmas. About 250 kids would come to the shop and we'd give the kids gifts and provide a Christmas experience. Every year we had the celebration on the same day, December 23. I didn't know why we picked that date, but one year Jim said, "It's my birthday." I said, "It's my birthday, too." Jim said, "Yeah, I knew that."

KEN MAGEE

Ken Magee grew up in the same Ann Arbor neighborhood as the Harbaughs, then spent more than 25 years working in law enforcement. He has amassed the largest private collection of U-M football memorabilia, some on display at Schem-bechler Hall. He is the co-author of The Game: The Michigan-Ohio State Football Rivalry *and* The Little Brown Jug: The Michigan-Minnesota Rivalry.

The Harbaugh family moved to Ann Arbor in '74. Little Jimmy Harbaugh was about 10-years-old and I was about 16. I was a friend of the Schembechler family, and sometimes the Schembechler boys and some of the neighborhood kids would ride our bikes to Michigan Stadium to watch the practices. Because we were with the Schembechler boys, we were allowed in the stadium. I was in the north end zone stands during a practice and kids were tossing a ball around. There was a little kid who was probably in row number 15 or 20 throwing the ball up to a kid in row 60. That little boy had a great arm. I asked one of the other kids, Geoff Schembechler, "Who is that?" He said, "That's Jack Harbaugh's son, Jimmy Harbaugh." I kept watching. Somebody threw the ball to Jimmy, and it went over his head. He sprinted down the bleachers to get the ball. I'm thinking, he's got a great arm *and* he's fast. Then he fell. His head landed smack-dab on a bleacher seat. Flush. I heard the sound. It echoed throughout the stadium. I thought, the fast kid with the great arm? He's dead now. I took a couple of steps toward him and saw him rise from the dead. He picked up his head. You could tell he was out cold, but he got on his feet. He was bound and determined to get that ball. I said to one of the other kids, "That's the toughest little kid I've ever seen." He picked up the ball, half unconscious, and threw it back to a kid halfway up the stadium.

TIM MARSHALL

Tim Marshall is the president and CEO of the Bank of Ann Arbor. A native of Indianapolis, he graduated from Purdue University and earned an MBA at Butler University.

At the Bank of Ann Arbor, we've done billboard campaigns that were spontaneous. When Michigan went to the NCAA Men's Basketball Final Four, they qualified on a Sunday afternoon. We had all hands on deck designing a billboard campaign for Coach Beilein and his team. We had the billboards up by Tuesday. We've also been very forward in terms of our utilization of social media. Last Columbus Day we posted, "We will not be closed for Columbus Day because Columbus is in Ohio."

In December of 2014, when it seemed as if all of the momentum was in place for Coach Harbaugh to be hired, the head of our advertising agency—Ernie Perich of Perich Advertising and Design—called me at home on Saturday. The announcement was going to be the following Tuesday. We worked all weekend. We got the creative done. We worked with the outdoor company Monday morning and got six boards aligned. We hit social media around 9 a.m. the day of the announcement. It was amazing, the amount of shares, the attention we got—the Big Ten Network, **ESPN***, as far away as the *Seattle Post-Intelligencer, The Washington Post.*

*Tim Brando was the original host of ESPN's GameDay.

One of the messages was "HarBO." That was a takeoff on Bo Schembechler. We've continued it. The boards are very simple messaging on the verbiage. It's all about trying to get people's attention. It's all about trying to get people to smile. It's all an attempt to add a little levity to what are normally rather dry and mundane advertising messages. We continued once Jim got here. We have a "Like and Love" campaign. One of our boards near the stadium was, "Like Jim loves Khakis. We love to help."

It doubles down into significant growth that we've been able to achieve as we've developed this very strong brand imagine. We're local. We can respond quickly to current events that are impacting our local community. And we can do it in a fun way. We're all about being part of the local community. It's a competitive advantage that other banks can't replicate.

PAUL CHUTICH

Paul Chutich was a childhood friend of Jim Harbaugh. His father owned Bimbo's Pizza in Ann Arbor which was a common gathering spot for Bo Schembechler, his assistant coaches and their families. Paul played hockey at Bowdoin College in Maine. He owns the Delkwood Grill in Marietta, Ga.

Jim's childhood and my childhood completely intersected. We did everything together. We went through first communion together at Saint Francis. We did our confirmation together. We played junior football together for the Packers, of all teams. Not the Wolverines. Then we played hockey together, and we were on the Tappan baseball team together. My main sport was hockey, and I played college hockey in Maine while Jim was playing football at Michigan. We still remained close, so whenever I was home from school, we'd have a good time and hang around together.

My best memory was of us hanging around the Michigan football practice field. We'd bug the players for sweatbands and try to get footballs. We got yelled at by Bo at least every other day. Bo didn't talk to you. He barked. "Get that kid out of here!" It wasn't nice language with Bo. He didn't mind throwing a few cuss words around.

I first met Jim when we were kids and I was hanging around all of the coaches' kids. We played football and hockey together. If I wasn't on his team it was always a bitter rivalry. Jim was the most competitive kid around. He wanted to beat everybody in everything. Jim was more competitive than his brother, John. John is the nicer of the two. I say that because Jim was so competitive that it would get in the way a bit. He was involved in a few playground fights, not fights where punches were thrown, just little scuffles. He had a lot of friends, but not on the field. I was a running back on the Packers team when Jim was the quarterback. I played only two years and then started concentrating on hockey. Jim quit hockey around the same time I quit football. We played against each other in hockey. We'd tangle and get into it, but afterward we'd still be best friends. He was good at hockey, as far as his knowledge of the game and his sense of the game. He wasn't the best of skaters, though. The reason he wore uniform number four a lot in his football career was because it was the number of his favorite hockey player, the Bruins' Bobby Orr.

Jim was a little bit cheap. We used to tease him. He had what we called Alligator Arms—he couldn't reach his pockets. When Jim was playing at Michigan, I'd come back to Ann Arbor and hang out with him and his teammates. We'd go to a drive-in movie theater and pack eight guys in the trunk. We were all cheap. None of us had any money, so we'd pack eight, nine guys in the trunk. Girls got in free, so we'd have a girl drive in with eight or nine guys in the trunk. Jamie Morris was in the trunk a time or two. Imagine Jumbo Elliott in the trunk. He was 6-foot-8 or 6-foot-9 and weighed nearly 300 pounds. He was in the trunk, too. Fortunately, we used a big old car, a Catalina.

There would be so many of us in the trunk that you couldn't move.

JOHN ELWAY

John Elway is a Hall of Fame quarterback who won two Super Bowls. He played collegiately at Stanford. Elway is currently the general manager and executive vice president of the Denver Broncos.

It was a long time ago, 1980 and '81, when I was a sophomore and junior at Stanford. Jim was in his final two years of high school at Palo Alto High School. He had transferred from a high school in Michigan when his dad became a defensive coach at Stanford. Jim would haunt our practices. There's one thing that sticks in my mind about Jim. When he would come to our practices, the one thing that you could not deny was the unbelievable confidence that Jim had. I remember thinking at the time that if this kid was at Stanford, I would be his backup! It didn't seem to enter his mind that he couldn't be the starter no matter where he was or who was the starter there. Nothing he has done in football has surprised me.

Chapter 3

BEAR DOWN CHICAGO BEARS!!

GRADE 6B

MR. McCARNEY
MATTHEW ANHUT
DEBORAH BLACKMAN
DAVID BROWN
JULIE CONLIN
EDWARD CRYDERMAN
STEPHEN DALY
KEVIN DECKER

JOHN DeVINE
ERINN DOUGHERTY
JOHN ELLIS
LORETTA FARRELL
WILLIAM FISTER
MILTON FUEHRER
KEVIN GAINEY
TRISHA GOODRIDGE

JAMES HARBAUGH
VALERIE KOVAC
ANDREW LAWRENCE
JOSEPH McCALLA
DAWN MALFESE
WILLIAM MARTIN
JILL MOSES

JULIE NIELSEN
VANESSA NOBILE
MICHAEL O'CONNOR
TIMOTHY OESTREICH
ELIZABETH OLSEN
ROBERT POLLOCK

KATHLEEN ROBRECHT
BARBARA RODDY
PAULA SPRING
JOSEPH SUPPLEE

DA COACH

MIKE DITKA

As the head coach of the Chicago Bears (1982-92) and New Orleans Saints (1997-99), Mike Ditka won 121 games and Super Bowl XX. He was an All-Pro tight end five times in his 12 NFL seasons. Mike is a member of the College Football Hall of Fame and the Pro Football Hall of Fame. His uniform number 89 was retired by the Bears and the University of Pittsburgh. After Jim Harbaugh retired, Mike Ditka sent him a signed picture with the inscription, "I still am—believe it or not—your biggest fan." The picture hangs in Jim Harbaugh's office.

I'm not going to tell you that Jim Harbaugh was the best quarterback I ever saw, because he wasn't. He was not Johnny Unitas or Joe Montana, and there's no doubt about it. But I will tell you that Jim Harbaugh was just about the most competitive individual I have ever coached. When it came to playing the game hard and getting every bit of talent he had and turning it into a player who could win games for you, Harbaugh was the guy you wanted playing for you.

From the moment he got here when the Bears drafted him in 1987, I knew he wanted to be a Chicago **BEAR*** and he wanted to do whatever it took to win games. That's what was so good

---

*In 1962, The Saturday Evening Post alleged that Coach **BEAR** Bryant of Alabama and Coach Wally Butts of Georgia colluded to fix a college football game. In 1967, the U.S. Supreme Court ruled in favor of the coaches. When asked what he was going to do with his huge settlement, Bear Bryant said, "Wally and I are going to start a men's magazine called 'Bear Butts.'"

about him. When it came to putting in the work, this is what he wanted to do first, last and always. It was like he was the best Jim Harbaugh he could be when he was on the practice field or playing games.

That's what you want as a coach. You want players who love the game, truly love the game, and prove it with everything they do. A lot of guys can talk it. A lot of guys who are really good players talk it pretty good. But to get a player who lives it every minute, that's really rare. That's why I love Jim Harbaugh so much. It's an indication about his character and what's going on inside his head and inside his heart. As a coach, you don't have to worry about a player like that. You know he's going to do things the right way every time he has the ball in hands. It's not that he didn't make mistakes. I told you, there were other guys who were more talented. But when he made a mistake, he worked hard to correct it.

He had all the measurables you look for in a quarterback when we drafted him. You assume that when you take a quarterback in the first round that he has the arm strength and the talent you need to be competitive. But you don't assume anything else. You look for a certain attitude that tells you as a coach that you're going to be able to depend on that player. I got more of that from Jim Harbaugh than I ever could have expected.

Now, I was not the easiest coach to play for. Everyone has their ego, and I have mine. I pushed hard when I was coaching and that was pretty well-documented. That's because that's how I knew how to coach. Was it always effective? No. Was it always the right way to act? Again, no. But I was going to coach the way that was true to my personality, and Jim understood that.

As a quarterback who understood the game so well and as an individual we trusted, Jim always had the ability to take any play we sent in and audible out of it. Sometimes it worked like a charm, and other times it didn't work very well at all. We had a famous game in 1992 against the Vikings where we were at the Metrodome, and we had a pretty good lead, 20-0, against them in the fourth quarter. All we had to do was hold on to the football, use some clock and not have any big plays against us and we would have walked out of there with a win. That was a very difficult building to play in, and we were playing well.

I sent in a play, and I thought it was a pretty good play. But Jim saw something when he went to the line and he audibled out of it. It obviously didn't work out because Todd Scott intercepted the ball for them and took it back for a touchdown. Everyone knows what happened after that. I was angry and I was upset, and I let Jim know about it. The cameras focused on me yelling at Jim, and that's what everyone remembers. As the years have gone by, I know full well that I shouldn't have reacted like that. At the time, I was angry and I wasn't about to just let that go. I reacted, and that was it.

If there was one player who understood that a coach is going to react emotionally, it was Jim Harbaugh. We called a play, he changed it, I reacted, and then we moved on. I was upset, but things didn't change between us. He was still the quarterback for the Chicago Bears and he still had the right to audibilize and change the play to what he thought it should be after that. Still, I wish I hadn't reacted like that. As you get older in this life, you live and you learn and you might do things differently the next time you face a similar situation. But the one thing you can't do is turn the clock back and change the way you did it the first time. That's just the way life is.

Jim had a really good career for us and he helped the Chicago Bears win a lot of games. I loved coaching him and after he left us, he did well with the Indianapolis Colts. That didn't surprise me at all. He moved on to a new environment, a new team, but he still had the same character. That's truly the measure of a man. When somebody has good character, they're going to do the right thing, prepare the right way and then execute the right way. That's what he did with the Bears and that's what he did as a Colt.

I knew Jim was going to be successful at anything he tried once he left the game. I didn't know it was going to be coaching. Despite being a quarterback and despite his background in the game, you really can't tell that a player is going to develop into a good coach—into a great coach—by the way he is as a player. But it turns out that's what he chose to do. I thought he could have been a company president or a CEO of a big business and he would have been successful.

He chose coaching and if you look at what he has done in his career, he has been successful everywhere he has been. He turned around Stanford and had great success there. Look what he did with the 49ers, it was really amazing. They were not a very good team when he took over, but that changed immediately.

Jim is very organized, very determined and very capable of winning no matter where he is. I think he's now in the right place for him. In pro football, when you're coaching, you're part of an organization and everybody has to be working together and believing the same thing. When that's not the case, it's not going to be enjoyable any longer. That's an important thing. You have to love what you're doing, and you have to enjoy your time on the sidelines if you're going to be the best coach you can be. I'm not so sure that Jimmy was enjoying what was going on with the 49ers in his last year there. Moving on was the best thing possible for him, and I think he found the best possible place to be at Michigan.

He's got that Michigan blood running through his veins and he wants that team to win. That means he's going to be as fully prepared to lead that team to victory as humanly possible every game Michigan plays. That's just the way he goes about his job. I hope he wins the national championship. That's his goal, and that's the reason he went there. It takes time and it takes work, but that's just the kind of person he is.

He may be much better off coaching college players than he was coaching NFL players. I think college players are a lot more receptive and a lot more coachable than those in the NFL. At a certain point, NFL players aren't always easy to coach. Money has something to do with that, but it's not the only thing. Ego plays a big role because at a certain point, you can't tell a player how to do his job anymore. You can give them a play and tell them to run it, but they play the way they do and that's it. With a college player, you have a lot more influence as a coach, and that's why I think Jim may have found the best place he can be.

Will he stay there forever? Will that be the last coaching job he ever takes? I can't read the future and I don't know what's going to happen three, five or 10 years from now. But I do think he's happy at Michigan, and I think it's a place that's great for him and a place where he can be successful.

When I talk to him, it's still a great joy to me. He meant a great deal to me when he was a player, and I'm so proud of him and happy for his success. I hope he has a lot more of it in the years to come. He's a good guy who does things the right way. It's called strength of character and Jim Harbaugh has got it.

THE WRITE GUY

HUB ARKUSH

Herb "Hub" Arkush is perhaps the most well-known football analyst in Chicago, and he certainly fits that description among non-former players. He has been talking and writing about the NFL and the Chicago Bears since the 1980s. Fans know him from his work as an analyst on the Bears' radio broadcasts, as a football insider and savant on WSCR-AM (The Score) and as the long-time publisher and editor of Pro Football Weekly. *But it was in his role as the color analyst on the Bears' WBBM broadcasts that Hub got to know Jim Harbaugh. What started off as a basic athlete-journalist relationship—with little to set it apart from the norm—quickly changed.*

Jim came to the Bears in 1987 when he was drafted in the first round. I got to know him the way I got to know all the rookies. Every player that gets drafted comes into town and meets the media, and being a part of the Bears broadcast team gave me the access to talk to him one-on-one and get to know him.

I could tell right away there was something different about him compared to nearly every other player I had met, and it was his competitiveness. It's a very competitive business, obviously, but he just had more of that than any of the other players I had ever met. It was striking. But I could also tell that he was a good guy and a nice guy. We developed a rapport and some of that may have been because I went to Michigan, so we had something in common.

In those days, there was no minicamp or Organized Training Activities—OTAs—so I didn't expect to see him again until training camp. But a month or so after the draft, I was coaching my oldest son's youth baseball team in Deerfield. I was looking at the stands and saw a familiar face. I thought the face looked just like Harbaugh's. I walked over to him and it was Jim. I asked him what he was doing there, and he said he was with his girlfriend and that her nephew was on the team. He asked me what I was doing there, and I said that I was coaching my son's team. Then I told him to get up out of the stands and coach third base for me. He did, and while he was with us for just a few games, it certainly helped me get to know him.

As training camp started that year, I could see that my initial impression about him being so competitive was absolutely right. The roots of the coach you see today were there as a rookie with the Bears in his first training camp. He wanted to do everything well, and he didn't want to make any mistakes. He wanted to win in everything he did, and that included the card games that the players had on the plane.

As Harbaugh established himself with the Bears, the work ethic he displayed as a rookie became even further ingrained in his preparations and in the way he played. You could just see how much he was putting into it and how hard he was working. When Jim was drafted, the Bears still had Jim McMahon and Mike Tomczak, so he didn't get the position right away. However, you knew that when the opportunity came, he was going to be fully prepared to play.

You could tell he had a great deal of admiration for Mike Ditka and that he was not the least bit overwhelmed while working for such a huge personality. He wanted to win for Mike, and he was doing everything he could to put the Bears in a position to win games for him.

Much was made of the sideline blowup that occurred when Harbaugh called an audible in a 1992 game at the Metrodome in Minneapolis against the Vikings. With the Bears leading 20-0 in the fourth quarter, Harbaugh audibled out of the play call and threw a sideline pass. The play turned out to be a disaster, as Todd Scott of the Vikings saw what was going on, jumped the route and intercepted the ball. He strolled into the end zone with a touchdown, and the Vikings had momentum. They went on to defeat the Bears, 21-20. Ditka blew up on the sidelines at his quarterback, and after the game, the media declared that Ditka's sideline tirade caused the Bears to lose and took something out of the quarterback. I always thought that was completely overblown. Jim had been around Ditka for a long time, and he knew what Ditka was like. It was not the first time Ditka had gotten upset. And I can tell you that there was at least one person who was even angrier at Jim Harbaugh than Ditka. It was Jim Harbaugh. He knew he had made a mistake that had cost his team badly. The last thing Jim ever wanted to do was hurt his team with a costly mistake. He didn't blame Ditka for anything. It was his mistake, and he knew the only thing he could do was continue to work hard and do better the next time out.

You could see that he was designed to become a coach very early in his career. While he was a very good player who would leave everything he had on the field, it was clear that there was never going to be enough football for Jim, and it didn't seem likely he would ever leave the game. Of course, much of that comes from his dad, Jack, being a head coach, and it's clear that it runs in the family. But Jim also played for Bo Schembechler at Michigan and Ditka with the Bears. I think that helped give him even more determination in his coaching style.

Jim never wanted anything given to him. He may be the head coach at Michigan now after a great run with the San Francisco 49ers, but he paid his dues every step of the way. He started off as an unpaid assistant with the **RAIDERS***, and he took

*The Oakland A's and the Oakland **RAIDERS** are the only MLB and NFL teams to share a stadium.

steps up the ladder before he finally became a very successful head coach at Stanford. After that, he had his chance with
the 49ers, and he made the most of it. The team was starting to
become quite talented when Jim was hired, and he was taking
over for Mike Singletary, who just wasn't prepared or ready to
become a winning head coach in the NFL. Jim was ready, and
he drove his players hard and got the most out of them. That's
what top-level **COACHES*** do. They get everything out of their
players that they can. I think it ended in San Francisco not
because of any real problem with the front office other than
him wanting more say with the personnel. It's the old Bill Par-
cells line about wanting to buy the groceries if you're going to
prepare the meal. That's all Jim wanted, and that's the same as
a lot of coaches feel.

Jim Harbaugh is not just the guy you see on the sidelines.
He has been the star quarterback, and he was the life of the
party many times off the field. I got to play in his charity golf
outing in Ann Arbor several times, and you see a much looser
and more relaxed guy than comes across when he's coaching.
He knows how to have fun.

---

*There are two current college football **COACHES** with statues of
themselves outside the stadium where they currently coach: Nick
Saban at Alabama and Bill Snyder at Kansas State.

CATCH THIS

TOM WADDLE

During Jim Harbaugh's run with the Bears, they were an average team with average to slightly below average talent. Harbaugh did not have a game-breaking receiver like Jerry Rice or Tim Brown who could make big plays. Instead, he had Tom Waddle. The effort that Waddle demonstrated endeared the wide receiver to his quarterback, his coach and Chicago's always hopeful football fans. Waddle got the most out of his career with the Bears, lasting six seasons and catching a career high 55 passes in 1991. Waddle has remained in Chicago since his playing career ended in 1994, and he has been an analyst on the NFL Network and on local Chicago television. He also hosts a popular radio sports talk show with partner Mark Silverman on AM1000, ESPN's radio affiliate in Chicago.

Jim was just a great guy to play with, and I really enjoyed working with him when we were both on the Bears. We had a good partnership because we both looked at the game the same way. I knew I had to leave it all on the field every time I went out there, and what happened the day before didn't matter at all. Jim had the same kind of attitude, and I saw it in him, and he saw it in me. I think that's one of the reasons we had a good partnership on and off the field. There was mutual respect.

I can tell you that's not something you always see from a first-round draft choice. Some guys don't go out there as if they could lose their job or as if there's something to play for every day. But Jim did. As we got successful, we started to get a little recognition. I remember we did an ad together for a popular clothing chain in Chicago, Bigsby & Kruthers. They had an ad painted on the side of a building. Jim was wearing a $2,000 suit, and I was still in my shoulder pads. It was great while it was up, and I think some people might still remember it. However, that ad wasn't up for long. Bigsby & Kruthers decided to replace us with Michael Jordan. I guess you can't blame them, and it was fun while it lasted.

Jim was the kind of guy who made you feel good about what you were doing. One time, I made a diving catch late in the game that led to us earning a win early in the season. After the game, we were running off the field, and Jim sprints up to me from behind and made a whole speech to me about the catch. "Tommy Waddle, do you know what you've done?" Jim asked. "You just made the game-winning catch for the Chicago Bears. That means you will never have to buy yourself another drink in the city of Chicago, because these fans won't let you go in your own pocket." Well, that wasn't the case, as I have bought many drinks over the year. But that's the kind of quarterback and teammate Jim Harbaugh was. He had a way of making you feel special about yourself and the contributions you made on the field.

That's what a great teammate is all about, and Jim was always that way. He did everything he could to get ready, and he was prepared. You could tell that he had the perfect makeup for being a **COACH***. Not because he was a yeller or a screamer, but because he always did everything he could to be prepared when he went on the field. That's what gives you the best chance of winning. I've seen him develop as a coach after his playing days, and he is clearly one of the best in the business. He's going to get the most out of himself and his players. Whether he was coaching at Stanford, with the 49ers or now with Michigan, that part is always going to be consistent. It's

*The highest paid public employee in 27 of the 50 states is a football **COACH** at a state university. In 13 other states, the highest paid public employee is a basketball coach.

like any other business. People see him working hard and doing everything he can to deliver a winning product, and so his players respond the same way. There's no secret there. That's human nature. Jim has always worked hard and been very talented. Those are the reasons for his success, and I'm sure he will always be successful in this business.

~ ~ ~ ~ ~ ~ ~ ~ ~ ~ ~ ~ ~ ~ ~ ~ ~ ~ ~

When Clemson University plays in a bowl game, most of their fans pay their hotel and restaurant tabs with $2 bills to show their economic impact . . . and increase their chances of a future invitation.

When Knute Rockne and seven others were killed in a 1931 plane crash, it was the largest disaster in U.S. aviation history up until that time.

NFL footballs are made in Ada, Ohio. Each team uses one thousand per year. The balls are made from cowhide, not pigskin. The balls used by kickers are different and are marked with a "K."

WHEN CHICAGO CALLS, YA GOTTA ACCEPT THE CHARGES

STEVE McMICHAEL

Steve McMichael played in the NFL for 15 seasons. The Pro Bowl defensive tackle was a member of the Chicago Bears from 1981-93. After retiring from the NFL, he has been a pro wrestler, the head coach of the Chicago Slaughter of the Continental Indoor Football League and an announcer on the Bears' pregame radio broadcasts.

The Bears drafted Jim in the first round in 1987, and the plan was that he was going to come in and start at quarterback. A couple of things hit me right away. Some quarterbacks are like delicate little flowers with an attitude of "Don't hit me, I'm the **QUARTERBACK***." There was none of that about Jim. He was all football player, all the time. He participated in every drill. That guy worked and worked and never stopped working. He practiced every day as if he wanted to be nowhere else but on that football field.

You respected him right from the start. I ran into a lot of people—both in my playing days and since—that know how to talk a good game. But when it comes to actually doing the work and playing a good game, they run, they hide, they make excuses and they don't perform. Jim Harbaugh was one guy who was just the opposite. I know people who say they love

---

*During the 2007 NFL lockout, **QUARTERBACK** Vince Young took a high interest loan to throw himself a $1 million birthday party. He filed for bankruptcy in 2014. He once bought out a Southwest Airlines flight from Houston to Nashville, all 120 seats, so he could fly alone. He blew $5,000 a week – $260,000 a year – at The Cheesecake Factory in Houston where he regularly took eight teammates to dine.

football and many of them are just saying the words. Some hate it, some like it, but very few really love the game. When Jimmy was in Chicago, he loved football. He loved being a Bear and he wanted to win more than anything else. I learned right away that he was his own man. You couldn't push him around or tell him what to do.

As the years went by, it was clear how much of a leader he was on our team. He did everything hard and he did everything the right way. He put a little extra into everything he did, and I think that's what leadership is all about. You don't have to tell anyone that they aren't doing things the right way when you go the extra mile and do them yourself. He never took the easy way out.

In 1991, nobody was expecting a lot from us. We had been a defensive team for so many years, but a lot of us veteran defenders were running on fumes. We needed help from the offense. Jim didn't have a lot of what you would call great talent, but he managed to get it done. Jim and wide receiver Tom Waddle carried the load. Those two were not Joe Montana and Jerry Rice, but they got the job done through sheer effort. The most important thing was that the offense held onto the ball. When you're old, and you've been on defense for half the game and your offense goes three-and-out, that's hell, baby. That would have been a disaster, as much as I was hurting. Jimmy wouldn't let that happen. He led the offense on some amazing drives. All our defenders were sucking wind. When it got to be third down for our offense, I would reach for my helmet. Jimmy would get chased and run for a first down that he'd make by six inches. Then it was third down again. This time he'd find Tommy, who would make an incredible catch as he was getting hit. You get three or four first downs, it's good for the soul. Forget the soul, it was good for this body. It meant I got to rest before I went on the field again. I wasn't 23 anymore. Our defense needed the break and Jimmy gave it to us. We won a lot of games that year that people didn't expect us to. We made it to the playoffs with an 11-5 record. We lost right away to the Dallas Cowboys, but getting to the playoffs that year surprised a lot of people.

One thing I couldn't tell was that Jimmy was going to become a coach. You can see that sometimes in a player, but what I saw was 100 percent a player—a guy who wanted the ball in his hands and a guy who wanted to make the play when the game was on the line. That's what you want from a leader and it all came naturally to him. He was a tough guy who didn't ask for any favors. If you think that's easy, you couldn't be more wrong. He was looking across the line at a bunch of Sasquatches who wanted to crush him. That's no different than any other quarterback, but what was different about Jimmy was that there was no fear to him. He knew defensive linemen and linebackers wanted to hit him and hurt him. But there was no cutting, running or hiding. He would stick out his jaw and say, "Give it your best shot." You didn't see many quarterbacks like that when I played, and I don't think you see many like that now. He was just a different breed of a quarterback and a different breed of a man. I mean that in a good way. He's only human, but sometimes I think he wanted to do it the hard way. He was happy to take the hit to make a play for the team, and he may have felt like he was cheating when it came too easy.

He's a really good coach now. I said that I couldn't tell he would be a coach after his playing days were over, but you could tell that he had the intensity to run the show. He was a good coach in college, he did really good things for the 49ers and now he's at Michigan. He's going to be very successful. Why not? He's been successful everywhere he's been. Jim's smart, he works hard and he wants it bad. That's what it takes to succeed, and Jim Harbaugh has always known that.

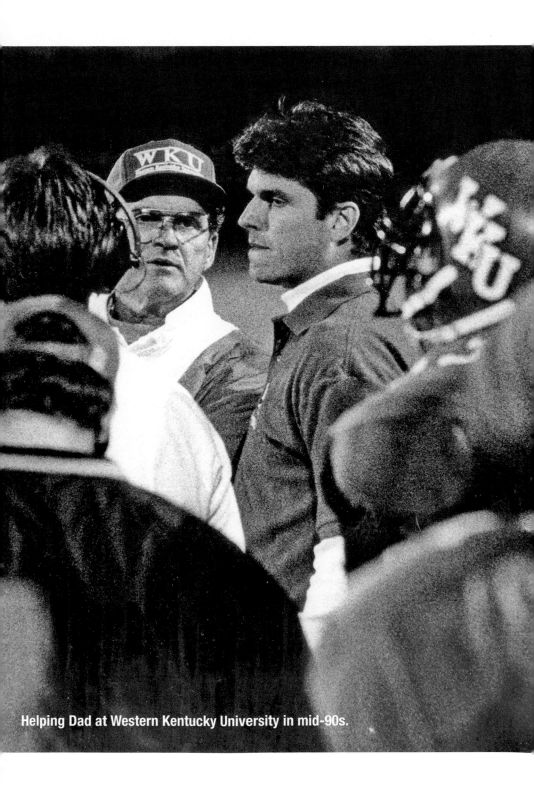

Helping Dad at Western Kentucky University in mid-90s.

Stanford Athletic Director Bob Bowlsby introduces Jim Harbaugh as new head football coach while Harbaugh champion Bill Walsh watches.

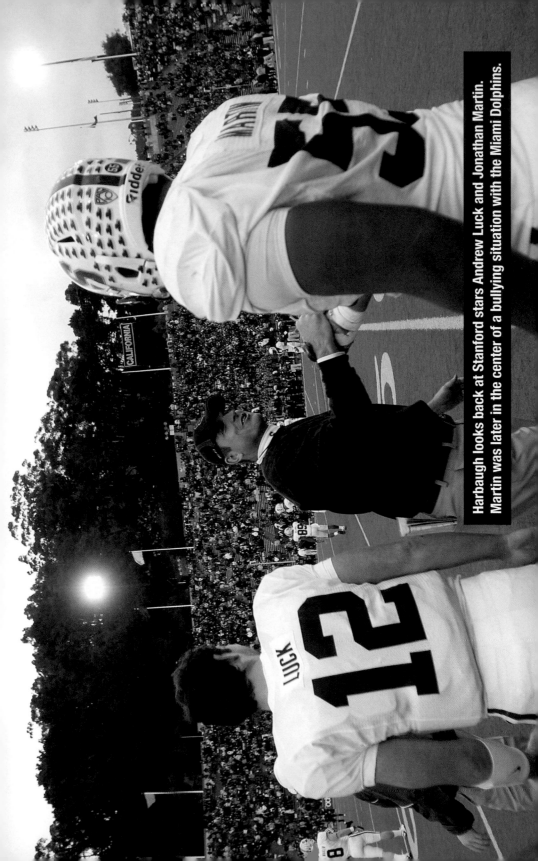

Harbaugh looks back at Stanford stars Andrew Luck and Jonathan Martin. Martin was later in the center of a bullying situation with the Miami Dolphins.

Panther Racing co-owner Jim Harbaugh welcomes General Colin Powell to Gasoline Alley at the Indianapolis 500. Hidden in the background are Nadia Comaneci and her husband Olympic champion Bart Conner.

Annual Missionary work in Peru

Peruvian prisoner wearing shoes and jacket he just received from Jim Harbaugh.

Huddling up for 'Peruball'

Brothers Jim and John Harbaugh relax at the NFL Combine in Indianapolis.

Hey, #4, make us #1.

Bank of Ann Arbor
Member FDIC

ADAMS

Jim Harbaugh throws the first pitch at Detroit Tigers game on June 30, 2015.

Palm Springs 2006: The last huddle ever
for Bo Schembechler and Jim Harbaugh.

Jim and Sarah Harbaugh

SUPER BOWL XLVII PREVIEW

10 THINGS WE THINK WE THINK

STAN MUSIAL

THE CATFISHY TALES OF MANTI TE'O AND LANCE

Sports Illustrated

FEBRUARY 3
49ERS vs. RAVENS
HarBowl Sunday

THERE WILL BE BLOOD

BROTHERS JIM AND JOHN
HARBAUGH FACE OFF IN A FIERY
SHOWDOWN IN NEW ORLEANS
P. 47

JANUARY 28, 2013 | SI.COM

TURN PAGE FOR
3 ADDITIONAL COVERS
INCLUDING SI's PREDICTION

Chapter 4

CALIFORNIA DREAMIN'

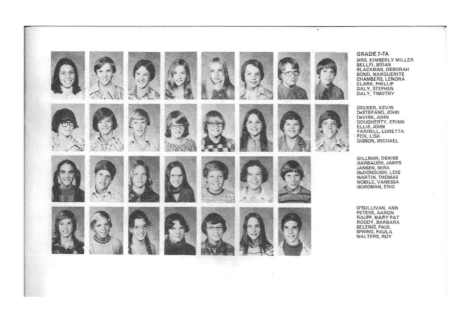

GRADE 7-7A
MRS. KIMBERLY MILLER
BELLFI, BRIAN
BLACKMAN, DEBORAH
BOND, MARGUERITE
CHAMBERS, LENORA
CLARK, PHILLIP
DALY, STEPHEN
DALY, TIMOTHY

DECKER, KEVIN
DeSTEFANO, JOHN
DeVINE, JOHN
DOUGHERTY, ERINN
ELLIS, JOHN
FARRELL, LORETTA
FOX, LISA
GIBSON, MICHAEL

GILLMAN, DENISE
HARBAUGH, JAMES
JANSEN, MIRA
McDONOUGH, LOIS
MARTIN, THOMAS
NOBILE, VANESSA
NORDMAN, ERIC

O'SULLIVAN, ANN
PETERS, AARON
RAUPP, MARY PAT
RODDY, BARBARA
SELENIS, PAUL
SPRING, PAULA
WALTERS, ROY

WAY OUT WEST,
OUT ON THE COAST

A COACH IS A TEACHER WITH A DEATH WISH

EARL HANSEN

Earl Hansen was starting his first year as head coach at Palo Alto (Calif.) High School when a gift named Jim Harbaugh walked into his office from Ann Arbor. Hansen left Paly in 1983 only to return in 1991.

I didn't know a lot about Jimmy when he transferred to Palo Alto High in the summer of 1980, just before his junior year. I knew he was from Michigan, and I talked to his dad, Jack Harbaugh, who was going to be the defensive coordinator at Stanford. They sent Jimmy over, and we sat down and talked to him to find out what he was about. He was obviously knowledgeable about the game. He was asking questions that most of our kids didn't even know existed.

"What defense do you run? Do you run a Cover 2? Do you run a Cover 3? What offense do you run?"

In his first practices, we could see how competitive he was, just very competitive with everything he did. At first, we made him do tackling drills like everybody else. He wasn't used to that, but he did it. Once he showed the team that he was a "real player," I didn't have him do that anymore. He was accepted. He was the new kid on the block, and athletically, he was outstanding. That was a really good team.

My first impression of Jimmy was that he was a little bit naive. He was coming into Palo Alto where kids are worldly. They're affluent, they travel, they do things. Jim's world was pretty much sports. He was all-league in all three sports—football, baseball and basketball. It wasn't just one sport for him.

After I got to know him a little bit, I thought he had a lot to learn, but he had a lot of support from the kids. They were good to him. They took him under their wings, showed him around and helped him. He's still buddies with a lot of those guys.

That year was the first time in our school's history that we went to the playoffs in football. Basketball was always strong, and that year or the next year Jim's team went to the finals. They had only one division in those days, so making the play-offs actually meant a lot. There weren't five divisions like there are today. There were just the top four teams and that was it.

After the first game, you could tell Jimmy was a pretty special talent. He threw three touchdown passes right on the money. The team the year before with the same guys was 1-9. We went 9-1 with one player difference, and that was Jim. The Palo Alto quarterback who was the MVP of the frosh-soph league transferred out the same year Jim came in. He was good too, but he wasn't anywhere near the same level as Harbaugh.

Jim went in with confidence, and you could see it. That's the big thing with quarterbacks, you've got to have confidence that you can do what you intend to do. Jim never felt that he wouldn't get a first down or wouldn't score. We could tell he was really good in practice, but we had to wait until actual games to see how good he really was.

We had our first scrimmage against Archbishop Mitty High School. They were always really good, and they were expected to do well that year. We just ran all over them. After that, the team's confidence was just sky high going into the season. We felt like we could play with the big boys. The scrimmage had refs, but no score was kept. Physically, we just pushed them up and down the field. Their coach was just distraught. You could see Harbaugh's competitive personality in that scrimmage. The way he conducted himself really did rub off on everybody. The confidence he went in with. The way he went into the huddle.

We knew from practices that Jimmy had great physical ability, but he had immeasurable qualities we couldn't really see until we started playing. He had the ability to inspire his teammates, and we could see that even in the scrimmage. He had a lot of very mature, very good athletes on that team. It was a combination of that, his getting used to his teammates and the confidence in how he called plays in the huddle. All of that worked.

We won the first game, which I thought we were going to win anyway. Then we played Los Altos. In those days, the teams to beat in our league were Los Altos and Wilcox. Los Altos came into our place thinking they were going to win— they'd slaughtered us the year before. They were favored to win the league like they were every year. We beat them, 28-14, behind running back Mark Ford—who went on to play at UC Davis—and Jim. They walked out stunned. From that point on, our team was just like "Go!"

Jimmy would always forget his keys and lock them in the car. He'd always come into the coaches' office after practice, looking around. I'd go, "Harbaugh's locked his keys in the car again." I kept a coat hanger for him so he could get in and get his keys. I think he still does it. It was an old car. He wasn't spoiled as a child, believe me. There wasn't much money those days in coaching. He had to work. I think that helped forge his work ethic. I'm sure of it. Jimmy had to toe the line. He had to do the right thing. He knew right from wrong, and he also knew he had great support. He had a very strong, very good family behind him.

Jim was extremely focused on football. Everything else, not so much. He was a great basketball player, too. He was a very physical player and a great scorer. He was the MVP of the league. Sports came first for Jim. Everything else was secondary. Jim was a good student, too. That was part of his thing, you had to do your job. That came from his parents, Jack and Jackie.

Jim never really experienced failure in high school. First, I don't think he believed in it. If something happened, he was not going to point fingers. If you beat him in a race, he was going to race you 100 times until he beat you. He's like **BOB HAYES***, the Olympic gold medalist sprinter and former Dallas Cowboys wide receiver. Eventually, he'll break you down. Failure is just not in his DNA. As a kid interrupting practice, he got yelled at by Bo Schembechler before I ever yelled at him. It was like water off a duck's back. He just goes back out there and does his thing.

He was very knowledgeable about the game, but he wasn't a know-it-all. He was very coachable, and he was a very hard worker. He would add his opinions to the offense when appropriate. His dad was a college coach, but he never once interfered. I'm sure there were times when he had to bite his tongue. Jack Harbaugh was a young coach, but he never interfered.

We could tell early on that Jim was a person of strong character. He's definitely someone who would stick up for the underdog. When you look at some of the recruits he brought in at Stanford, some of them weren't heavily recruited, and they turned out to be highly successful. He likes to look at a player's character, not just the physical skills.

The bottom line with Jimmy is that he knows how to win. He has a goal. His goal isn't to be anything but a winner. He's not interested in the press' opinion. You're not going to get a lot from him if he doesn't want to give it.

He carried himself around campus like a star. You have to have a little bit of cockiness to be a good quarterback, but not over-the-top cockiness. There are knuckleheads who don't make it who have tons of talent. But you have to have

***BOB HAYES** was so fast that he's considered single-handedly responsible for the creation of the zone pass defense.

confidence, and you have to show it to be a good quarterback. If he ever went over the line, that's where his teammates were so good with him. They'd be like "C'mon, Jim." No confrontation. It was the perfect atmosphere for him. That really was a special team we had in 1980. There were a lot of great kids on that team I'm still in touch with today.

We didn't win it all, but it was the first time Palo Alto had ever been to the playoffs in football. We lost to Live Oak, the eventual champion. We had an opportunity to win or tie at the end—and that was on me, not Harbaugh—and if I knew then what I know now, we would have scored. We missed an opportunity, barely. It's one of those games I'll never forget. Norm Dow was the head coach at Live Oak back in the day. They won the championship going away. The first round of the playoffs that year really was the championship game.

There was a huge difference between Jimmy's junior and senior years. We lost about 1,000 pounds on our offensive line, so it was a lot different. Our skilled position players were still good, but you need a line. Any quarterback needs a line. Even Jim Harbaugh.

There was one game nobody will ever forget. We were playing at Gunn at the end of Jimmy's senior season. It was raining so hard it was coming down in buckets. They had a crown on the field, so water just rolled to where we were on the sidelines. My feet were under water. We were wearing white uniforms. We'd run a dive play and everybody would come out of the pile-up muddy, but before we got out of the huddle, the uniforms were clean. That's how hard it was raining. It was one of the few times we won the toss and said, "We'll kick." I knew they wouldn't be able to move the ball, and we would have field position. The rain was really coming down. Jimmy was five-for-five on short passes, and we won the game.

Jimmy didn't change much when he was here. He was pretty well developed by the time we got him. He was football mature when he got here, but socially, no. That changed while he was here, though. That's part of being a teenager. Dealing with adults, he was always very good. He was always respectful. It was always "yes, sir" and "no, sir." Even then California kids weren't like that. They were respectful, but not like Midwestern kids were.

~ ~ ~ ~ ~ ~ ~ ~ ~ ~ ~ ~ ~ ~ ~ ~ ~ ~

In the TV show "B.J. and the Bear," Bear was a chimpanzee named after Bear Bryant.

Roger Maris once held the national high school record for most kick returns for a touchdown in one game – five, at Bishop Shanley High School in Fargo, North Dakota. Maris received a full scholarship to play for Bud Wilkinson at the University of Oklahoma, but quit after two weeks.

HIS FUTURE IS HISTORY

KY SNYDER

Ky Snyder was the athletic director at the University of San Diego who gave Jim Harbaugh his first head coaching job in 2004. Snyder is from Tempe, Ariz., home of Arizone State Univversity, but played football at San Diego State.

The one thing I've learned about Jim is that he is very strategic. He's got a game plan. Before he applied for our head coaching job, it was something that he had actually mentioned to Monsignor Dan Dillabough, vice president for Mission and Ministry on our campus—even while he was an assistant coach with the Raiders. Jim had just said, "Hey, if there is ever an opening there for that job, that would be a great place to be." He had a home in Coronado. He still had it when he was at the Raiders. Obviously, he got to move back into his home in Coronado. He had that from his playing days here in San Diego. It was part of what he wanted to do. He knew he wanted to be head coach. I'm not sure if he had a game plan to do that in the pros or in college, but he did understand that he probably could move up the ranks faster in college than through the NFL. The biggest thing with Jim is that he is very, very smart, and he has a game plan in all that he does.

I interviewed Jim, and it was what you would expect from Jim. He came in with a game plan—a book that was put together on how he would build the program. He recognized that we didn't have the resources that a lot of other schools had, and he had game plans for how to be creative to take advantage of our environment and how to use the network of people he knew to build a coaching staff. It's one of the things that is overlooked. You don't see it in the media very much, but every place Jim has been, he has had an incredible staff around him. He is so good at building his staff. He did the same thing here. The fact that his dad, Jack, came and was an assistant coach for two years helped Jim tremendously. He knew his dad could help him with being a head coach and learning all of the stuff that he had to do. That's why I say Jim has really got a game plan hidden behind each step he takes.

We actually had a very good pool of talent and interviewed other people for the job. There were others that brought a book or a plan like Jim did, but Jim's was unique—it took advantage of our assets and our community. Most of the others' plans were around developing the team. Jim's was broader than that.

Jack Harbaugh is great. The whole family is great. That's one of the beauties of the Harbaughs—it's an incredible family. We had a game at Princeton when Jim was here. John came up because he was at the Eagles as a special teams coach, and John held Jim's wires for his headset during the game. That's just the family. John figured out a way on a Saturday to pull himself away from the Eagles, pop up to Princeton—and he's on the sideline with his brother. It was really neat. One of the things I always enjoyed was having lunch with Jim and Jack. I did that a number of times. I even said to them at one point, "You two are more like brothers than father and son." Yet, Jim always had the respect of his dad as a father. Jack is a great father. He's a great family man, but he is also a great mentor.

I remember when Jack told me he was going to leave. Jim's last year with us, Jack was not on the staff. We were sitting in our stadium and we were talking, and I said, "You're still helping Jim. Why are you leaving? What's going on?" He put his hands together in a closed cup, and he lifted it to the sky. I said, "What's that? You're releasing the little bird?" He nodded. I said, "I get it. I'm good. Thanks for coming." The whole family is just an incredible group to be around.

I knew that Jim was a winner, and I knew he was a motivator. When he was a player, he was a field general on the team, he was a coach on the field. It was natural to him. Jim has this ability to just connect with people and rally people. You could call him the Pied Piper. They call it the "it factor." He has that "it factor," that ability to rally people. When he called me about Jim, I told Stanford Athletic Director Bob Bowlsby that Jim's greatest asset is his ability to elevate everybody's game around him. Whether it's players, other coaches, administrators, alumni, sponsors, Jim just has this innate ability to elevate everybody that he comes into contact with.

The year before Jim went to Stanford, there were a number of teams that were talking to him, just after the second year here. I told Jim, "Listen, I get it. You're not long-term here, but pick a good opportunity for yourself." Jim waiting the extra year was smart. Stanford was a good fit—especially coming from here—because he had to deal with academic standards here, and it was going to be the same thing up there. It was a good fit, and it was good timing for Jim to go there as well. Jim is one of those really unique coaches, because he's a motivator and he's an Xs and Os guy. Typically, you'll get one or the other, but he's got both.

I don't think you can help but feel respect for Jim as a person and as a coach. He comes at it from the players' perspective, he understands what they're going through. We're all getting a little older, but he was not that far out when he started, and he just has this youthful enthusiasm that is so catchy. Jim has all sorts of different slogans, and some of them just stick with you. Jim-isms, we'll call them. I have one in my household now, from him at Michigan. If you recall, when Jim was introduced as the head coach at Michigan, he stumbled going up onto the platform and almost fell. But he caught himself, straightened up. The very first thing out of his mouth was, "A lesser athlete would have fallen." In our house, anytime anybody stumbles, and this is all my kids saying this as well, but my wife especially, we say, "A lesser athlete would have fallen." Or, "A lesser athlete wouldn't have survived that." That's just Jim. You see something like that and that's Jim right there. That's Jim.

He doesn't think that there is anything he can't accomplish. When you talk with the players, that's what they love. That is the inspiration. That is the vision that Jim provides to everybody he is around. We say it around here, "Why build a fence around what you think you can do?" Jim's way of approaching that is he is always looking to get better at every step.

It wasn't like we were in the depths of darkness before Jim came in. We had a good program. But certainly what Jim did for us is he took us to another level, in both success and in exposure. That was one of the great benefits that came with him as well—he brought exposure to us.

It was a fun ride with Jim Harbaugh. We still talk about it. It was a fun ride. He's one of those unique people who comes around every once in a while. It was a great time for our program, because I was new at the job, and we were able to elevate the stature and the visibility of the campus together. Jim was very helpful for USD, and I know each step of the way he is going to be successful. He is going to be successful wherever he is, always. That's just who he is.

I haven't seen Jim much since he left here. We talk and text. Even when he was with the 49ers, there were times when I'd get in early—he gets in early, too—and we would text back and forth at 6 o'clock in the morning, about different things, games, and stuff like that. I went up and saw him at the 49ers a couple of times. He showed us around the facility. Jim helped me get set up to host an alumni reception up there for our people in the East Bay. It's fun to be with him. Ironically, one of the times we went up to see him, Jack was there, too. They were just back from a taping with Judge Judy.

Anybody who is a head coach—and I would say Division I, II or III—is very competitive. They are very competitive. Jim has blinders on, on what he wants to do. Maybe sometimes that can rub people the wrong way, but he is very motivated and very competitive. Everybody is, in their own way, when they get to that level. When you're in that upper tier, all those guys are extremely competitive, and Jim just lives it in every aspect of his life. If we're walking to the drinking fountain, he's going to want to win and get there first. I've heard the same thing of Michael Jordan—it didn't matter what it was, he was going to compete. That's how Jim is. He wants to be the best at everything.

In Ann Arbor, Jim is going to win.

~ ~ ~ ~ ~ ~ ~ ~ ~ ~ ~ ~ ~ ~ ~ ~ ~ ~ ~

Seattle Seahawks' coach Pete Carroll's roommate at the University of the Pacific was Scott Boras, the mega sports agent. Boras played minor-league baseball for the St. Louis Cardinals . . . as did former Illinois basketball coach Lon Kruger.

O.J. Simpson's cousin is Ernie Banks. Their grandfathers were twin brothers.

IT'S NOT HOW BIG YOU ARE, IT'S HOW GOOD YOU ARE

J. T. ROGAN

Despite being an outstanding foot-ball player at Coronado High School in suburban San Diego, J.T. Rogan was lightly recruited. Through help from intermediaries, he was able to "walk on" at the University of San Diego during Coach Jim Harbaugh's first season. After his record-breaking career at USD, he accompanied Harbaugh to Stanford as a Graduate Assistant. He is now a sportscaster/sportswriter in his hometown.

Coach Harbaugh arrived at the University of San Diego in the spring of 2004. I graduated in the spring/summer of 2004 from Coronado High. That's when Jim became the head coach of USD. He had actually lived in Coronado previously. He had made a home there when he played for the Chargers.

I had known that he had been in town prior to accepting the job there. Once he was there, there was a little bit of a Coro-nado connection. When he got the job, Coronado residents were really chewing on him to take me over there to USD. I was lightly recruited. I was basically not a good enough athlete and not a good enough student to get into the Ivy League. If I were a better athlete with my grades, I would have gotten in, or if I were a better student, but had been a little bit more of an athlete, I would have gotten in. I was just kind of through the pyramid recruiting scale, so they could take a couple of really good athletes with bad grades or a lot of average athletes with really good grades. I kind of fell out of the mix.

I had pretty good stats that year. I had over 30 touchdowns. I had over 1,700 yards rushing. I was among the rushing leaders in the county behind Arian Foster. I had a good year. I was all-state, small schools, according to *Cal-Hi Sports*. I'd done well, and people in Coronado were telling him, "Hey, you've got to take this guy. You've got to give him a shot." He heard that so many times that he actually told a mutual friend that I wasn't good enough to play college football, and he was just tired of hearing it from the entire community.

I go over to USD in the summer of 2004, and I'm certainly interested in going there and being recruited by him, but I've got to make the money work because it's a non-scholarship school. I take my highlight tape and try to diagnose the situation. I see Coach Harbaugh. He pops in the highlight tape and watches about 10 or 20 seconds of it in between things, always trying to be efficient, reducing drag, all terminology that he would use. I'm standing there. My dad's there. He starts squeezing my neck and my shoulders and my biceps. That's not atypical to him. He certainly likes to physically feel the guy. Sometimes guys overstate their weight, or guys are wearing baggy clothes. You can't really see what you're getting. He wanted to have a known commodity. That's his style, his way of doing things. He's like, "Okay, all right."

When he was feeling my muscles, it surprised me. It's not common for a man to put his hands on another man. But he's in the position of leverage, right? I want what he's got—the opportunity to play college football. He's squeezing me and grabbing me and groping me. It's certainly not anything inappropriate, but he's trying to size up the body. He's trying to see what the frame is like, what the potential is, how you can build it out. That's a real straightforward way of doing it, right? It's common. They did it with multiple recruits. They would tell you that. It's a common practice.

When I got into USD, they brought in 110 guys, and I wasn't one of them. They can only bring in 110 guys. There are only so many lockers, only so much space. There are restrictions that the NCAA has. It wasn't exactly like he took a flyer and gave me a chance. The circumstances worked out so that he would be able to bring me in. John Bowlen, the son of the owner of the Denver Broncos, was rendered maybe medically ineligible. He didn't pass the physical. I was able to get into camp at USD after maybe two days. I redshirted my first year. I was behind a great running back in Evan Harney. But the next year, Evan hurt himself in the summer, and I was able to take the reins with the starting position and keep it for the duration of the Harbaugh tenure.

I heard through the grapevine he said early on that I wasn't good enough to play there. I mean, I was 5-foot-9, 165 pounds. I didn't find this out until after my career. This wasn't something that was a hindrance to me. I had had enough people tell me that I wasn't good enough—that I wasn't big enough or whatever—throughout my lifetime that I certainly didn't take offense to it when I found out about it. But like I said, I didn't hear about it until after my career was over.

So much about being a running back is just having innate qualities—your ability to avoid tacklers, to have great vision, to run through contact and being tough and physical. Honestly, all of those traits I was able to use in spades as a kickoff returner. I ended up leading the nation in 2007 in I-AA in kickoff returns. I was an All-American kick returner. They said that I wasn't fast enough. But with kick returns, I was given a 20-yard running head start to get up to top speed. Once I got to top speed, I just navigated the holes, and it was really easy. I was able to use all my skills that way. I like to think that I had some elite characteristics, even though I wasn't necessarily an elite running back.

It was a grind, trying to figure out the mettle and the true will of his team. I went from being somebody who he thought wouldn't play and couldn't play to somebody who he really valued and appreciated having on his team. We still have a great relationship to this day because of it. Since I wasn't a part of the first 110 guys, now he'll call me Mr. 111. I was on the short list of guys that he wanted to bring in, but didn't commit to and couldn't commit to bringing in on Day One of training camp. I actually ran into him in Coronado like a day or two prior to training camp. He said, "Just be ready. We want to get you out there. We don't have a spot for you right now."

His dad, Jack, ended up being the running backs coach. Jack is just my favorite coach of all time. Jack is just a saint and a genius and knows the game so well. He was able to bring me in as Mr. 111, and the rest is history.

A lot of people might take exception to Coach Harbaugh's personality and find him to be flammable or difficult or over-bearing, but why do you play football? To quote Herman Edwards, "You play to win the game." That's all he cares about, and that's what he communicates and conveys to his players. Everything he does is in the interest of winning. Even more than that, sometimes it's in the interest of winning in a domi-nating fashion so that then you can create a bravado about your team. It's not arrogance. It's because you do all the hard work, right? We worked hard, and it was important to us. We valued the grind, and we knew that he had inspired us and motivated us to get to where we were. The sum of our collective parts was much greater than the individual values. The way that he inspires and challenges and motivates and leads—there are so many different traits. Sometimes it's challenging you as a man. Sometimes it's saying things that are so outrageous and crazy. The offhanded remarks he makes are sometimes just comi-cal. He said that he's never been sick a day in his life, and he doesn't tolerate sickness. It's just crazy, but it's so great to be a part of, if winning is important to you.

I wasn't surprised when he made that quantum leap to the Pac-12. He had been interviewing with other programs the year prior, but the right opportunity had not presented itself. North Texas was one of the places he had been interviewing.

The Stanford opportunity is really unique. Not only that, he took David Shaw, our then-offensive coordinator at USD, to go with him to Stanford. David had played at Stanford himself. Stanford was a really appealing opportunity to him. That was the type of landing that he was looking for.

We had all known that his trajectory and his desire was to coach in the NFL. He had made that clear. Just as everybody's faced their ambitions early on, that was apparent to us. We weren't immune to the fact that it wasn't going to be 10 years of Jim Harbaugh at the University of San Diego. He was aggressive. He was coaching to win and playing to win, so his leap—his quantum leap up to Stanford—wasn't shocking by any means.

At Stanford, it was a little bit of a grind. He went from 4-8 to 5-7 to 8-4 to 11-1, and then he was out of there. I talked to him throughout the whole process, went to his wedding, was at his bachelor party. I was around the program a lot, especially in the last year when I coached there. The success that he had wasn't shocking to me. If you're 1-11, you have a culture of losing, right? You've got to get your own recruits, change the attitude, the culture and the expectation. You've got to reform some administrators who are used to the status quo. There's a lot of work that goes into really turning a program around. USD, he took a good program, made it great and kept it there and was able to really change the culture. We went 7-4 and 11-1 and 11-1 in his three years there.

It was good coaching with him at Stanford. He had many brilliant, genius coaches there, so it was relatively impossible for me to contribute on the level of others. I tried to add value as much as I could and be there for him to bounce ideas off of, talk about different motivational tactics, what I'm seeing from different players, etcetera. It was awesome to see the preparation and planning while trying to polish the running backs. They had produced so many running back talents out of there. I mean, after Toby Gerhart even, like Ryan Hewitt, Owen

Marecic, Stepfan Taylor, Tyler Gaffney and Jeremy Stewart. Those were all guys that I got the opportunity to coach. It was a great time, kind of the golden age certainly most recently, not to mention on that team, Richard Sherman, Coby Fleener, Zach Ertz and many others that went to the NFL.

He'll do all right at Michigan. The cupboard was certainly more well stocked at Stanford. His motivation, inspiration, tactics and his supporting coaching staff will not allow them to fail. The days of being under .500 are gone while he's there.

The last time I saw Jim Harbaugh was when he spoke at his son's graduation at Coronado High School this year. After he signed a ball for a gentleman with Lou Gehrig's disease, ALS, we talked for about two hours. There was him, Jack and Jackie, and then his son, Jimmy.

We've got a huge hill at USD that many now call Harbaugh Hill. From the Jenny Craig Pavilion, you look out, there's a huge hill with a great vertical rise. He just had the players keep running up the hill and then circle all the way back around and run up it again. His biggest thing was, "Don't stop running. No matter what, keep your feet turning. Don't walk." In trying to show that he could do it, too, he was running up it. He was slowing down, losing speed or whatever, and ended up vomiting on himself. But he just kept on running up the hill and finished. He got to the top. That's the type of thing you see, and that's another club in his bag of motivational tactics.

Here's a story about his drive. He had a mission. He said, "Look, I'm going to do a push-up every day until I can do a hundred." We'd be in our stretching line when he started out. He could do almost 40 push-ups. He'd try to do one more—at least one more than the day before—because his dad's got that adage, "Every day you're either getting better or you're getting worse." His goal was 100, and he ended up busting out over 100 push-ups. In true Jim Harbaugh fashion, he's explaining how he got to do over 100. He's changing his hand positions and working different muscle groups and everything. There's always like an angle to trying to compete and finding a way to win. It's like a microcosm for his skill set in the pros. He didn't have the strongest arm. He certainly wasn't the fastest runner. But he just willed himself to do it. He found a way to win, which has been a common theme throughout his life. It has served him well, obviously, in the coaching profession.

His first wife still lives in Coronado. I saw her at the graduation. Her name's Miah. They have a daughter together, Grace, who will be going to Coronado High School. His son, James, was class president and graduated from Coronado High and is going to Michigan. James played football in Pop Warner and absolutely hated it. He is very much into performing arts and theater and is the farthest thing from a football player that you can imagine. It's been a great learning experience for Jim, how to see and handle somebody who has completely opposite interests.

IS ARIZONA A FOUR-YEAR SCHOOL NOW?

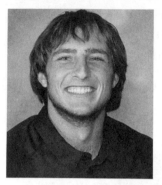

ERIC BAKHTIARI

Eric Bakhtiari was an All-Conference linebacker at the University of San Diego under Coach Jim Harbaugh. He had stints with six NFL teams from 2008-2012, including Harbaugh's 49ers. Eric's brother, David, is an offensive lineman for the Green Bay Packers.

I first met Jim Harbaugh in the spring of 2004. They fired our coach at the University of San Diego during the season, right before a game. I don't know why or how. They were bringing all of these new coaches in for interviews. They put two players from each class—freshman, sophomore, junior, senior—on this committee board. I was picked. I have no idea why. I didn't play as a freshman. I wasn't slated to play as a sophomore or anything like that.

I'm a huge football fan—oh my god, here comes Jim Harbaugh. He showed up and he was very intense, like the way he is today. He has never changed the beat of his drum or who he is. He talked about wanting to make a culture of winning USD football. He brought with him sample playbooks that he took from the Raiders. On the bottom it said, "Property of the Oakland Raiders." Coach Harbaugh and Coach Drevno were the two candidates that I really wanted to be head coach. Tim Drevno was the USD offensive line coach and offensive coordinator who is now the offensive line coach and offensive coordinator of the Michigan Wolverines.

I'm originally from Burlingame, which is 20 minutes south of San Francisco. I applied to one college on time, and that was University of Arizona. I applied in the really early acceptance period and got accepted six weeks later, in the spring of my senior year. I did the freshman thing with the family and bought a bunch of U of A gear. I was going to the U of A—it was signed, sealed and delivered. I had my dorm and everything. Then my buddy was like, "Dude, let's go visit one of our friends in San Diego."

I didn't know this, but my mom hated Tucson. She wanted not to visit me, so she bought me a plane ticket to San Diego. Plus, I wasn't going to play football at U of A. I didn't think I was good enough to play in the Pac-10 at the time. We went down to USD, and I saw the campus and I saw San Diego and the weather. I was like, this place is cool. USD had late acceptance, up until the end of March, so I had time to apply. I was thinking maybe I could play at USD, they're I-AA. I had a pretty good last year of high school, and maybe I could still seize the opportunity. I got accepted. I switched from Arizona, and my mom was ecstatic.

Harbaugh kept everyone on edge. We worked so hard. The first day it was like go-go-go and you're like, okay, are we done? Even like the warm-up to our workout. Jim would show up wearing shorts. Coach Dave Adolph was the defensive coordinator, and he used to coach with Woody Hayes. He would always wear pants. Coach Harbaugh would say, "Why do you always wear pants?" Coach Adolph said that it was because he wanted to be prepared, no matter who he had to meet with. Coach Adolph would meet administration or the owners or scouts of a football team or whoever. "You never have to get changed, and you can go straight from practice all the way up." Harbaugh ditched the shorts and started wearing pants, the chinos, the Dockers-type pants.

I loved the way he coached. It really rubbed some people the wrong way, but they weren't there. He was really hard on some guys. I don't know if he was ever hard on me. I couldn't tell. All I know is that we were winning, and we were getting better. That's all I cared about. As long as he's doing that, he can do whatever he wants. He can say whatever he wants. I loved the way he did it. Some people might be like, oh, it's so stupid, it's so dumb. It was always entertaining. It was never boring. You worked hard. What are you there to really do? Why are you playing football if you're not there to win? Why are you playing football if you're not there to get better?

There is only one person at the top of the mountain at the end of every year, right? Thirty-one other teams are disappointed. In the history of football, no one has ever gotten there without a coach. If someone can tell me what to do and work me harder and harder until we're the best, or we're the best that we can be, I have no problem with that.

We had this really big hill. At the practice field off to the side, through this little canyon, you can see this huge, gigantic hill. Harbaugh one day asked, "Do you guys ever run that hill?" Yeah, I did it on my own when I used to live in the dorms. It's tough. It probably takes about a minute to sprint up, if you sprint. It's even more formidable than it looks. At the next workout, we all ran to the hill and then he had groups sprinting against each other. He would join us on some of the workouts. He would run the hill. It is intense. It was not easy to run up the hill. The coaches were at every station, yelling at players. Some guys were hiding in the bushes because they didn't want to run up the hill anymore. Doing it once was enough. We had to do it like four, six times. Jim was running with us. He just threw up all over himself and didn't break stride. We called it Harbaugh's Hill after that.

He put the idea of playing in the NFL in my mind. He was the one who really told me that I could be great, and not just good. I hadn't really considered it until he put that in my brain. I just wanted to be a contributor. I wanted to be someone that showed up and people could rely on if the starter went down or make a couple plays here and there. I didn't think that I could be what I ended up being. He was the one who first told me that I could.

We were at a postspring practice meeting, where he meets all the guys. We were meeting in this Podunk office, because he didn't have any offices. It was like a room right next to the library, so there were all these books everywhere. He said, "I just want to let you know I think you could be a good player for us." There was a pause. Okay. I understand. Then, "You could be a great one." He's like, "We are really expecting big things of you. I'll hold you to a high standard, and I know your teammates will hold you to one, too. I hope you're ready for that." I was. When he put that on me, he gave me that vote of confidence. I wasn't good in high school. I wasn't highly recruited outside of high school. I didn't come to USD and everyone was saying, "Oh my god, we got this player." I was nobody. I was a walk-on. I just somehow, someway found a way, and he saw something in me that everyone didn't, and I was able to produce.

He left my senior year, to take the job at Stanford. We looked into transferring there, me and Josh Johnson. I didn't have a redshirt year, so I would have had to sit out. He had my potential position coach call and tell me, "We looked into it, we want you here. We think you could start in the Pac-12." I thought that was a joke, because those are the big boys, right? Later, he said, "You don't have the eligibility to do it. But we'll be watching you, and if you need anything, call us."

I finished out my senior year. I led the nation in sacks down at USD, with 20. Then Coach Harbaugh offered me a chance to come train there, train for the draft with Coach Shannon Turley, who is still there, who is from my hometown. I ended up not doing it, which was a big mistake. I should have done it. They invited me to train, to do my combine training with my former training coach who was there. I didn't do it. That's on me. That was a regrettable mistake.

When I did get to the NFL, it opened up the doors for me, and I could come and play football there. Or train in the weight room, so it was right there. I got free training even during the lockout years when I was with the Chiefs. We couldn't go to Kansas City because we were locked out, so I would go to Stanford and train. They were always really good to me. Before my brother started playing at Colorado, Harbaugh was interested in getting David to come play for him at Stanford.

I suffered a concussion in Kansas City and was given an injury release. When I saw what Jim was doing in his first year in San Francisco, I wanted to play with him again. I called him a couple of times. I was invited to a mass tryout and did that. Then they were like, okay, you're invited to come to this workout for the rookies, where they bring a bunch of rookies in. I don't know how I had eligibility to do that, but I did it. Then I got a contract after that. I was on the team off and on throughout the Super Bowl year. He was great to me.

When my brother came out and was going through his NFL draft process, Jim wanted to draft David, because he knew we were a football family. He knew me, and David obviously had a good career for himself in college. But the Packers beat him and my brother has been a key lineman for Aaron Rodgers the last three years.

USD was great, because of Coach Harbaugh. We still get together, because what we had was really special. At USD, we turned ourselves into real champions. We forged something. We got national attention. It was Harbaugh's first gig, and everyone who was on that staff went on to much bigger places—half of them are at Stanford now.

Jack Harbaugh is the best. Jack is an unbelievable human. He is always smiling and happy. He tells the best stories. He is just infectious; he's got one of those infectious father figure, grandpa demeanors. I bet those kids love seeing Grandpa Jack. When I see Coach Jack, I get excited, give him a hug. I'm smiling. I'll bet his grandkids are the same way.

Jim was really involved in everything. When Facebook first came out, he went on Facebook. He would go on Facebook to look at what his players were doing. If we were drinking, he would print out the pictures and bring them to practice and punish us. Facebook was not a good idea at the time. I don't think any other coach could have done what he did at USD, in terms of winning all those games. Jim is a different coach. He's a different guy. He took over football at a predominantly white school that had never won at the level we did. We were really good. He recruited amazing guys. He coached us up. He got the most out of players like me who were just borderline. He put together a great staff. He made sure every link in the chain was strong.

We all got together at a team reunion in 2012. We go to USD. We give speeches, and we talk about the good old days. It was good to reminisce and see all the guys and the coaches. The coaches were all at San Francisco then. Jim got there. People were calling him "Jim." And he was like, "Guys, guys, let me stop you guys. It's Coach. Coach Harbaugh." He wants to be addressed as coach. He always will. Always call him Coach.

He said, "I had a moment of clarity one night. Did I push those guys too hard? Was I too hard on you?" Because he was a rookie coach, he didn't know how hard he could push us and how much we could take. He was figuring it out, too. As we were figuring out what kind of players we were, he was figuring out what kind of coach he was. What is acceptable to do? What is unacceptable? He said, "I thought about it. Was I too hard on these guys? Was I unfair? Now I look at all these trophies and everything we won and everything we accomplished collectively and individually, and I never lost sleep over it."

A lot has been documented about him, so the Michigan players should not be surprised. Like me, we didn't know any better. We had no idea what we were getting ourselves into. Stanford was surprised. San Francisco was surprised. Everyone was surprised. But the thing that people shouldn't be surprised about anymore is winning. Look everywhere he has been—every place that he went to is now better for having had Jim Harbaugh there.

They've got some tough competition in the Big Ten. But believe me, it may not be this year, but as sure as I'm standing here—that's a Harbaughism, "as sure I'm standing here" — they will be at the top of that conference and the top of college football in a few years. He turned places like USD, Stanford and the 49ers around—and turned them around relatively fast—because he has such an aversion to losing. It permeates through him. Everything he does is highly competitive, highly intense. It's conversations. The way he eats. The way he thinks. That's why certain people are rubbed the wrong way by him. Everyone can say, "We need to do things this way, this way, that way." If you want to win, if the only thing you care about is winning, hire Jim Harbaugh. Someone once said that winning is more important than breathing. That's him. Once he wins the Super Bowl or the national championship, I don't know if there will ever be a break. I don't know if there will ever be a satisfaction. Because then he'll have to do it again.

Jim Harbaugh's a neat guy. He's really interesting. He's a good man; he's a really good man. He is really loyal, and he takes good care of his players. I have nothing but kind words and admiration for him.

I'm glad I didn't go to Arizona. I definitely made the right decision. San Diego is now a second home to me. I have a lot of good memories there and wouldn't trade it for the world. My buddy who convinced me to go out there the night before, he didn't even end up going there.

STRAIGHT OUTTA OAKLAND

JOSH JOHNSON

Josh Johnson played with his cousin, Marshawn Lynch, at Oakland Technical High School, then became a record-breaking quarterback at the University of San Diego. He played in 26 games (including five starts) with the Tampa Bay Buccaneers and served as the back-up QB at Cleveland, Cincinnati and San Francisco (reuniting with Coach Harbaugh).

I was part of Coach Harbaugh's first recruiting class at the University of San Diego. He recruited me personally. I decided to go there because of his love of football and his passion for the game. When he came to my high school, I had the same love of the game. It was exciting. He is more of an extrovert of showing his love for the game. and I tend to hide mine. But the things he is willing to do! We were in a classroom and he was talking about things that I had never even experienced in football. I said, "Explain what you're talking about." Then he started. He grabbed pencils, he grabbed whatever he could use to show an offense, to put up a defense. He has an appetite for football, an appetite to teach it, an appetite to want to get better. I just liked him right away, who he was. Everybody knew who he was. But meeting him in person, we just hit it off from the beginning. I gravitated to that, because I found somebody that loves football just as much as I do.

I wasn't recruited by any other big-time schools, but I was talking to some other small schools. But once I met him, I knew that's where I should be. He saw that I was physically going to grow. I don't know how he knew that. He met my mom, he met my dad. He said, "I've seen your parents and their size, and I feel like you're going to grow a lot." He predicted something that I didn't even think was going to happen.

Once I got to San Diego, he pushed me. He really taught me how to play quarterback on the general level. He taught me how to play with my eyes, how to understand what's going on. How not to be thinking negatively, how to break the game down to where you can simplify it in your mind and let your natural moves take over. I probably wouldn't have made the NFL if I had gone to another school. I don't know, honestly. I know it would have been a lot different.

When I had a bad game or was down, his philosophy is you go evaluate, you be honest with yourself on where you can get better—and you fix it. Then let it be. We always had a 24-hour rule. Whether it was a win or a loss, we worried about a game for 24 hours; after that, you moved on. Within those 24 hours, you had all that time to fix it, or you've got all that time to enjoy it. He trained us up that way, and it's a good philosophy.

When I got to USD my freshman year, there was real quarterback competition. Jim was always trying to find somebody to push you. Before I had the success I had, he was telling me guys were coming to take my spot. He wanted to see how you handled it, to see if you were going to keep going. Once I had success, he didn't try to say that a certain guy was going to take my spot, but he kept bringing in recruits to push me. That's his thing. He always said, "Iron sharpens iron." That's his deal.

I know he spoke positively about me with the NFL scouts and teams, which is all I could really ask for. He was at Stanford at the time. He left USD before my senior year. I always knew he was going to leave. I knew he was too big for San Diego. He was too good of a coach to be here very long. I knew somebody would pay him to come for his expertise, because of what he was doing. What he did with us was amazing, just to get us to .500, let alone a national championship. I know the way he's coaching is based on what I believe: if you know how to get the best out of your players and put them in the best position to be successful—imagine doing that with D-I athletes? The "best of the best," you would say. I knew eventually—we all knew—he was going to leave. It wasn't a shocking thing to us.

He kicked me out of practice when I was frustrated my first year. I threw my helmet on the ground. I was having a real bad day. He sent me home from practice for that. It was just something that I had to learn—me coming from Oakland and being expressive. It's something that as a quarterback, you never let that type of stuff get you that frustrated. You're a leader on the team. You've got to shake it off and bounce back. Take your helmet off and slam it on the ground in practice? I would never do that now, understanding that I'm a quarterback. But when I was 18, I had to learn.

He's going to do awesome at Michigan. He probably has to get his recruits in there, but he'll do the same thing he's done everywhere else he's been.

All of us at USD hung in there and were able to do what he wanted, and we paid the price because we were grinders. He knew that. That's why he recruits grinders—because he's going to grind you, and he wants guys that are going to give 100 percent all the time. If you let him grind you, you're going to end up playing for him, because you know it's going to get results. That's what football is all about. Football will test you.

I ended up with Jim at the 49ers in 2014. It was a great experience. It was good to actually play for him again as a pro quarterback, to be around him. His coaching style and systems didn't change. He was always trying to figure out a way to win. You appreciate that as a player. He's always trying to figure out ways to get better. How can we get better? How can we do this better? He lets you be yourself as a quarterback.

It was always good when you would stop in. He keeps a good rapport with his old players. It's not like guys are calling him 24/7 or seeing him 24/7, but he's always available. It's probably a little harder for him now, because he's got all of these different players and he's had so much success all over the place. Jim has had an impact on so many different guys' lives now, because he's had so much success as a coach.

I love Jack Harbaugh. Jack is very enthusiastic and always has stories to tell. A good Jack Harbaugh story at USD is his story of Freddy Soft. It's not a real person, it's a made-up person. When the dog days of football season are coming and you don't want to do something, you need to push yourself. When you decide to say, "I don't want to do it today," Jack says that's the little guy on your shoulder called Freddy Soft. He's telling you not to push to get in shape. Don't ever let Freddy Soft win! Jack always had a smile and was always lively. Always.

I would rate my decision to follow Jim Harbaugh to USD a 12 out of 10. A 12. He changed my life.

A PLAY-TONIC RELATIONSHIP

JAMES MCGILLICUDDY

James McGillicuddy arrived at Stanford in 2005 from Worcester, Mass., but the defensive lineman's playing time at The Farm was derailed by injuries. It took two surgeries and a groundbreaking medical procedure to get James into a game for the first time as a junior in 2008. He is currently Chief Operating Officer at Sourcegraph in San Francisco.

I was former Stanford Coach Walt Harris' first commit and played my first two years there for him. My last season with Coach Harris, I had a knee injury, so I had a redshirt year and a medical redshirt year before I started playing for Coach Harbaugh.

Coach Harbaugh and his staff definitely changed the culture at Stanford in an incredible way. Shannon Turley, who was the strength coach at the time, made an incredible impact. Coach Haubaugh took a team that was 1-11 and made the players believe that they could beat the best team in the country, which was USC. We went out and did that. He's a winner. Jim Harbaugh loves to win, and he is relentless in making sure that he and his teams win, and that's really admirable. As a result, he puts together championship teams.

It was Christmas Eve, and I was walking into Christmas Mass with my family in Massachusetts. I got a call from Lance Anderson. Anderson was the defensive line coach at the time and the recruiting coordinator, more or less. He was my position coach when I played defensive line. The call went like this: "Hey James, this is Coach Anderson. I'm here with Coach Harbaugh. Do you want to say hello?" I was like, wow, here's our new coach working on Christmas Eve. That's pretty fantastic. It sent a good message that he was excited to be here. He basically said, "Hey James, Coach Harbaugh here. I'm really excited and honored to be your coach. We're going to build a champion-ship team, and we're going to need as many amazing people as we can, so get ready to work hard and win championships." That left a really good impression. I'd say it sent a message of hope. And since he was working on Christmas Eve, it showed that it was not going to be easy. It was going to require a lot of sacrifice, but we have the right folks, the right coaching staff, and we're going to get it done. He's putting in the work, why wouldn't everyone else?

I was injured at that point. I had knee surgery, and I wasn't playing at that time. I returned from my injury in Coach Har-baugh's second year, but I was always around in his first year. I was in meetings and went to games. I couldn't practice, but I was doing rehab and whatnot. It was evident that he was changing the culture. He was making people believe, and people bought in—not just on the team, but in the athletic department, in the administration and also the student body. Success begets success, and he made a believer out of every-one. He made everyone love what they were doing by putting up results. Results speak for themselves, and when you start winning, people love that. Stanford's fan base—I love Stan-ford and I love our fans—but if you're not performing as well as people expect, the stadium gets a little empty. Coach Har-baugh put his money where his mouth is, and people started believing.

Jim's a great guy. He definitely loves football, he loves coaching, he loves competing, and he loves winning. His humor played well. Not everyone's going to like you, but often-times with the best leaders and the most successful people, not everyone likes them.

It was hard work, but he gave us the foundation to make practices and games fun most of the time. It's never fun when you're losing, but when you're winning, it makes up for all the hard work. The combination of Coach Harbaugh and Strength Coach Turley in the offseason had us focusing our eyes on the prize the entire time. Some of the stuff in the offseason, when you're up at 6 a.m. running around the track or on the field, that's hard stuff. But the bonds that were created and the vows that we made to each other to be a championship team were very memorable. My other memorable experiences that involved Coach Harbaugh involved the greater team. Obviously, beating Virginia Tech in the Orange Bowl was huge. It proved that our program was back. Beating Notre Dame in 2009, that was an awesome moment, and beating Oregon that year was awesome, too.

Coach Harbaugh essentially called out Pete Carroll at the Pac-12 media day leading up to the USC upset win in 2007. Coach Harbaugh said, "We're coming after USC. Why wouldn't we want to beat USC?" Everyone was like, you're crazy. Then leading up to the game, Coach Harbaugh was like, "Hey guys, I put my mouth out there. You guys better back me up." It was just a typical workweek. Then game day came and even though I wasn't there, from what I heard, there was a great atmosphere in the locker room. Everybody came in amped up and ready to go. USC was the No. 1 team in the nation, and we beat them.

Coach Harbaugh had a pretty big personality. As soon as you started interacting with him and have a few meetings, you knew this guy was here to win. He meant business. He wanted us to be winners, because it's good for everyone. That was pretty apparent early on.

His success in San Francisco was expected, and he'll win at Michigan, as well. He'll win a national championship or a Super Bowl in his career. He's pretty relentless in his pursuit of building championship programs. He always does what's best for the team. He's not about what's best for an individual. That's a really great thing about him. He always looks out for what's best for the team. And he's always reevaluating and reassessing players that will put the team in the best position to win. The NFL is quite a bit different than college. In college, you either buy in and you adapt or you're not there anymore.

In the NFL, some of the players are making more money and are worth more to the franchise. In some of these organizations, the coach has to adjust to the player.

He had so many great one-liners, and he could use them to diffuse a lot of tension. His speeches were pretty funny, where he would literally quote Richard III or a Shakespearian play about St. Crispin's Day. He would say some funny things. It was one of the things he'd do. He quoted people and told stories and talked about different stories we all heard as children. It was motivating, and it showed that he could connect with the players. All the stories and parables served a purpose to motivate us, and they made us closer as a team.

LOTSA LUCK

OLIVER LUCK

In early 2015, Oliver Luck became the NCAA Executive VP of Regulatory Affairs after serving as athletic director for four years at his alma mater, West Virginia University. He played for the Houston Oilers from 1982-86. His son, Andrew, was the No. 1 recruit coming out of high school when Jim Harbaugh landed him for Stanford. Andrew now stars for the Indianapolis Colts.

Andrew was at Stratford High School, which is a school in the suburban west side of Houston. He was recruited fairly heavily as a quarterback. Initially, he cut down his list pretty tightly to a handful of schools, based largely on academic performance. He ultimately ended up taking trips to Stanford, Cal-Berkeley, Purdue, **NORTHWESTERN*** and Rice University in Houston—that's where my wife, his mom, went to school. Some kids have a tough time narrowing it down, but he narrowed it down right off the bat. Every kid is different, but he had a pretty good idea that he wanted to go to a school that was not just good at playing Division I football, but could offer a rigorous academic curriculum. That's a decision that he made on his own, and he stuck to it.

I had met Jim a couple of times. I wouldn't say that I knew him well. We had a friendly relationship, but he wasn't a friend. He was more of just an acquaintance, somebody you bump into every now and then at some NFL event. I was always an admirer of him when he was playing, because I thought he was

---

***NORTHWESTERN** has never played a game in the NCAA men's basketball tournament. However, it has twice hosted the Final Four.

the classic overachiever. He wasn't the most gifted guy athletically, but he certainly created a very nice professional career.

Jim came to our house to recruit Andrew, but only once, and it was only after Andrew had committed. Andrew had taken a trip out. We took two trips. He and I took a trip to look at Stanford and Cal when he was a junior. Then, the summer before his senior year, he went out with his mom for a quarterback camp, the Stanford quarterback camp. Then he committed to Stanford before the start of his senior year. At some point during basketball season of his senior year, Jim came to the house. Not so much to recruit Andrew, but to visit. Andrew had already committed, so there wasn't much recruiting going on. Jim just wanted to talk about expectations. It was the one time that Jim came to the house. I suppose it was a recruiting trip, but Andrew's decision had already been made.

Jim is a very personable guy. He is a very competitive guy. My wife had very positive impressions of him. She had met him before, during the football camp that summer. At the end of the day, she felt very comfortable with Jim. Ultimately, it was Andrew's call, so my wife would have supported whatever Andrew would have decided.

Andrew enjoyed every minute of being at Stanford—academically, athletically and socially. It was a perfect spot for him. He made a great choice. Jim did an absolute tremendous job of teaching the quarterback position to Andrew. A guy like Jim—who played the NFL game for 14, 15 years and had coached successfully at San Diego and before that with his dad for a number of years—provided a great learning experience for Andrew. It wasn't just Jim; he had an excellent staff of guys. Greg Roman was out there, and is now a coordinator in the NFL, Willie Taggart, the head coach at South Florida, Derek Mason, head coach at Vanderbilt, David Shaw, head coach at Stanford. There were a lot of really good coaches, including Jim, who were able to influence Andrew. That was when he really developed as a quarterback.

I went to about two-thirds of Andrew's games at Stanford. My wife got out to some on her own, as well, and sometimes we went together. Andrew is the oldest of four kids, and the other three were also competing in sports, so it was hard on the weekends. It was a great experience. I often didn't see Jim in Palo Alto, maybe for literally 10 seconds after a game to shake his hand and congratulate him. We didn't really talk that much. I didn't ask for sideline passes or anything. I just wanted to sit in the stands quietly and watch the game.

When Andrew signed with Stanford, they were 1-11, but they had hired Jim. That summer was when Andrew committed. Ultimately, Andrew chose Stanford for three reasons. One, the academic profile of the school—obviously, the top or very close to the top of Division I schools. Two, the new coaching staff led by Jim. And three, the belief that Stanford could turn it around. They've had very good teams in the past. They've been to the Rose Bowl numerous times. They've had a bunch of top draft choices. But they also have had times when they've really struggled. Andrew had a belief that the coaching staff was going to be able to turn it around, and they did. They went from 1-11 to middling in Jim's first two years, then to 8-5 and a trip to the Sun Bowl. The next year, Andrew's junior season, they turned it totally around and went 12-1 with a big win in the Orange Bowl.

I never interacted much with Jim once Andrew was out there, maybe once toward the end of his career. Not because I didn't like him. He's a great guy, and I really admire him.

I have three other kids. Andrew is number one. Number two is a daughter who graduated from Stanford in 2014. She is now working in San Francisco. Another daughter is a senior at Stanford. Then we have a high school son, who is a senior in high school. He's a soccer player, and he's planning to go to Yale. He'll be in the class of 2020. He attends high school in Morgantown, W.Va. My wife and I decided not to bring him to Indianapolis for his last year. That would have been tough on him. He's captain of his soccer team, which won the state championship last year. We thought it would be mean-spirited to yank him out and put him in a new high school his final year. They're all smart kids. They take after my wife. She's a city gal. I'm just a West Virginia boy.

~ ~ ~ ~ ~ ~ ~ ~ ~ ~ ~ ~ ~ ~ ~ ~ ~ ~ ~ ~

Marion Motley, Alan Page and Dan Dierdorf are all Canton natives and are enshrined in the Pro Football Hall of Fame in their hometown. Page worked on the construction crew that built the Hall while Dierdorf and his father attended the groundbreaking ceremony.

Tony Dungy, former Indianapolis Colts coach, is the last NFL player to throw and make an interception in the same NFL game. He was a defensive back and a backup quarterback for the Steelers.

Peyton Manning's father, Archie, is regarded as the greatest football player in the history of the University of Mississippi. In honor of Archie's uniform number, the posted speed limit on the Ole' Miss campus is 18MPH.

Chapter 5

AN ECLECTIC ENDING

THE HARBAUGHS' OLD KENTUCKY HOME

PAUL JUST

Paul Just has been involved with the athletic department at Western Kentucky University for 50 years. The Kentucky native and WKU grad served as the school's sports information director from 1978-2002. He was recently inducted into the College Sports Information Directors of America Hall of Fame.

When I first heard that Jim Harbaugh might be involved in coaching at Western Kentucky, my first reaction was how is that going to work? How could he have the time for that? He donated a lot of his spare time, making phone calls and, when he could, making house visits to recruits' homes. Whenever he had a chance, when he had an opening in his schedule of any kind, he was either here or on the road, wherever we were.

He was an excellent recruiter. His time was so limited that he couldn't be at practice very often. He was such a good recruiter because of his personality. Plus, his name recognition went a long way. The one I hear about most often was getting Willie Taggart for us. If you've never seen Willie Taggart play, go find some film. He was some kind of exceptional athlete. I saw every game he played. He just totally amazed me. Jim played a key role in recruiting Willie out of Manatee High School in Bradenton, Fla. Willie is a head coach now, at the University of South Florida. Willie stayed on here and was an assistant coach after graduating. He worked his way up to become the offensive coordinator. When Jim took the job at

Stanford, he offered Willie a chance to join him there—which he did. Willie went out there for three years.

Because he was playing with the Indianapolis Colts, Jim was in and out a lot. But, of course, in his season we usually saw him when he had an open date. There were limitations. We came within a hair's breadth of losing football in the spring of 1992, but football survived. Because of severe budget cuts across the board, football survived, but it had to take quite a cut. Jim offered to help out, and he came on board as a volunteer assistant. He had to take all the NCAA tests and everything before he could be termed an assistant and be qualified to formally represent our football program in recruiting.

Jim was always telling me that we ought to throw the ball more. Typical quarterback. Jack sure liked the running game. We passed the ball a good amount, but Jim always felt like we could pass it a lot more and do some things better. Anyhow, that was always a friendly argument between them.

He made suggestions and assisted in camps. He did a lot for us on the recruiting scene when we needed athletes and were short on coaches to be able to get out and make contacts. Of course, Jim's name recognition was really strong in the high school football world at that time. He just did a wonderful job helping us in that regard.

We would see him on open Colts dates. One time we went over to play at Marshall. They were still I-AA at that time. Their great player was Randy Moss, and they were, gosh, they were ranked way up there. Jim met us there that day. It was a televised game, so I spent most of my time trying to make arrangements for him to get on the air for interviews. But he managed to spend most of the actual game itself on the sidelines with his dad. Jim was more than willing to help with anything you'd ask him for. Most places we'd go, if he was there, there would be somebody who wanted to talk to him.

He would stay at his dad's house. Jack and Jackie lived just a few blocks from campus. Jack is real well regarded down here. He's the second winningest coach in our school's history. He went through some awfully tough times in the early years here, particularly in '92. Who would have thought that 10 years later we'd be a national champion? Jack retired after that year, and then the opportunity came up at Marquette to be on the athletic staff. He and Jackie moved to Milwaukee.

After we nearly lost football in '92, it was amazing the support that came from everywhere. When the regents voted to keep football, we still took a big budget hit. We didn't have enough money to have a full coaching staff. That's when Jim was a volunteer. You were allowed only so many assistant coaches. Jim, as a volunteer, filled one of those slots. We were short day-to-day in practice. We had a couple of retired assistant coaches who volunteered as well.

One thing we needed was equipment. We had to scratch and claw for things like that. Jim signed a deal with Fila and part of his deal was that Fila would outfit our teams. I don't remember the particulars of the deal, but we wore Fila uniforms and Fila shoes. That really was a major plus for our program. We had been searching for equipment and uniforms, while trying to stretch our budget, and suddenly we were the nicest-looking team in the country.

Another happening that's fascinating about that fall of '92 is we actually had college football coaches around the country buy season tickets to our games, including some rival schools' coaches. A lot bought season tickets to help our program. It was a real testament to Jack Harbaugh. Coaches rallied, not wanting to see a long and established program axed and a great coach and a great guy like Jack Harbaugh go out like that.

Jack had a sign over his outer office door that said, and I may be paraphrasing, those who remain—or those who stick with it—will be national champions. That sign hung over his door for years, even during those tough years. It took time. It took 10 years. It took having to rebound from going near rock bottom to making things happen. We've had a good tradition here in football for a long, long time. Jack took the steps he had to take and built the program slow and steady into a nationally ranked I-AA program. And, eventually, in 2002, a national championship. The entire Harbaugh family is real special.

~ ~ ~ ~ ~ ~ ~ ~ ~ ~ ~ ~ ~ ~ ~ ~ ~ ~ ~

Until recently, Michigan had more golf courses than any state in the Union.

Tigers manager Jim Leyland was once a second-string catcher for Perrysburg High School, in the Toledo area. The starting catcher was Jerry Glanville.

Bear Bryant coached against two schools, three times each, that he never defeated: Notre Dame and Alabama. While coaching at Kentucky and Texas A&M, he never defeat the Crimson Tide... Bryant often joked that if he ever quit coaching he'd probably "croak within a week." He died 28 days after his last game.

THAT'S BOB WITH ONE "O"

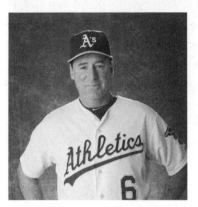

BOB MELVIN

Bob Melvin just completed his fifth season managing the Oakland A's. He led the A's to three consecutive playoff appearances (2012-14). Bob also managed the Seattle Mariners (2003-04) and the Arizona Diamondbacks (2005-09). He was named the National League Manager of the Year in '07 and the AL Manager of the Year in '12. He was a catcher in the big leagues for 10 seasons with seven teams.

Jim played on the same American Legion team I'd played for two years earlier, but I didn't meet him until he was with the San Francisco 49ers. I followed his career and pulled for him because he was here locally in Palo Alto for awhile. I first met him when he came out to see one of our games and I invited him into the office. He came to one of our games at AT&T Park and we spent some time together before we played the San Francisco Giants. We hit in the cage that day, so we spent a few hours talking in the office. I went to a couple of 49ers practices and some games, and hung out with him in his office pre- and postgame. I was on the field, 10 or 15 yards from him, watching the games at Levi's Stadium. Our relationship developed pretty quickly, and we spent quite a bit of time together.

We bounced some ideas off each other. We're in different sports, so it's a little different in terms of your preparation—we play every day and they play once a week—but we got some good ideas from each other. What stuck out the most was his passion for what he does. I watched how he motivates players and gets them to focus each and every game.

Jim coached first base for the A's in a spring training game. That came about because he took such good care of me during the football season and the experience that he gave me, whether it was being on the field for practices or on the field for his games. I wanted to be able to do something for him that would be in the same realm. During spring training, it's a little more informal for us. You can have guest guys on the field, and I just thought of putting together a day for him where he was in uniform and part of all our pregame activities. It was my idea to let him coach first base for a couple of innings. I had him watch our first base coach for a couple of innings and I went over what the first base coach does, and then I let him go out there. He watched two innings and then went out and coached the rest of the game. I thought he'd be out there for a couple of innings, but he wanted to be out there for the rest of the game.

We won in nine or 10 innings in walk-off fashion and he was part of the whole celebration on the field. It was a great day for him and a great day for my team to be around him. He said a few things to my team before the game. It ended up being a great experience. He talked about what he thought of the **OAKLAND A'S*** from following our team. He said, "When I think of the Oakland A's, I think of jungle lions." He got into why he thought that.

He didn't have a lot to do on the field. As the first base coach, he wasn't giving signs, but he was into every pitch. Every time a guy got a hit, Jim gave the player a high five and chatted with him a bit.

*M. C. Hammer (Stanley Burrell) for several years was listed in the **OAKLAND A'S** media guide as "Executive Vice President" with a salary of $7.50 a game. He was named "Little Hammer" by Reggie Jackson for his resemblance to Hank Aaron. At the same time, Tom Hanks was a Coca-Cola vendor and Debbi Fields of Mrs. Fields cookie fame was a ball girl for the A's.

THE SON ALSO RISES

SHEMY SHEMBECHLER

Glenn Edward "Shemy" Schem-bechler III is the president of GES Advisory Co. in Columbus, Ohio. Yes, Bo Schembechler's son lives in Columbus, Ohio. Most of Schembechler's career-has been scouting for NFL teams (Seahawks, Bears, Redskins and Chiefs). He's known as a patient and cooperative man.

Jim's four or five years older than me, so when Michigan played in the Gator Bowl in 1979, he was in charge of babysitting me and some of the other kids. He would have been 15 or 16 years old then. Jim took us up to his room, and we threw the mattresses out the window into the outdoor pool below. After that, Jim never got to babysit us again.

When he was young, Jim got thrown out of practice by Bo for getting in the way. Jim loved being in the middle of everything, just as he does today. He probably thought he was the head coach when Bo was. My dad always thought he'd be able to get Jim to play for Michigan when the time came, as long as the decision was made before signing day. But he didn't offer Jim a scholarship until very late in the recruiting process. Bo said all the time that Jim would never play a down at Michigan because he was a pain in the ass to coach. Jim brought his free spirit to the position.

When Jim broke his arm against Michigan State in 1984, we knew that he was going to miss the remainder of the season, and there was a possibility that he was going to miss spring football, too. My dad visited him at the hospital the night after the game. Jim got really emotional. If I were him, I'd have gotten emotional, too. The way the program was set up, players were constantly challenged to maintain their role as a starter, and they were always challenged. When guys got hurt they feared that they would never get a chance to play again. That was exactly how Jim felt. As my dad was leaving the room, tears were streaming down Jim's face. Jim said, "Bo, please don't forget about me." It was important to Jim to be the starting quarterback at Michigan. Bo knew how to handle situations like that. I went with my dad to the hospital and was waiting outside Jim's room. Bo didn't know I was listening. Those conversations were intended for the coach and his player only. The door was open and I heard it.

Jim had a lot of talent. You don't go in the first round of the NFL Draft without talent. He had a good arm. He was a good athlete. He could change direction. He knew how to bide time. I'd go to practice and Jim would warm-up on me, throwing a rocket ball to me, a high school kid. My hands would hurt after the warm-up.

A lot of Jim's coaching philosophy is espoused from my father. Even though Jim has his own coaching style, there are a lot of things about his coaching acumen that was impacted by my dad. Jim has his own personality, which is quite different than my dad's. Jim is a little goofier. My dad was never goofy. Jim, especially when he was younger, would try to figure out ways to push the envelope and be on the edge of getting in trouble, but not get in trouble. My dad was exceptionally good at toeing the line. When you play and coach with and under Woody Hayes, you didn't want to cross Woody. Woody Hayes would lambaste you. When my dad came to Michigan, many of his leadership traits came from Woody. On a campus like Michigan, even though discipline was held at a premium, Bo allowed his players to have their own personalities more than Woody did. My dad would never push the envelope. My dad never got arrested, never even considered crossing a line. Even though people like to say that my dad was a clone of Woody— just like they say that Jim is a clone of my dad—they all bring their different personality types to being successful. Living in Columbus with the name Shembechler, I tell people I love Woody Hayes and they leave me alone.

All the players were scared of Bo. He knew how to manipulate them from a motivational standpoint. Sometimes that meant you weren't going to play. Guys were petrified about that, but they also were petrified about what my dad might to do them from a disciplinary standpoint. All the players brought their own traits, their own personality and their own passion and desire to be good. My father would say that he helped foster those skill sets and taught them how to be men, how to be honest, how to work hard and how to be there for their families. That's the impact that my dad had on them. My dad was very good at identifying character and talent as a combination, and some guys weren't as talented as others. He knew the types of kids that were predisposed to be successful and would buy into the team philosophy regardless of how talented they were. When you bring a group like that together that puts the team first, you have a high probability of success.

Let's be honest. Michigan football hasn't been what it should be over the last decade or so. With Jim coming to Ann Arbor a lot of questions are going to be answered. I'm getting re-excited about the Michigan-**OHIO STATE*** rivalry. There is a real possibility that the Big Ten Conference will return to what is good about the league with Michigan and Ohio State leading the way.

*Howard "Hopalong" Cassady, the 1955 Heisman Trophy winner from **OHIO STATE**, introduced George Steinbrenner to his wife on the Ohio State campus when Steinbrenner was an assistant football coach there.

BUENAS NOCHES, COACHES

TED MARCHIBRODA

Ted Marchibroda spent 12 seasons as an NFL head coach, including stints with the Baltimore Colts, Indianapolis Colts and Baltimore Ravens. He also spent seven seasons in the radio broadcast booth with the Indianapolis Colts as a color commentator. He is one of two head coaches—and 12 people total—in the Colts Ring of Honor.

I remember a lot of conversations I had with Jim Harbaugh, but none stands out more than one we had on the plane ride home from **NEW YORK*** early in the 1995 season. We had just beaten the Jets in overtime in the second game of the season. Jim had come in with us down, 24-3, early in the third quarter, and he brought us back for the win. Craig Erickson was our starting quarterback, but Jim had been doing a good job out of the bullpen. I called for him to come up to the front of the plane where I was sitting and asked him to sit down. I told him that I was thinking about starting him the next week against Buffalo. I thought that he had done such a fine job coming on in relief that he deserved to start. But I wanted to give him some options, too. I told him I could start him or I could just let things go the way they had been going and continue to start Erickson. I told him that maybe I could start Craig for the first quarter and see how things were going and then go to him very quickly or we could see how he did in the starting role. I really wanted to know what he was thinking. I was a

---

*In 2003, an inebriated Calvin Klein crossed the Madison Square Garden court to talk with the Knicks' Latrell Sprewell as he was getting ready to inbound the ball. A few months later, **NEW YORK** City passed an Interference with a Professional Sporting Event law.

little bit surprised at his response. He had been in situations before where the starter felt like he was being undercut by the backup and that was one thing he didn't want to do. He supported Craig and wanted him to succeed. He was never one of those players who were sitting around hoping the other would fail. He wanted to be supportive. That was on his mind, too. He thought about it for a few minutes and said, "Coach, I'm a hero with the way things are going right now, but at the same time, I can't lie. I'd much rather start." That was what I was hoping he'd say, and the next week I started him against the Bills.

Through the years, I've thought about that conversation and I think the whole thing may have loosened him up a bit. It showed Jim that someone believed in him. When he came in with the Bears, he came in under a lot of pressure. It was both being the quarterback of the Bears and also being there with Mike Ditka. He had been under pressure all of the time, and then in the end, he was kind of made the scapegoat in Chicago. It was like he had something to prove in Indianapolis, and he had put more pressure on himself to do just that. When he got the chance to start that season and he felt like somebody believed in him, you could tell it impacted him immensely.

Later on, during that same plane flight, I called him up to the front one more time and I told him I had decided to start him. He told me the darnedest thing. He said, "Coach, I feel like I'm throwing the football better than I can right now." That surprised me. I had never expected to hear that from a quarterback, and I'm not sure it's really what I wanted to hear. I told him that he was doing such a great job and I didn't want him to do anything differently. I told him not to pull any of the horns now, just keep doing what he had been doing. I told him I wanted him to go out there and let 'er rip. I believe the feeling that he had a coach who believed in him made a big difference for Jim, and he was ready to go out and show what he could do.

Jim became known as Captain Comeback in that season because he brought us back from behind at least three times, and he almost pulled off a miracle finish in the AFC Championship Game, too. We never felt we were out of a game when Jim was leading the offense. A few weeks after we beat the Jets when Jim had brought us back from 24-3 down, he did it again in Miami. That time we were down, 24-3, at halftime, and we got the ball first in the second half. We were on our 28-yard line with 11 minutes to play, and it was fourth-and-one. For some reason, I just had it in my mind that the way the momentum was definitely in Miami's favor that if we punted it away and gave the ball back to Dan Marino right there, and if they scored, the game would be over. I had a little voice in my head saying, "Don't give the ball back to Marino." We went for it. And Jim was really good on that drive. Four times on that drive we had fourth-and-one, and all four times we went for it. Jim hit Floyd Turner for a touchdown at the end of that drive, and we ended up coming back and winning that ballgame. Jim was never afraid of fourth-and-one. That was the toughest call I ever made in my coaching career, and I don't think I would ever make it again.

That 1995 season was really a great year. I had two really great years in football as a coach. The 1975 Colts in Baltimore was one and the 1995 Colts in Indianapolis was the other. They were very comparable with each other. We weren't supposed to do anything, and we went into the playoffs something like 15- to 18-point underdogs. We probably should have gone to the Super Bowl. Those guys gave us everything they had, and it was just a wonderful time to be coaching great athletes like that. With Jim, you just felt so good within yourself, because you knew with a player like that, you were going to be able to get everything out of him. Then he, in turn, was getting everything out of the other 10 guys on the field. They were all certain about one thing—their quarterback was going to be ready to go on Sunday afternoon. Jim was going to give you the most that he had all of the time. He had some teeth knocked out on a sack. The players were pretty sure he was done for the day, but he just spit out a little blood and went right back in the game.

Not only did he play, but he played well. That was one of those times when his teammates perked up and took notice.

That was one thing I came to really realize about Jim as time went on—the respect he had from his teammates. He was one of them. He knew it and they knew it. That's really important with a football team. Jim was really good. I think he loves football as much as any guy I've ever seen. He just seemed like he lived it. He never questioned anything. He'd never second guess. He'd do what he was told, and he enjoyed doing it. He really did. I felt like he had the respect of the players more than any player I've seen.

Jim has always been a football guy. He lived it. He breathed it. In 1995, we brought in Lindy Infante to be the offensive coordinator, and he had a whole new offensive system. Some of our quarterbacks struggled with it a bit, but Jim never had a problem. He was never behind. He was always on top of everything. What helped him when Lindy came in was now he had both of us to lean on, and he could bounce stuff off of both of us. He got everything twice. But he enjoyed every minute of it. He really did.

I've been a little surprised at how well he's done as a head football coach. It's not that I didn't think he could do it, but more that I never really gave it much of a thought. I knew he had an interest in it because of his father coaching at Western Kentucky. I knew it was in his blood, but for the most part, he was so focused on being the best player he could be at that time that I was only thinking of him in terms of being a good quarterback. I do remember he had some coaching responsibilities on the side even when he played for us at Indianapolis. I don't mean responsibilities within the Colts, but helping his dad at Western Kentucky. I saw Jim in the training room getting treatment before or after a practice and he'd be sitting there on the phone. I said to one of the trainers that it sure seemed like Jim spent a lot of time on the telephone, and the trainer told me that he'd use that time to make calls for his dad to players

Western Kentucky was recruiting. He felt like that was dead time, so he wanted to help his dad. I know that working with his father was something that meant a lot to him. I think he enjoyed every minute of it. He was doing his father a favor, and that was something that was very important to him. Jim has always been a family first kind of guy.

I've enjoyed following Jim's career since he went into coaching. I used to call him once or twice every year just to wish him good luck and let him I know I was thinking about him. I'm really happy for him now at Michigan. It's a funny thing for me. When I grew up in the late 1930s, my favorite player was Tommy Harmon. He played for Michigan and was the greatest back in the country. Now it seems like the name Harbaugh has taken over for the name Harmon. Similar names, but for me those are the two guys I think of when I think of Michigan.

I thought he did a great job as an NFL head coach, too. We talked a few times when he was the head coach of the 49ers. He said, "Coach, you and I had the best jobs in the world and that's to coach a professional football team." Then he added, "But you know it always comes back to bite you." I didn't know what he was talking about, but it wasn't too long after that when the talk started coming out of San Francisco with the problems he was having there. I really thought he handled that whole situation about as well as anyone could.

Jim Harbaugh is always someone you root for because he works hard, he's an honest guy and he's a straight shooter. He loves football as much as any player I've been around.

RACECAR SPELLED BACKWARDS IS RACECAR

TERRY LINGNER

Television production executive Terry Lingner and Jim Harbaugh were part of an ownership group of six that formed IndyCar team Panther Racing in 1997. The team's car finished second at the Indy 500 four years in a row (2008-11). Lingner was among the first production staffers hired at ESPN in the late 1970s. In 1989 he founded Lingner Group Productions, a sports broadcast production company.

I lived very close to the Indianapolis Colts practice facility. My home was walking distance to where they practice, so we had Colts players coming and going all the time. Jim was living in our neighborhood and both our sons played soccer, so there was a relationship. He enjoys auto racing, and I've made my career in broadcasting racing. We eventually became partners in Panther Racing. We were both foolish enough to put our money into a racing team.

I'm an old ESPN guy and I've been in sports my entire career, so I'm around world class athletes a lot. What I always appreciated about Jim was that he was really active in the community. I don't remember him saying no to anything. He was also very active with philanthropic endeavors. While he was in Indianapolis, it was kind of Jim's town. He brought a lot of class. Everybody talks about his intensity, but I never saw that. I've seen it on the sidelines on television, but I know him to be more casual. He certainly likes to win, but he wasn't this fanatic that people make him out to be. He's a guy who cares about winning. Even after he left Indianapolis, he stayed involved in

Panther Racing. A lot of people on the racing team were kind of awestruck that he liked the sport. It was a conscious effort on our part not to say, "Hey Jim, we're going to pitch somebody at Acme Speed Shop and we need you there." We were flattered that he wanted to be involved, but he was at the peak of his football playing career, so we weren't going to distract him.

Jim was always humble. He would look you in the eye, shake your hand and tell you, "Good job." That would motivate and show the rest of the team that what they were doing was important and appreciated. That's what you want out of a leader. His involvement had far reaching implications. He drove the pace car at a **RACE*** and loved it. He was a positive influence on everybody.

NFL players make a lot of money. They're fairly well insulated. Why in the world would Jim say, "Yeah, I'll throw in with you and I'll do something way out of my comfort zone." Most athletes let their handlers take care of their money or they throw the money into restaurants. I can't think of any other athlete at his level that has such diverse interests.

He wasn't above immersing himself into the culture of the city, both in IndyCar and in the city itself. He was this great looking guy, well spoken, definitely raised the right way, somebody that the community loved to rally around. Jim's entry into IndyCar was a product of his engagement with the city. When clearly the top priority was playing football, I'd see him at the shop and wonder, what's he doing here?

*The Indy 500 was made 500 miles long because the originators wanted the **RACE** to last seven hours. The track is known as The Brickyard, but only one yard is brick—the start/finish line.

BEHOLD THE MAIZE AND BLUE

BRUCE MADEJ

A native of Dearborn, Mich., Bruce Madej went to work for U-M in 1978. He spent 34 years with the athletic department in various roles, serving as the school's sports information director from 1982-2010. Madej received an honorary "M" from the Letterwinners M Club, The Champions Award from Wolverines for Life and co-authored the best-selling book, Michigan: Champions of the West.

Jimmy is not Bo Schembechler. He is not Mike Ditka. He is not Jack Harbaugh. He is Jim Harbaugh. What I like about Jim is that Jim has never pretended to be anybody else, ever. He has been Jim Harbaugh all the way through. When they hired him, the first day, I said, "Well, they've got themselves one of the great football coaches, no doubt, but my god, Jimmy is not going to be one of those people that is going to jump when they say, 'Okay, Jimmy, you really need to do this.'" Jim's going to do what Jim thinks is right. Jim's going to make mistakes and he will learn from them. But I'm going to tell you, he's got integrity. You know what you're going to get when you've got Jim Harbaugh. He doesn't try to be anybody else. Certain coaches would ask me when they took over as a head coach, "How should I do things?" The answer is, "Don't try to do anything different than what you are yourself." That's Jim Harbaugh. Jim is Jim Harbaugh, period. I know that sounds silly, but it's the truth and it is so important.

He knows what is important on and off the field. On the first day of school here in Ann Arbor, he took his kids to school. He took them to St. Francis, the same school he attended while growing up in Ann Arbor. That's Jim Harbaugh.

Realize that a Michigan quarterback was not going to throw the ball a lot with Bo Schembechler as the coach back then. He had great running backs, great linemen, great receivers and great coaches. But, you know, at quarterback, we had Rick Leach, who was absolutely one of the best option quarterbacks you could have. Steve Smith, a great quarterback, an option quarterback. Dennis Franklin, a great option quarterback. The list goes on. Well, Jimmy really wasn't that type of an option quarterback. He came in and, all of a sudden, Bo and Hanlon have a drop back passing quarterback. Harbaugh was the man who started Michigan as "Quarterback U," and we started throwing the ball.

A game I remember well was in 1985. We were playing at Iowa. We were high in the national polls, and they were high in the polls—it was a No. 1 versus No. 2 matchup. We had a third down-and-six play, and the crowd was just screaming, hollering, and going nuts. This was back in the day when the referees held up play until the crowd quieted down. And there was Harbaugh, running the team like he was sitting in the middle of the library. He was cool, calm, collected, just letting the crowd go crazy. He wasn't going to put the ball in play until he knew he could run the play with a good chance of it being successful. He just stood over the center. We're not talking about 30 seconds. We're talking a good four, five minutes. He was letting the crowd go nuts until they calmed down. Then he took off, he got back, the pressure came. He started to roll to the left, and all of a sudden, as he was rolling, he knew he was in trouble. He threw a shovel pass into the middle of the field that was behind Gerald White. White corralled it and went in for a touchdown. I can tell you point blank. I don't ever remember anybody ever throwing a shovel pass with Bo Schembechler as the head coach. I saw that, and I was thinking to myself, holy Moses, what's Bo going to do? Bo had to be going nuts. Of course, Bo was going nuts. It was one of those things where he probably said "NO!" then, "Oh, great play."

But Jimmy was always the guy who would create that type of play. Jimmy was the type of guy when we played Florida State, early in the game, what did he do? He went right down the field, and he threw right at **DEION SANDERS***. Right at him. The pass was incomplete, but he threw right at him, opening up the field right off the bat. And from then on, it was a game of Jamie Morris and Thomas Wilcher, especially Morris, and we beat Florida State.

He was just damn good all the damn time. He was smart about what he did all the time. We got to his senior season and had a great season going until Rickey Foggie and Minnesota got us one week before the Ohio State game. Two days later, we were going into the press conference before the Ohio State game, and here was the guy who had done everything right. He didn't vary from the script at all. He knew what Bo wanted. He knew what was good for his team. He knew exactly everything that was going on, and he was the perfect player to talk to the media. Then out of the blue, at the Monday press conference at Weber's Inn, Jim Harbaugh said, "We're going to beat Ohio State." I'm telling you, I'm sitting there going, "What did he just say?" I couldn't believe it. That was so untypical of any of the players at Michigan, but Jim Harbaugh especially. I had to make sure that I caught Bo before he got up to talk, because I wanted Bo to know exactly what Jim said. I immediately went back through the service area and found Bo walking through the workers doing laundry and folding sheets. I had to grab Bo. I said, "Bo, you're not going to believe this. Jim Harbaugh just guaranteed a victory against Ohio State." Now understand, I was scared just telling Bo that, right? Bo looked at me. He said, "You sure he said that?" I said, "Bo, he guaranteed a victory against Ohio State." I was expecting Bo to explode. I was expecting Bo to say, "What in God's name is Jim Harbaugh

*Dallas Cowboy football players who once had Topps baseball cards include **DEION SANDERS** and quarterbacks Quincy Carter, Chad Hutchinson, and Drew Henson.

doing? How did you allow him to do that?" But Bo, all he did was he looked at me. He said thanks and walked into the press conference. He did not even flinch. I went into the press conference with Bo. Of course, what do you think the first question is? "Did you hear? Your quarterback has just guaranteed a victory over Ohio State." Bo said, "Well, what did you expect him to say?" That was it. Nothing more, nothing less. In the locker room that night, from what I heard, Bo said, "I have a quarterback who says that we're going to beat Ohio State. Now your job is to make sure that this quarterback is correct." Of course, we won the game and all ended well.

Probably the toughest time for Jim while he was at Michigan was when he broke his left arm against Michigan State in '84. We were controlling the game and Jamie got hit and fumbled the ball. Harbaugh went diving for it and in the ensuing pile up, Jim broke the arm. When that happened, I went over to see Nick Vista, the SID at State, and told him, "Nick, not only are you going to win the game, we are going to have trouble going .500." We had already lost the defensive leader of our team for the season, Tony Gant, and now our offensive leader. Those words turned out to be prophetic. State came back to beat us and we had the toughest season in Bo's history. Some media were actually questioning if Bo should give up coaching. They were saying he might be done. Heck, we lost Harbaugh and Gant and to get to .500 was tough. And we did finish the season 6-5 and played BYU in the Holiday Bowl the year BYU won the National Championship. To this day, I maintain if Harbaugh was healthy, BYU would not have won the National Championship.

When we had Jim's introductory press conference, when Jim saw me, he grabbed my arm and gave me a big hug, "Bruce! How are you doing?" I think he was surprised to see me there, but in his eyes, you could see he was happy to see me. They had to keep pushing him toward the press conference because it looked like he was about to start a longer conversation. It was like he would just as soon talk to me than he would go to the press conference. And when you look at Jim's eyes, I believe you can actually see his personality. It reminds me of a running back that takes a look around at the line, looking for the holes always—thinking and enjoying himself. Just look at Jim Harbaugh's eyes when he is at a press conference, coaching on the sideline or just talking with people. The one thing I do know is Jim is always looking at how he's going to improve that football team, what he's going to do to help that football team.

Jim is not one of these guys that you're going to see on the front page of *GQ*, because Jim is Jim Harbaugh. Jim likes to go to Cracker Barrel. Jim likes to take his **BASEBALL*** mitt to baseball games. That's Jim. He doesn't need all this. It's kind of funny, because he gets all this hype, and it's almost like Jim doesn't care if he gets this hype. He really doesn't. He's a football coach. Michigan's hired a football coach. That's what they got, and they got a damn good football coach.

His teammates have a special bond with him. That's something that I see a lot of with Bo's players. Jim is not Bo Schembechler, but he learned from Bo. Jim is not Mike Ditka, but he learned from Mike Ditka. Jim is not his dad, but he learned from his dad, and that's what's so neat about Jim. He literally has tried to learn from almost every situation that's out there. Maybe it's a tough situation where a teammate might be injured. Maybe it's a situation where he didn't get a shot at being a coach at a certain time. Maybe it's a situation where he didn't get a chance to be a quarterback the way he wanted to be a quarterback, but he learned from it. He grew from it. That's what he's trying to instill in these players.

When you saw Jim after the season opening loss to Utah, there was no despair in his voice. It was, "Okay, here's what I've got to do. Here's what I've got to do. Here's what I've got

---

*In Major League **BASEBALL**, there are an average of 46 foul balls per game. About 16 of them go in the stands.

to do. Here's what I've got to do." When you looked at his eyes in that press conference, that's all he was thinking about. He was thinking about where he's going to find that next spot to improve that team.

Jim says things that make you go, "What?" Other times, they're very deep. Jimmy has a way of saying things the Jim Harbaugh way. It's not a Bo Schembechler way, Ditka way or Jack Harbaugh way. It's his way of saying it. When he talked this past year about starting the season and how excited he was, he was trying to relate it to the birth of a child. He was talking about coming out of the womb. It was just so different, but every time I think about it, I think, well, that's Jim.

When a little kid asked him about being quarterback, Jim Harbaugh grabbed the kid. Jim loves kids. When you see Jim around kids, he loves kids. I'll say this, and I don't mean it in a derogatory way, Jim is really a big kid. He really is. He's got the heart of a kid. He's got the enjoyment of a kid. He's got the love of a kid. He's a big kid who loves what he's doing. Try to remember when you were 10- or 12-years-old, and you loved something. You find it very difficult to recreate that feeling because of your age. It seems as if Jim Harbaugh is able to recreate that. He's able to recreate that feeling, and that's a special feeling. That's because he understands who he is. He understands the culture of sports. He understands the importance of sports in life. He resonates that when he talks to somebody or he steps on the field and coaches. It's fun. That's what sports is supposed to be. That's what resonates when you see Jim Harbaugh.

When they hired him, I was just damn happy they got Jim Harbaugh. He really was the one person who could tie everything together that we need to do at Michigan. I'm excited about it. I really am. I'm 63. Jimmy's 51. It's 12 years. I know his dad and his mom. I know Jack so, so well. Jack and I have stayed in contact all through the years. In fact, Jack and Jerry Hanlon and I, we went out for beers a couple of months ago.

We really didn't want to talk about Jim. We just wanted to talk about football. That's what's so good about the Harbaugh family. When you go out with the Harbaughs, you don't have to talk about the Harbaughs. All you have to talk about is things that are enjoyable to talk about. That's one thing you've got to say about the Harbaugh family, they're just sports fans in general. When you're talking sports, Jack's face just lights up. Even Jackie's face lights up.

John Harbaugh is so much different than Jimmy. They're two different guys, period. They had a press conference the week of the Super Bowl. Jimmy and John were playing each other that week. There was a teleconference with Jack and Jackie. Reporters were asking questions, and a guy came on the phone, and said, "I'm so and so from the Baltimore whatever, some newspaper, a website. I want to ask Jack and Jackie, who's your favorite son?" All of a sudden, you heard Jackie in the background. She was laughing and said, "What am I going to say? What am I going to say?" Jack was trying to say something. The reporter asked the question again, and Jack said, "Is this you, John?" And it was John Harbaugh having fun.

That's what I love about the Harbaugh family, and I think Jim's penchant for having people enjoy themselves combined with his coaching strengths will allow him to have a great run at Michigan.

JIM HARBAUGH IS JUST A REGULAR GUY WHO SOME DAYS WEARS A CAPE

TODD ANSON

Todd Anson grew up in Mount Pleasant, Mich., and graduated from Michigan law school in 1980. As a California Big Law lawyer, Anson served as a Managing Partner at a law firm that pioneered representation of leading technology companies. His pro bono work led him to represent Nobel Peace Prize recipient Mother Teresa.

Jim came to play for the San Diego Chargers in 1999 and moved to Coronado, Calif., and became our neighbor. Our sons, his Jay, who's now the Michigan tight ends coach, and my Ryan, were teammates on Coronado Pop Warner teams.

Long before he was honored as the NFL Coach of the Year or the College Football Coach of the Year, he was playing quarterback for the Chargers, attending Coronado High School football games with my family, and attending his son's Pop Warner games, when he could make them. He used to show up on sunny days in a white floppy hat, and he'd always be pulling for the local team's quarterback. When a kid went down—in Pop Warner these are nine, 10-year-old boys—he'd scream, "Pop back up! Pop back up! Don't show them that they hurt you!"

We later became neighbors. He lived right next door to us. We spent hours watching what we called "The Jack Bauer Power Hour," the old *24* television series with Kiefer Sutherland. Because he was busy coaching, he couldn't keep up with the show on a weekly basis. So, every year for his birthday, we'd send him the prior season's DVDs of the entire series of *24*.

Jim is a natural born leader. This guy is one of the most mentally disciplined and toughest people that I have ever encountered. He believes that leaders have to have broad shoulders, and you're there to take the arrows and protect your troops. You're there to build them up. He has this saying, "Make yourself small and make others big. Be humble. Build up your players. Those are the guys who have earned the respect and the adulation, not the coaches."

He's a 14-year NFL quarterback, Big Ten Player of the Year, All-American and Academic All-American, but also a coach who can't get enough of having his father around him on his sidelines. Every time a coach got sick, took a different job in the middle of the season or Jim found himself without a coach, who would he hire to fill in? His dad, Jack. He loves having Jack Harbaugh around him. They talk almost daily. Here's this big-time achiever and alpha male who is still so anchored to his father. Most people who know them well will tell you that Jack Harbaugh is Jim's "True North." He's his compass and his sounding board on almost a daily basis. On every important decision in life, Jim talks with his dad.

I've said many times that the Harbaughs have the best Rolodex or contact list in football. You've got Jim. You've got Jack who won a national championship at Western Kentucky and spent his career in football. You've got John who's a Super Bowl winning coach. Among the three of them, they source coaching talent and player talent better than any NFL franchise.

I've been around lots of professional athletes and lots of tech entrepreneurs who have achieved extraordinary success, but there's always been something different about Jim. He's one of these guys that you pay attention to the minute he walks in the room, and I don't care whether or not you're talking about a group of Pop Warner parents, or you're talking about a group of NFL Hall of Famers. You can't help but be aware of Jim Harbaugh when he walks into a room. He just commands attention. There's something unique about him. He inspires people, and he's a talent magnet. That's probably his greatest skill as a coach. People who are ambitious and have outsized goals for themselves in football want to be around him. They want to associate with him. They want to learn with him. They want to sort of have him cast his spell on them.

Jim took the USD job against Al Davis' admonitions. "Don't do it! You'll be an NFL head coach in three to five years." What did Jim do? He left Oakland because he wanted to be a head coach now. He took an $80,000 a year job when NFL head coaches were making millions. He cares about the money, but the money does not define him. He defines himself and without regard to the money.

While Jim was working with Al Davis and the Raiders, he went to high school games and scouted talent. He took the USD job knowing that there was a tall, skinny kid at Oakland Tech High School, which has produced Clint Eastwood, Rickey Henderson and Marshawn Lynch. The kid was a quarterback who spent most of the game handing off the ball to Marshawn Lynch.

The quarterback was Josh Johnson, an inner city kid from a single-parent family with not a lot of means. Jim recruited him to private, Jesuit USD with its $44,000 a year sticker price. Josh couldn't afford to go there on his own. Jim said, "We'll do what we can to get you merit scholarships and help. In any case, you'll only need to go in debt two years because, after two years, I'll be able to get you a scholarship to any big-time school in the country that you want to go to."

Jim pumped up the kid as a guy with NFL potential at a school that had never had a guy invited to the NFL Combine, let alone an undrafted free agent come out of it. Nobody went to USD who was thinking about playing professional football. Josh could throw the ball 70 yards and was a 4.5 40-yard dash guy. He was a string bean, but still growing. In Josh's sophomore season, he led USD to an 11-1 record. Jim met with Josh and said, "Okay, it's time for you to move on." Josh was befuddled. He said, "What are you talking about, Coach?" Jim said, "I told you when you came here you'd only need to go into debt for two years, and then I'd get you a scholarship to anywhere you wanted to go. I can get you a scholarship to places like Oklahoma, anywhere you want, a school in any major conference." Josh said, "Coach, I'm not leaving." Josh played four years at USD and has spent the past seven years in the NFL.

When Jim was announced as the new head coach at Stanford, I attended the press conference and sat next to Bill Walsh. He took the job without even asking what the pay would be. When asked about his life and football, Jim said, "Well, I was born. I planned to play as long as I could, coach as long as I could, and then die."

Before he took the Stanford job, he had been offered both the Tulane and **NORTH TEXAS STATE*** jobs. He had to pass on both of those jobs, which were a step up from USD, without any assurance that he would get the Stanford job. But when he received a call from Bill Walsh telling him that he "couldn't guarantee him the job," but "guaranty" that Jim would be "in the final three" candidates considered, Jim passed on two sure things, upgrade jobs, and took the Stanford interview. He's a risk-taker. He believes in himself.

I know exactly how Jim won at Stanford. He used the academics as a tool. Jim encouraging Andrew Luck to major in engineering was the reason why he got him. When he was being recruiting, Luck asked, "Coach, can I major in engineering and

---

***NORTH TEXAS STATE** University is nicknamed the Mean Green after Mean Joe Greene. It's the only Division I school whose nickname is derived from an actual person.

play football for you at Stanford?" Jim said, "Of course, you can." Luck said, "Coach, I don't believe you." "Why don't you believe me?" "Because Texas and Oklahoma are recruiting me, and they both have told me that I can't major in engineering and play quarterback at their school." Jim said, "I have 16 engineering majors on my roster right now." By the time he left, that number was 23 or 24.

Every year, Jim needed about 25 guys. Every year there are about 10 or 11 guys that have Stanford, Harvard, Yale academics. They're going to get in those schools without a sport even though they have Big Ten, Pac-12, SEC athletic tool sets. Those 10 or 11 guys find their way to Stanford just by identifying them and a little bit of recruiting effort. At the time Jim took that job, he calibrated that there were about 150 guys nationally that he could recruit that had the academic package to go with the athletic package. He needed 14 or 15 of those 150 guys, because 10 or 11 were going to sign themselves up just because Stanford is Stanford academically and because they compete in the Pac-12.

In his mind, he was competing to get about 10 percent of a pool of about 150 guys. What did he do next? He figured out that what was holding guys back from admission into Stanford was they weren't taking the minimum required four AP classes and getting at least B grades in them. He started looking at guys in 9th and 10th grade who might develop, and he started getting the word out to guys in their sophomore year that they needed to have four AP classes with B or better grades to get into Stanford, and otherwise have the ability to play. He felt that he tripled the size of that pool to 450 kids. Then he needed to get 15 out of 450 guys. Do the math.

His quarterbacks have been exceptionally smart. Todd Mortensen was the guy who came down from BYU and was his fifth-year senior starter his first year at USD. He's a lawyer in New York now. He was a high school valedictorian. He had a 4.0 at BYU, played four years, but didn't start. Jim picked him up as a fifth-year senior. He got a master's degree at USD with a 4.0. He became the first guy ever in the history of USD to be romanced by the NFL, and hung around on development squads for three or four years, including with the Lions. All the while, he took his GMATs and LSATs and Penn admitted him into the law school and Wharton School of Business. He ended up getting a JD MBA at Penn.

Andrew Luck, Alex Smith, Todd Mortensen. They're all about 135, 140 IQ guys. These quarterbacks in Jim's system are incredibly smart. Jim told me when he was at Stanford that no NFL team could have in place an offense as diverse as the one Stanford had because the kids were so smart. He turned intelligence into an asset. He believes that you have a greater chance of winning with a really smart team.

The night after the 49ers beat the Packers in a season opener, I was with Jim in his office when he showed me a little blue and gold flip book that was about the size of two credit cards. Bo had given it to him when he was a senior. Everybody on the Michigan team had to write down five personal goals and five team goals. One of his personal goals was to be a good person. Among his team goals were wining the Big Ten title and national championship. He had the 49ers do exactly the same thing. A lot of people say that you can't coach professionals like college players. I think Jim proved that you can. His fifth personal goal for the 49ers that year was to be fearless in the face of adversity, controversy, or threat of being fired. In other words, he was going to coach that team the way he thought was best, whether it put his job on the line or not.

I took a photo of him that night to remember the occasion. He had changed into a blue Mr. Goodwrench mechanics shirt with "Jim" stitched over the pocket. He was holding up this book in his office at one in the morning after beating Green Bay.

This past summer Jim did an "Aerial Assault" quarterback camp in Ann Arbor. He had 250 campers exposed to 11 NFL quarterbacks. One day in Michigan Stadium he had the U-M baseball coach hit balls to the football campers who he loaned baseball gloves to. Jim was watching them field ground balls and fly balls and throwing it to the cut-off man who was Bears QB Jay Cutler. Bill Walsh had told Jim that the quarterback on a high school team should be the best athlete in the school. Jim was looking for athleticism, not quarterback skills. Jim could immediately eliminate half of those kids after watching them field fly balls and ground balls.

Some of the things that he's done since he's been on the job at Michigan are simply brilliant. The "Summer Swarm" rotating camp tour that he did was phenomenal. He knows that there are a lot of kids who can't afford to get to a football camp halfway across the country, let alone one a few miles away at their local university. So he literally put the Michigan program on the road, creating opportunities for kids all across the country. They had 10 or 11 camps scattered around the country that allowed kids to showcase themselves to the Michigan coaches. I think more than 4,000 kids took advantage of these camps. A Texas kid wasn't sure he could come up with the $40 to attend the camp in Dallas. Jim told him, "I'd really love to have you there. Can't you mow lawns or rake leaves or get odd jobs to come up with the 40 bucks?"

When he was accused of doing the camps to get around the recruiting rules, he countered by inviting coaches from every university in the country to attend the camps that Michigan was paying for and his coaching staff was running. Any coach who wanted to come was allowed to come, whether they were from the Big Ten, SEC, the Pac-12 or wherever. Only a few of the BCS-level schools sent a coach. The "Swarm" shows how innovative Jim is. I hope that the NCAA doesn't ban the camps because what they will be saying is, "We're allowing our head coaches who don't want to hustle, who want to be lazy, to put that ahead of the interests of all of these kids."

Jim and his brother, John, are on a crusade to support and prop up the sport of football. I think they see the game as being challenged with the concussion issue and the expanding popularity of other sports. They want to make sure the game is preserved. They want to make sure that the game is safe. And they want to call attention to the game they love as much as they want to win and out-recruit the other schools.

Jim famously said when he got back to Ann Arbor that his favorite restaurant in the world was Cracker Barrel. He liked being back in Ann Arbor because there aren't Cracker Barrels in California. I'd never been to a Cracker Barrel. I was visiting him last spring and said, "Okay, we have to go to Cracker Barrel for breakfast." He lit up. It was eight o'clock on a Saturday morning, and there were 50 or 60 people that posed for photographs with Jim. He was signing Cracker Barrel hats, menus, you name it. He won't say no to anybody. He understands his role completely. It was heartwarming to see how well he treated everybody who approached him, respectfully, always telling them he'd be happy to pose for a photograph with them. He didn't say no to a soul. Jim likes all the little trinkets, candies, toys, and other things for the kids at Cracker Barrel. It's like taking the kids to the carnival. Another thing that Jim likes about it is it's not expensive.

During the season, Jim is focused. I call it his "football bunker." His cell phone is shut off more than it is on. It's almost shocking to see a guy of his intellect keep himself that narrowly focused, but he's all in for football every moment. It's amazing how focused he's able to keep himself for a guy who has diverse interests in history, in his family, in his kids, and other sports.

Jim was coaching at an All-Star game in Las Vegas when he met his future wife, Sarah. After the game, several of the other coaches and friends were going out. Jim said, "I think I'm just going to have a quiet night." He went by himself to P.F. Chang's for dinner. He was sitting at his table when he saw a really pretty woman sitting at the bar eating alone. He was just starting his meal when she got up and walked out. He later told me, "My arms and legs were just moving before I could even think." He headed out the door and called out to her and asked if he could introduce himself, which he did. She felt comfortable enough that they exchanged contact information. She asked what he did, and he said he was a coach. I don't know whether he ever made it back to finish his lettuce wraps. I do know that they dated for months before she knew who he really was. She confided to her brother, John, who's now close to Jim also, that she was dating a coach. John asked who, and she said, "His name's Jim Harbaugh." John said, "He's not a coach. He's a former NFL quarterback." She said, "No, he's not. He's a coach." In all that time, he'd never told her that he'd been a famous football player.

Jim was very interested in the **KANSAS*** job before he took the 49ers job. He was interested in that job because it would put Sarah close to her family. He's building a house in Ann Arbor for his parents and Sarah's family to stay in when they come to town. It's right next door. He loves having his family around. His life is so demanding, and he's so focused on football that the closer he keeps his family, the more time he gets to enjoy them, and they get to enjoy him. It's just his definition of how you have a semi-normal life in an ultra competitive profession.

Jim understands that there's something about coaching at Michigan that's different than coaching the 49ers. Tim Kawakami, who covers the 49ers for the *San Jose Mercury News* said, "No NFL team's fan base can compare to the passion that

---

*The **KANSAS** City Chiefs have nothing to do with Native Americans. They were named after Kansas City Mayor H. Roe Bartle, nicknamed "The Chief." Bartle helped lure the AFL's Dallas Texans to Kansas City in 1962...so owner Lamar Hunt renamed the team in Bartle's honor.

the Michigan fans have for their team. With them, it's almost a religion."

For Jim's first game as head coach at Michigan, I was at the team hotel in Salt Lake City. FOX Sports promoted it in the weeks leading up to the game by crossing the country with the "Harbus," a bus wrapped in khaki filled with Jim Harbaugh look-a-likes. I was in the lobby of the hotel at 6:00 a.m. and ran into Rick Leach, the former Michigan QB great and 10-year Major Leaguer. He said, "I've been trying to get a sideline pass for today's game. It would mean the world to me to be on the sidelines when Jim takes the field for the first time as coach."

Rick Leach was Jim Harbaugh's hero when Jim was a kid growing up in Ann Arbor. There's a famous photo of Jim as a Michigan ball boy on the sideline, running over and patting Leach on the helmet after Leach scored a touchdown. The families were close, and Rick really wanted to be on the sidelines at least for a moment when Jim first took the field to coach Michigan. Leach spoke at a pep rally before the game, and the Michigan AD, Jim Hackett, drove Rick into the stadium in a golf cart. Rick was on the field when Jim came out. After the game, Rick sent me a text message: "To have the Harbaugh family back at Michigan had the feel of making my life complete....Being on the field and taking a picture with Jim Hackett and Coach Harbaugh will never be forgotten! Go Blue!"

That's how much it meant to him to have Jim back coaching at Michigan. A 10-year Major League veteran and star Michigan QB acting like a giddy little boy over Jim's return to Michigan. Michigan football does that to you. There's nothing like it.

WHEN THE ONE GREAT SCORER COMES TO MARK AGAINST YOUR NAME, HE'LL MARK NOT IF YOU WON OR LOST BUT HOW YOU PLAYED THE GAME

(WITH APOLOGIES TO GRANTLAND RICE)

FATHER JOE UHEN

Father Joe Uhen has been at the Santisimo Sacramento Parish in Piura, Peru, for 22 years. "Padre Joe" is a graduate of Notre Dame University. His parish sits in the desert region of Northern Peru, about 35 miles from the Pacific Ocean. People around the world send $25 food packages to families living in nearby villages. For more information on Padre Joe's parish visit the parish website: http://www.santisimo.org/us-content/index.html.

Jim Harbaugh started visiting our parish in Piura, Peru, within a year of taking the coaching job at Stanford. Jim learned about the Santisimo Sacramento Catholic parish from his friend, John Dennison, who lives in Palo Alto. Jim stayed at John's guest house shortly after he arrived at Stanford. My sister lives in Palo Alto, and she and her husband are friends with John. They brought John down, then John brought Jim the next year. Now Jim comes every year.

They don't know Jim as a celebrity here. At our school we have 870 students from preschool to high school. We've told the kids who Jim is and that he's a great coach. They understand what that means because everybody down here understands soccer and the World Cup. We tell them he's a great coach who plays for the American football championship. The kids go wild. They've gotten Harbaugh T-shirts. Jim is impressed by the excitement and enthusiasm of the kids. They're thrilled to see him, so it's mutual. We play a little football in our little stadium and have a great time. When we visit the local prison, we tell those guys about Jim and they appreciate him playing football with them. At the prison, he always leaves without any shoes. He gives his shoes to one of the prisoners. He also gives away his sweatshirt. He gives away whatever he has and walks out wearing a T-shirt and a pair of sweat pants. He does that every year. He always gives away whatever he can to the prisoners. We play real football inside the prison, and the guys enjoy taking photos with Jim. They don't know much about him, but his humanity is engaging.

Jim has a genuine love for people, especially for the poor and those who are most in need. Jim has a way of empowering those he meets, myself included. He invited me to a Stanford practice and to help celebrate a Mass before Super Bowl XLVII in New Orleans. He has a great outlook on life. He's open to having a positive interaction with everyone he meets.

Jim was delivering some food packages in a very poor area. A lot of the homes don't have electricity. Jim went into one house and saw a man on the ground. He was not in a good way. You could see he was almost dying. Jim picked up the man in his arms and carried him to the truck and drove the man to our hospice. The man lived in the hospice for more than a year. When Jim came back the following year, he saw the man again. The man passed away after that visit, but the last year of his life was much better because of Jim.

When he arrives, we first go to the market to buy groceries for the orphans. It's a typical Peruvian open market with vegetables in bushel baskets and sacks of rice. He'll load a few sacks on his shoulder and carry them to the truck and then tote a bushel basket of cauliflower. We load up the truck with groceries and take it to the orphanage. The girls at the orphanage teach Jim the local folk dances like La Marinera and El Tondero.

Jim loves to play football with the kids. We'll go to a neighborhood that has a dusty, sandy soccer field, and the kids will come running. We'll have 80 kids. It's a little unorthodox, but we divide the kids into teams and just run around and tackle each other. Jim puts on a **PUNT***, pass and kick clinic. Most of the kids don't know how to catch the ball or how to punt. We have prizes and always give away soccer balls to the kids.

Jim notices little things. I had a young man named Renfro who didn't talk to anybody, but helped at Mass. He was an altar boy. He didn't have a lot going on in his life, so he came and hung out at the church. Jim picked up on that. He began to talk to the boy and got him talking a little bit. Jim said, "Why don't I help you get a scholarship so you can study at a better school?" Renfro was able to get a better education. He finished high school and now is in a trade school learning computer science. He said, "I'm thinking of becoming a priest." The kid wasn't connected to anything or anyone until Jim spent time with him.

Another time, Jim connected with Franz, a young street kid. Franz always watched cars. He said, "If a motorcycle parks up here by the church or somebody comes up in a car, I'll watch it for you and you can give me a Peruvian sol." A sol is worth about 25 cents. Jim said to Franz, "Come in and take a shower. Have you ever had a shower?" Franz said, "No, not a real shower. I've had a bucket of water I've washed with, but never a shower." Jim brought Franz into his room on our church campus and got him his first shower. Franz was in the shower

*Pulaski Academy, a Little Rock, Arkansas, high school, has punted four times in four years…They never field a **PUNT**…All their kickoffs are onside kicks. They have won four state titles in the last 10 years.

singing away, the street kid enjoying his first shower. Jim is bold about reaching out to people and helping them feel empowered, making them feel like they're part of the team, that we're all in this together. Let's all do what we can to move forward. He does that with just about everybody he can. There's a family with a special needs child. The father is a carpenter who works for me as a handyman. The child, Mathew, is about three years old. He can't walk or speak. He has three older brothers and sisters who are young, too. Jim took all of them out to dinner then played with the kids.

Jim can become very personal. In these three cases, he's developed relationships with the kids and their families. He also goes out and builds houses, plays football in the prison, visits the hospice and goes to school with the kids. He even goes into the classroom and encourages the kids. He gave a talk at the drug rehab center. Jim said, "Let's just try to do a little bit better today than we did yesterday. What else can we do?" He contributes. He makes an impact as a human being. We have about 600 people from the U.S. come to this parish every year. Jim is one of them, and he's made a wonderful impact doing what he can without all the color of being the Jim Harbaugh that we see on TV. He's just himself and enjoys being himself, helping the people that he can.

Jim's visits to Piura are chronicled in *Peruball: Jim Harbaugh in South America*, a documentary produced by Comcast Sports Net. Dave Feldman, a friend and former high school basketball teammate of Harbaugh's who now works at CSN, told Jim, "Give me some time so I can do a story about you." Jim said, "OK, come on down to Peru. You can help me build some houses and you can help me play football with the kids." The documentary was filmed during Jim's visit in May of 2014. Comcast sent a cameraman, Dave Feldman, and a producer. They all joined in with building houses and bringing in food packages.

Some of the kids at the parish have seen *Peruball*. They see themselves on the video and they don't know what to think. It's surreal in the sense that they see a video of Jim building houses, delivering food packages and playing football. Jim has found a way to share part of himself among the poor in Northern Peru. He's a rock star missionary.

~ ~ ~ ~ ~ ~ ~ ~ ~ ~ ~ ~ ~ ~ ~ ~ ~ ~ ~

When Tom Zbikowski, an All-American defensive back at Notre Dame, made his professional boxing debut at Madison Square Garden in the summer of 2006, his opponent was Robert Bell from Akron. Bell entered the ring wearing an Ohio State jersey. Bell was knocked out 49 seconds into the first round.

Ohio State beat Michigan 50-14 in 1968. Ohio State went for a two-point conversion in the fourth quarter. When asked about it, Woody Hayes said, "I went for two because I couldn't go for three."

In the 1979 baseball draft, the Kansas City Royals selected Dan Marino in the fouth round and John Elway in the 18th round. That same year the Royals hired Rush Limbaugh for their group sales Department. Limbaugh left in 1984 for a radio opportunity in California.

WAIT...THERE'S MORE
JIM HARBAUGH!!

AN ADDITIONAL BONUS CHAPTER
COVERING HIS CAPTAIN COMEBACK
DAYS AND OTHER GOOD STUFF IS
YOURS FREE. SAME FORMAT!

www.gostealthisbook.com/
jimharbaugh

Other Books by Rich Wolfe

For Cardinals Fans Only—Volume I
Remembering Jack Buck
I Remember Harry Caray
Ron Santo, A Perfect 10
Jeremy Lin, The Asian Sensation
For Cubs Fans Only
For Cubs Fans Only—Volume II
For Notre Dame Fans Only—
   The New Saturday Bible
Da Coach (Mike Ditka)
Tim Russert, We Heartily Knew Ye
For Packers Fans Only
For Hawkeye Fans Only
I Love It, I Love It, I Love It (with Jim Zabel, Iowa announcer)
Oh, What a Knight (Bob Knight)
There's No Expiration Date on Dreams (Tom Brady)
He Graduated Life with Honors and No Regrets (Pat Tillman)
Take This Job and Love It (Jon Gruden)
Remembering Harry Kalas
Been There, Shoulda Done That (John Daly)
And the Last Shall Be First (Kurt Warner)
Sports Fans Who Made Headlines
Fandemonium
Remembering Dale Earnhardt
I Saw It On the Radio (Vin Scully)
The Real McCoy (Al McCoy, Phoenix Suns announcer)
Personal Foul (With Tim Donaghy, former NBA referee)

For Yankee Fans Only	*For South Carolina Fans Only*
For Red Sox Fans Only	*For Clemson Fans Only*
For Browns Fans Only	*For Oklahoma Fans Only*
For Mets Fans Only	*For Yankee Fans Only—Volume II*
For Bronco Fans Only	*For Mizzou Fans Only*
For Michigan Fans Only	*For Kansas City Chiefs Fans Only*
For Milwaukee Braves Fans Only	*For K-State Fans Only*
For Nebraska Fans Only	*For KU Fans Only (Kansas)*
For Buckeye Fans Only	*For Phillies Fans Only*
For Georgia Bulldog Fans Only	

All books are the same size, format and price.
Questions or to order? Contact the author directly at 602-738-5889.